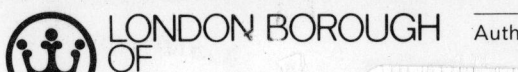

# NO TEARS TO FLOW

The hand that signed the paper felled a city;
Five sovereign fingers taxed the breath,
Doubled the globe of dead and halved a country;
These five kings did a king to death. . . .

The five kings count the dead but do not soften
The crusted wound nor stroke the brow;
A hand rules pity as a hand rules heaven;
Hands have no tears to flow.

DYLAN THOMAS

# NO TEARS
# TO FLOW

*Woman at War*

RENA BRIAND

HEINEMANN MELBOURNE LONDON

WILLIAM HEINEMANN LIMITED
Melbourne   London

National Library of Australia
Registry Number Aus 69 2431

Registered at the G.P.O. Melbourne
for transmission by post as a book

Printed and bound by J. C. Stephens Pty Ltd
Melbourne   Victoria

# TABLE OF CONTENTS

# ILLUSTRATIONS

# FOREWORD

When people first asked me why I wasn't writing a book about my experiences in Vietnam, I admitted I didn't feel qualified to tackle such a task. My ego swelled rapidly as they continued to flatter me as a prospective author, and I found myself talking about 'my book'. Then I had to write it — to save face.

This book is not intended as a military or political analysis of the situation. I discarded politics as nonsense at the age of eleven, after ploughing through three pages of Karl Marx under the initial error of thinking it was a book by Karl May, popular German author of over sixty novels on the Wild West. That's the kind of trouble I've always had with names. In fact, some names that should be in this book are omitted because of my lousy memory . . . others are omitted because they belong to friends who might be compromised if they were identified.

This book is mainly the story of a woman journalist freelancing in a war zone. The episodes are factual, though they are not in chronological sequence. It would be rather difficult, and I think extremely dull, to write up nearly three years of South-East Asia in diary style. I have included a short outline of the history of Vietnam — because I understood better the confused situation there once I knew something of the country's background.

The incidents described are typical of the way a person lives under war conditions. Few 'authorities on Vietnam' have lived right among the people and incidents look quite different when seen from an expense-account room at the Caravelle by a person who regards eating at a local joint as 'slumming'.

My warmest thanks are tendered to friends who helped me during difficult times; and to the courageous people of Vietnam who have taught me patience and human values. My gratitude also to Lam, for his research on the history of Vietnam; to Le Ngoc Cung, AP Saigon and Michael Perry, Melbourne, for photo finishing; and to J. M. Dent and Sons for permission to reprint 'The Hand That Signed The Paper' from *Miscellany* by Dylan Thomas.

Photos taken with Nikon F on TRI-X, Kodakcolor and Ektachrome.

For R.T.G.

# HISTORY OF VIETNAM

The Vietnam problem is not simply defined by clashes of the Ho Chi Minh regime against supporters of whoever is currently in charge of the South. There are many 'small wars' fought south of the 17th parallel. For example, there is the frequent trouble arising between religious groups. Most publicised have been the confrontations of Buddhist and Catholics, which at times resulted in the taking-up of arms. Vague struggles between Buddhist sects also cause problems.

The main barrier against a unified South, however, is caused by the various minority groups of different ethnic origins, groups which look upon the Vietnamese regime as foreign invaders.

To understand the complicated situation, one must know at least a brief outline of the country's history, and realise that while most Westerners regard Vietnam as an ancient nation, the Republic south of the 17th parallel has actually been colonised only comparatively recently by the Vietnamese.

Originally, the Indo-Chinese peninsula was populated by an Austro-Indonesian race similar to the inhabitants of New Guinea. Thai, Mongolian and Indian invaders pushed these aboriginal tribes into the inhospitable mountain regions, where their descendants are today known as the Montagnard tribes.

Indian migration created the Khmer empire, which today remains as the kingdom of Cambodia, and which comprised the southern part of Vietnam until about 300 years ago. A half-million Cambodians still live in Vietnam's Mekong Delta and are known as Khmer Krom.

About 200 A.D. a melange of indigenous Austro-Indonesians and seafaring Indians founded the once-powerful Champa Empire, along the coastal stretch of Central Vietnam. The Cham were seaborne raiders, whose powerful fleet of swift ships frequently penetrated into the Red River Delta. In 1177 they sailed up the Mekong and sacked Angkor. The Cham in turn were eventually colonised by the Vietnamese, who steadily advanced southwards. The Viets proved expert in the acculturation and genocide of their conquered opponents, and all that remains of the Champa kingdom are about 50,000 Indian-featured Chams living as artisans and fishermen in the valleys of Phan Rang and Phan Ri. In the cities, the large colony of Chinese, mainly businessmen, keep as a group quite apart (similar to certain migrant groups in Australia). The various Montagnard tribes and other small groups usually have little contact with the Vietnamese, and in the main speak only their own language (there are forty-seven minority languages in Vietnam).

It would be difficult enough for a country with a fair social structure to rule such a variety of groups. Since the Vietnamese Government has made no effort to improve the standards of these people, it is impossible to expect their loyalty in a time of crisis.

But now, to the history of the people we know as the Vietnamese—

During the second century B.C., the birth of a new civilisation took place in the Valley of the Red River. It was a mixture of Sino-Tibetan, Indonesian, Thai and native Viet strains, with roots in various Asian religions and philosophies. Legend has it that the one hundred venerable ancestors of all Vietnamese sprang from the union of a Dragon-god and a beautiful fairy princess. The Viets originally occupied parts of what is now south-eastern China and the northern part of the east coast of the Indo-Chinese peninsula.

In 207 B.C. a number of small independent states were conquered by Chinese generals who had broken with the Ch'in emperors. Combined with two Chinese provinces, they formed the independent kingdom of Nam Viet ('SOUTH [ern country of the] VIET'). In 111 B.C. this kingdom was victoriously invaded by the Chinese army of the Han Dynasty. For the thousand years that followed, China controlled the country almost continuously, and exacted tribute from the settlers of the area. At times, the Viets rebelled against the Chinese burden, usually unsuccessfully.

In 39 A.D. the Chinese beheaded a local chieftan, Thi Sach. His widow, Trung Trac, and her sister Trung Nhi managed to eject the Chinese garrisons for a short period. Like Joan of Arc in French history, the two Trung sisters, mounted on elephants, led 80,000 of their countrymen to a victorious battle against the Chinese garrisons, which had grown careless over the years. The sisters were proclaimed queens of the country. Three years later the Chinese returned with a large force. The Vietnamese committed the fatal error of confronting the Chinese invaders in the open field (not far from the spot where, almost 2000 years later, General Giap and his ill-trained followers were defeated in a battle against experienced French regulars.) Seeing their army slaughtered, the Trung sisters committed suicide by throwing themselves into the Hat River.

Two more unsuccessful rebellions followed, one of which was also led by a woman. While the powerful Tang Dynasty reigned in China, resistance was hopeless. The Chinese renamed the country An Nam (Pacified South), a name proclaiming the shame of their defeat, and forced Chinese civilisation upon its inhabitants. Amazingly, the Vietnamese kept their national identity despite a thousand years of oppression.

By the year 938 A.D. when China's Tang Dynasty tottered, the Viets had gathered enough strength to rid themselves of the Chinese yoke, and renamed the country Dai Co Viet (The Great Viet State).

But the expulsion of the Chinese masters did not bring peace to the people. Rival chieftains continued warfare amongst each other. The annexation of the south began with the fall of Indrapura, the beautiful Cham capital. And meanwhile the cautious Viet rulers continued paying triennial tribute to China.

The Mongolian hordes of Kublai Khan were defeated by Tran Hung Dao in the thirteenth century (a celebrated epic in Vietnam's history), a new Chinese invasion was ejected by a peasant named Le Loi, and Vietnam was the strongest state of the Indo-China peninsula by the time of the great Le monarchs in the fifteenth century. A period of brilliant progress followed, during which arts, craft, agriculture and commerce flourished.

A general, discontented about his emperor's pre-occupation with cultural aspects, assassinated Le Cung Hoang in 1527. This brought the country to civil war that, except for brief spells of unity, lasted for almost two centuries. The feudal Trinh lords ruled the northern part, while the south was occupied by the Nguyen rulers, both claiming to protect the interests of the Le pretender.

In 1630, the Nguyen built two huge walls across the Quang Tri plain — barely a few miles north of the present dividing line, the 17th parallel. Thus, for over 100 years, the country was divided. The Nguyen continued the conquest of the Mekong Delta. At the same time, Western missionaries arrived to bring Christianity to Vietnam and one of them, Father Alexandre de Rhodes, invented the present Vietnamese writing.

In 1772, the misery of the peasants started a revolt in Central Vietnam, led by three brothers from Tay Son, a village near An Khe. After many battles they defeated the Nguyen. The most brilliant of the Tay Son brothers adopted the name Nguyen Hue. He then conquered the Trinh and smashed a powerful Chinese invasion force, considered the greatest military feat in the history of Vietnam.

The last of the original Nguyen family, Nguyen Anh, had flown to Thailand after his defeat by the Tay Son brothers. He had a loyal friend in a French missionary, Monseigneur Pigneau de Behaine. Nguyen Anh sent this missionary to France, together with his son

Prince Canh, to ask help from Louis XVI to recover his kingdom. In 1786 the unity of the Tay Son brothers began to break up. Nguyen Anh profited from this situation, returning from Thailand with his loyal troops. In July 1789, ships arrived carrying three hundred buccaneer-type French adventurers, and supplies for Nguyen Anh. In return he had to resign his sovereignty over Hoi-An and Con Son Island in favour of France, and had to allow the French a monopoly of trade in the Southern Territory. With the help he received in the exchange, Nguyen Anh re-unified his country. In 1802 he proclaimed himself king and mounted the throne as emperor Gia Long. He established his capital at Phu Zuan (Hue) and changed his country's name to Viet Nam.

The captured Tay Son families and their generals were given atrocious treatment before being killed by the 'torture of the elephants'.

Gia Long's internal politics brought back peace, but continued the dictatorship of absolute monarchy, and was impermeable to progress. He used Western help to recover his position, but did not try to profit by the contact in order to modernise his country in conformity with the contemporary trends. Asia, with its immense resources in manpower, its huge prospective consumer market and its backyard economy, held a great attraction for the Western world. By requesting French assistance, Gia Long unwittingly opened the door to an excellent opportunity for France to establish trade bases in Vietnam.

But the Imperial Court did not adapt to the situation which it had permitted to come about. A flexible policy, giving satisfaction to the French need for trade outlets would have been of benefit to Vietnam's economy. With early gradual modernisation, the nation would have increased its power of resistance to foreign domination. But the Nguyen maintained the traditional policy — authoritarianism, discrimination and isolationism.

Poverty and misery brought on popular revolts. Instead of co-ordinating the nation against the invading French, the Imperial Court asked for French help to put down internal revolts. Emperor Tu Duc surrendered to the French with the Treaty of 1862, in order to have more soldiers at his disposal. France's armed intervention resulted in the establishment of a protectorate over the whole territory of Vietnam.

Although their administrative policies led to deep resentment by the Vietnamese, the French did much to advance the standard of living in Vietnam. They built canals, dykes, roads and railroads, churches and hospitals. Crops were fostered and vast areas of farmland irrigated. The Pasteur Institutes throughout Vietnam were

largely instrumental in stopping the recurrent outbreaks of epidemics of smallpox, cholera and other diseases which had plagued
the nation. Many Vietnamese were sent to France for advanced
education. A small middle-class emerged, consisting mainly of businessmen and intellectuals. Nevertheless, the Vietnamese were no
more content to live under French rule than they had been under
the Chinese.

Their spirit of independence, though trampled on for centuries,
had not died. Many brave resistance leaders, too many to be mentioned here, attempted to free the country, but all plots and uprisings failed.

In 1941, the Japanese Forces came to control Indo-China and a
group known as the Viet Minh took advantage of the conflicting
situation, and rallied a large following. French and American officers
parachuted into the Viet Minh Zone and began their underground
activities against the Japanese. The Viet Minh gave the signal for
general attack on 13 August 1945, when news had reached them of
a pending Japanese surrender to the Allies. On 16 August, the Viet
Minh announced formation of the 'National Liberation Committee
for Vietnam' and for the first time Ho Chi Minh was introduced
to the people.

Three days later Ho's forces took Hanoi and Emperor Bao Dai
abdicated. Ho's forces were largely supplied with US arms, and the
Americans backed his stand against French rule in Vietnam. On
2 September 1945, Ho Chi Minh proclaimed the 'Democratic Republic of Vietnam', with himself as president.

On 6 March 1946, an agreement was signed in which France
recognized the DRVN as 'a free state with its own government,
parliament, army and treasury, forming part of the Indochinese
Federation and the French Union'. The French troops still in
Vietnam were to be withdrawn gradually, complete withdrawal to
be accomplished by 1952.

But acts of hostility and incidents of armed violence between the
Viet Minh and French settlers and military still residing in Vietnam
nevertheless continued, and on 19 December 1946, President Ho
ordered a general attack against the French. The Indo-Chinese War
had started. And it was to last seven and a half years, during which
time several hundred thousand soldiers and civilians lost their lives.

Faced with the superior French forces, Ho's troops immediately
withdrew into the highlands. They adopted the guerilla strategy of
Mao Tsetung, attacking isolated units, and sabotaging, harassing
and terrorising the enemy while avoiding major battles.

After the Communist Revolution in China in 1949, Peking provided the DRVN with military equipment, supplies, and training

for their growing army. Heavy use of Chinese Communist artillery and massive attacks resulted in the defeat of the French at Dien Bien Phu on 8 May 1954. Ten weeks later the Geneva Accord ended hostilities in Indo-China. Vietnam was divided at the 17th parallel. The South became the Republic of Vietnam, under the leadership of Bao Dai, followed by Ngo Dinh Diem, with Saigon as its capital. The North became the Communist-controlled Democratic Republic of Vietnam, with Hanoi as its capital. The Geneva Accord provided for free elections to be held throughout both parts of Vietnam in 1956, to enable the population to determine which ruler they wanted to follow.

Diem, backed by the United States, refused to let the elections take place in South Vietnam, well aware of the difference between his popularity and that of Ho Chi Minh. In protest, guerilla groups formed in the south, supported by their comrades in North Vietnam.

The Southern regime called for US assistance and history is now repeating itself in Indo-China.

# I

## *THE TARNISHED PEARL*

Vung Tau beach — the ocean calm, murky and swarming with jellyfish.

Nevertheless, the water was the only refuge from the searing heat thrown back off gleaming sand, so I put on my goggles and paddled through layers of small rippling waves, watching for poisonous tentacles as I went.

I dived, surfaced and almost collided with a man.

'Hullo there . . .'; a banal enough opening sentence from him.

*How green his eyes are*, I thought as I gave a casual 'Hi' in response, then turned and swam towards the beach.

He followed.

'You a nurse or something . . . or maybe from one of the embassies?'

There was a definite Aussie drawl.

He was deeply tanned, and jet-black hair clung Napolean-fashion to his head. Almost at the beach, I found my feet on the sea-bed, half-turned, and caught the look of surprise on his face as I briefly answered, 'Neither. I'm a freelance photographer.' I joined my friends on the beach and forgot him.

After all, I had more on my mind than those lonely soldiers who tried to strike up a conversation with one of the few English-speaking females in Vietnam.

At that time men, to me, had only one use. . . . I judged them solely by the value they would have as subjects for my camera lens: Depressed faces staring through pouring monsoon rains, the agony of war portrayed on the distorted features of the wounded, bodies that were twisted in death or crouched behind bushes for protection; ghostly silhouettes disappearing into the morning mist on patrol; the joy shown on the face of a soldier reading a letter from home; the sympathy of a medic treating a sick child.

Other than that, men had become of little importance to me.

Not that I was a career-minded female who had come to Vietnam to leech on the misery of others, building up a reputation as a war photographer. Quite the contrary — I had come to Vietnam to join my charming but restless French husband, Jean, and my first few weeks there were spent as a housewife in Saigon.

That was all I ever wanted to be — a housewife. For me, being married to an adventurous husband, whose aim in life seemed to be travelling from place to place, was excitement enough . . . especially when it landed us in a spot like Saigon with war raging around us.

The Pearl of the Orient — that was Saigon's sobriquet. The dirtiest, foulest pearl one would ever care to see. Dirt, bad smells and over-crowding was nothing new to me. . . . I'd been in India and had seen plenty of that. The difference was that I had been warned what to expect before I went to India, but friends in France who knew Saigon had envied me the prospect of going there, and had longed to return to its beauty. Those friends had been there befo  the start of the 'Vietnam Incident'.

If Graham Greene and Somerset Maugham had sat on the terrace of the Continental Hotel in recent days, it is doubtful if they would have recognised the city they knew and immortalised. Even Tu Do, Saigon's main street leading from the Majestic Hotel by the river past the Caravelle Hotel to the Cathedral, was littered with foulsmelling garbage, human excrement, used sanitary napkins. The only pseudo-bright spots were the garish bars, neon-signs flashing Las Vegas-style names: Stardust, Flamingo, Playboy. Young Vietnamese girls hovered in the doorways, some pretty in their native ao-dais, others pathetic in copies of American frocks — designed for a Jane Mansfield, but here hanging flatly on Twiggies. They had one aim: American dollars, the maximum they could get for a minimum of giving. Greed for dollars had infected the cab and cyclo drivers too. Their famous 'I-have-been-robbed' act took on new frenzy as they shouted angrily after their GI customers. Saigon's dignity and mystery drowned in a sea of green bills.

Dollars brought more than double the official exchange rate for anyone willing to take a chance and dispose of them other than through a bank. While the official rate was 72 piastres to one US dollar, you could get anything up to 200 piastres at an Indian book or perfume store ('going to the Bank of India' was a popular expression), or at a dingy little Chinese tailor's shop in Cholon. There were many willing to take the chance of being caught, even though detection meant heavy-handed bribing of officials if the blackmarketeer wanted to keep out of Vietnamese jails (which most of them did, because the jails were rightly described as hell on earth).

During my first few weeks I had little to do but wander around the

Typical scene of my district: Taxis, cyclos, vendors, *boyess* with straw hat, Chinese women with bound feet, girl in ao-dai.

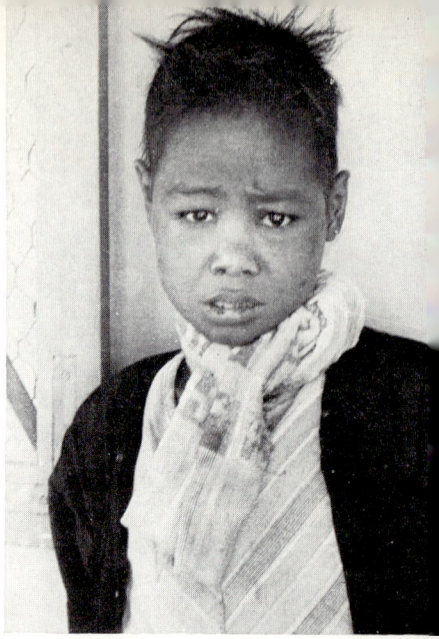

Montagnard woman whom I taught to prepare a baby's bottle.
Dr Harveson's jungle boy: the eyes of a frightened animal.
Light filters through the bamboo walls of a Montagnard longhouse.

The Boudoir.
The Lone Marine. (*AP Photo*)

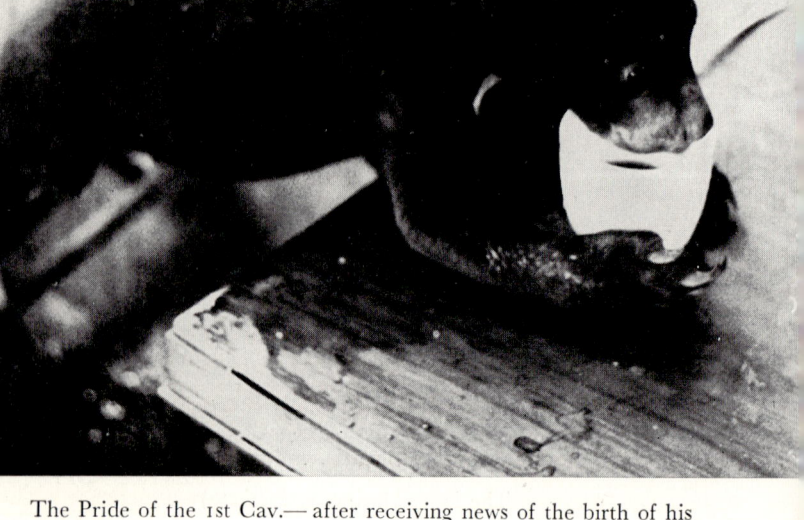

The Pride of the 1st Cav.— after receiving news of the birth of his
ninth child.
During Saigon riots a boy challenges the lens with raised hand.
Uncle Sam cures his hangover with coffee.

streets soaking up the atmosphere, watching thousands of refugees who teemed in from villages in battle zones to seek the comparative safety of Saigon. Side streets and alleys were packed with them. Few were lucky enough to have relatives with room to spare for them; the others lived on sidewalks, their meagre goods stuffed into a burlap bag or a cardboard box.

They cooked at the roadside on primitive terracotta stoves, squatted there to eat what they had prepared, washed their laundry in tin buckets and threw the dirty water into the gutters to wash away the excreta they had deposited there.

They had nowhere else to go.

Some, even amidst the appalling conditions, maintained a certain personal dignity despite the indignity of their life. On Bac-Si Yersin Street, near Central Market, I saw one old man carefully spread a piece of newspaper on the edge of the pavement, squat to attend to Nature's needs, then wrap the result in a neat parcel to be tossed into the gutter.

Saigon had no public toilet facilities for such people as these.

'Outdoor cafes' in Saigon were the sidewalk meals cooked on small fires in carts standing at the edge of the pavement or transported there in baskets suspended from poles, and sold to workers and refugees. A few piastres would give these people their daily meals. I used to walk past soup-wagon pedlars pushing their hand-carts through town and idly watch the customers who paid for and ate their meal on the spot.

I had no way of knowing then that the time would come when I would gladly hand over a few coins for my daily meal like these refugees. When that happened I was an object of more curiosity to them than they had ever been to me for a Western woman who regularly bought her meals on the streets was an unbelieveable sight.

The area Jean and I lived in swarmed with refugees and was a regular hangout for the cyclo pedallers who lived on the streets of the downtown district. Our building stood on Nguyen Van Sam, across the street from No. 2 Police Station, and around the corner from the most famous Black Market housed in the walls of a burned-out theatre. Two blocks north was Central Market where executions took place, and two blocks to the south was Rach Ben Nghe, a side-arm of Saigon River. Across this river, from our fourth-storey roof-top garden, we could watch the action through strong field glasses in the early evening, just as people elsewhere might watch TV at suppertime. How detached I was then, and how unaware that soon I'd be in the midst of such action, and that my indifference, my detachment, my sheer ignorance would give way to fear, anger, frustration — and compassion.

3

Our apartment building wasn't much by Western standards but compared to the crowded ramshackle housing that surrounded us it stood out conspicuously. Even then, at the beginning of 1965, it was difficult to find accommodation in Saigon. Our quarters were upstairs on the first floor and consisted of a huge studio apartment with a blue-tiled floor. Two prized assets of the apartment were its hot water system and an air-conditioner next to the bed. During the irregular functioning of the electricity both were a boon.

We also had Chi Hai, our quiet, friendly little Vietnamese 'boyess' (maid). For the equivalent of $10 a month she kept the place clean and helped me shop at the market for food. I prepared the meals myself, as Jean liked my cooking.

But I guess even his favourite dishes couldn't keep someone as unstable as Jean,—and the day came when I returned from one of my excursions about town to find a note.

He had gone.

I had known about his escapades with local bargirls but never thought he would leave me, just like that.

I sat down and had a good long cry, then bathed my swollen face in cold water and took stock of my situation. My purse revealed the equivalent of $2.40 and the rent was due the following week. It cost us almost US$100 for rent even allowing for exchange at the black market rate.

That evening I got half a bottle of whisky from the huge stock Jean had left behind, drank it, and passed out on the bed. The next few days are nothing more than a hazy memory. I systematically emptied the bottles he had left, pouring the contents into water glasses and gulping them down. Whisky, gin, vodka (some liquors I actually disliked), down they all went. I vaguely remember talking to my reflection in the bathroom mirror, tearing my hair at the base of my skull where it felt as though it would burst open, passing out on the bed . . . reviving and reaching for yet another drink. Finally came the morning when I looked in the mirror and saw an old woman of sixty. That was the end of that episode.

I stared at my image and realised that, if I looked like that, people could easily say that Jean was right to leave me. After standing under the shower for a long time, I swayed downstairs and bought a bowl of soup from a street stand.

I didn't care about the staring neighbourhood. I hadn't eaten anything solid and warm for days and was feeling sicker than I had ever felt in my life before. At first the covert glances from passers-by were undisguisedly hostile, and muttered remarks indicated that some watchers thought I was completely out of line following their example, eating from the sidewalk stalls. But the streets of the poor have an efficient grapevine system and word soon got around that my husband had moved out and I was flat broke. Spreading of the news was inevitable from the moment I told Chi Hai that I couldn't afford to keep her as my maid any longer — a foreigner doing her own housework was unheard of in Vietnam. People in the streets became used to my presence and quite friendly when they realised I was there, like them, through sheer necessity. Quite a few spoke French, many of them fairly fluently, as they had worked on plantations or served under the French regime.

The day after I pulled myself together I went looking for a job. Finding one wasn't easy because I simply wasn't trained for anything. In Canada I had worked as a research writer for CBC educational programmes — but my typing wasn't good enough for secretarial work. And Embassy or USAID posts, even had they been available, called for shorthand. Sales personnel and similar jobs were filled by Vietnamese employees . . . the salaries paid to them wouldn't meet half my monthly rent bill.

I started doling out my resources in pennies — saving even these by living on two bowls of soup a day, bought for eight cents each at the street stall outside my apartment building.

I walked miles through town, hitched rides on American jeeps whenever possible. Fortunately casual invitations to have a drink with the GIs came very easily. The boys patronised their military clubs and liked to have company. And when I was hungry I only had to murmur something about going home to eat, and my escorts would wave for a hamburger or a more substantial meal to be brought to the table. Nevertheless it was a hand-to-mouth existence, with little prospect of security. My first break came when Captain Canty, officer in charge of AFRS* asked, 'Would you be interested in handling a broadcast session for the troops? It's a request programme, and I'm sure they'd love to hear a female voice from this end. We need an answer to Hanoi Hanna.'† He was quite frank about the job's limitations: 'We don't have a budget to pay for it, so there'll be no salary. But at least you can eat in the mess with us. That will save you money.'

It was fun. I was so lacking in experience that a disc jockey would have recoiled in horror just listening to me — but the men loved it. The programme was called 'Marlene' and though I'd had no broadcasting experience at all I just took a deep breath, thought of the troops as 'one man', and started talking to him.

The letters that came in proved it was the right approach.

*Armed Forces Radio Service.
†A female broadcaster on the other side who was being used as a propaganda weapon; the Tokyo Rose of Vietnam.

Dear Miss Marlene, You don't know what your sweet voice does to us out here in the foxholes — and I hope you don't know what we are doing to you. . . . — Dear Miss Marlene, When you said 'lean back and relax to an hour of your favourite music' I forgot where I was sitting right then, and ended up with my back in the mud, too.

After getting that one I readjusted my remarks and said things like 'Kick off your muddy combat boots and make yourself as comfortable as possible out there'.

Some wanted letters in reply to theirs, some sought photographs. Doing the programme answered one part of my current problem. AFRS was located on the first floor of the Brink BOQ, a block from the Continental Hotel and I could walk there from my place in about fifteen minutes. There was a coffee machine in the front office, complete with biscuits, and someone would take me to the rooftop restaurant for lunch. They also supplied me with necessities such as soap, shampoo and cigarettes from the PX.

At least I was eating. I still needed a paying job to meet my long overdue rent, and although fortunately my French landlord was understanding, I couldn't expect his patience to last forever.

At the Associated Press office Ed White, the bureau chief, gave me a glimmer of hope: 'We could use someone like you around here — translating from French to English when Government officials are interviewed, doing some research into background material for articles. And there's need for a bit of book-keeping. You could probably handle it all right but I'll have to get the OK from New York first.'

The answer, when it came, was a curt, 'No women staffers for Vietnam.' I sat down at a desk and cried. I'd built all my hopes on that job.

Horst Faas, the sturdy German in charge of AP's photo department, took pity on me. 'Do you have a camera?' he asked. 'And can you take a picture worth a damn?'

His idea of a good picture probably differed from mine since he'd recently won the Pulitzer Prize for photography.

But I was desperate: I had an old Kodak Retina IIIc, and people had always liked my photos. My travels with Jean had given me experience in building a bluff on more flimsy platforms than that. So Horst Faas gave me four rolls of film and the first of my instructions: 'Go down on Nguyen Hue and photograph GIs buying those crappy souvenirs. Get names, ranks, home towns. If the pictures are any good we'll buy them for use in the boys' hometown papers.'

On Nguyen Hue I felt conspicuous and embarrassed. The Vietnamese street photographers who worked there gave me odd glances, suspecting I was trying to take their business away. They were friendlier when I explained my pictures were for American newspapers.

I snapped away happily and wrote down details.

Horst liked the pictures and I had a month's rent in my pocket. 'You could take more shots around the camps if you like. You know, human interest stuff. Guys unwrapping parcels from home, filling sandbags, feeding stray dogs, playing with Vietnamese kids.'

My old Kodak might have served to get me into the scene but it certainly wasn't the answer for a permanent set-up.

Ed White came to the rescue. He knew someone who had a Nikon F he wasn't using — and the owner was willing to sell cheaply and let me pay it off as my money came in.

It took a day to get my MACV accreditation (the press card which allowed me to enter camps and use military transportations) and the next day I was on a night flight to Danang, the only place in Vietnam with a regular Press Centre.

The C130 arrived at 11.30 p.m.

In the shed at the airfield soldiers slept on their backpacks, waiting for further orders. The troops I had come with flopped wherever there was room while I sat on the only chair, waiting for transportation from the airstrip to the Press Centre.

It took nearly two hours to arrive — a jeep driven by a Captain of Mexican origin.

'Jesus, lady, you *are* for real!' he exclaimed when he saw me.

He was apologetic about the delay and quite nervous at the sight of me.

'They told us a woman was waiting for a lift but we thought someone was having us on. The guard kept phoning back to ask when we were coming . . . and we finally realised that maybe it wasn't a joke, so we'd better check it out.'

And then I heard for the first time the question which was to be repeated a thousand times: 'What the hell makes a girl like you come to a place like this?'

Too tired to launch into explanations, I yawned, and he didn't press the question.

He glanced at me, dressed in my usual street clothes.

'The jeep's a bit dirty,' he said dubiously. 'How come you aren't wearing fatigues?'

I explained I had none, and he remedied that next day by getting me a set of fatigues and a pair of jungle boots, 'the only sensible outfit out here'.

Danang Press centre, situated on the riverbank, consisted of a few barracks with cots, an office for the PIO*, and a small restaurant

*Press Information Officer.

with a bar, a jukebox and two poker machines.

At breakfast I met several journalists and one asked, 'You coming on the medical am-track mission with us?'

I was willing; a medical mission sounded harmless enough.

A half-hour ride on a weapon-carrier brought us five journalists and the several marines in the party to the amphibious vehicles based at a camp outside Danang.

Monsoonal rain was pelting down as we left and a marine handed me a poncho.

'Riding inside or on top, lady?'

Asked what difference it made he drawled, 'Waal . . . if you sit inside you keep dry but you get roasted alive if we hit a mine going downriver. Sitting on top you get mighty wet and you could get hit by a sniper . . .'

I began to have second thoughts about the harmlessness of a medical mission. Wondering if he was exaggerating I challenged him: 'Surely they wouldn't hurt anyone on a medical mission, would they?'

'Oh, it's not so much us they're after ma'am,' he assured me. 'But Charlie* pays 50,000 piastres for every am-track destroyed, and that's more than an entire sampan village earns in six months. So you just figure things out for yourself. . . .'

I sat on top of the am-track, scared stiff every mile of the way.

As we trailed through rice paddies children and peasants spotting me crouched among the marines laughed and pointed, exclaiming, 'Ba, Ba!' ('A woman!')

I smiled, waved back, and hoped they weren't too keen on earning that 50,000 piastres.

After about two miles of caterpillaring our way over the dirt trail the am-tracks rolled down the bank into the river. They submerged, leaving about a foot above the surface. Waves splashed over us: luckily the other journalists had provided me with a plastic bag for camera equipment and film; they'd been on these missions before and knew what to expect.

At our destination outside the sampan village, two am-tracks halted while a third stood guard a bit further up the river. The Vietnamese interpreter's voice boomed through a loud-speaker telling the villagers to bring their sick to the medics for treatment.

I began photographing small sampans detaching themselves from the larger ones the people lived in and swarming towards us, then snapped the medics treating the people, mainly children, on top of the vehicles. My fears vanished as I worked. Meals with the poor

*Despite claims by other journalists, in my time many fighting men referred to the VC as Charlie.

in the streets of Saigon had given me a feeling of alliance with these people and I was pleased to see they also warmed quickly towards me.

Soon I was regularly accompanying various units on missions, a strange twist of fate for someone who had wanted only to be settled and content with her husband — but who had been unexpectedly launched into a career as a war photographer.

Whenever I wasn't out on a field assignment I spent my Sundays on Vung Tau Beach. A fashionable resort in French times, it was now the R&R centre for forces in Vietnam, including the Viet Cong who mingled anonymously with the local population. There was no fighting at Vung Tau, except for the occasional clashes between 'Friendly Forces' — such as a GI and a Vietnamese Ranger shooting it out over the favours of a local bargirl.

The town beach, called Front Beach, was too polluted for swimming but a short distance away were miles of pure sandy beaches, called Back Beach by the troops, with huge dunes stretching almost to the water's edge. An unwritten law divided the beach into several sections. Nearest the town was French Beach with the picturesque Black Rock rising like a fortress out of the water. The remnants of the French colony spent their weekends there. A little further, lined with an array of fly-covered huts where they served drinks and excellent salt-and-pepper fried crab was Vietnamese Beach. Then came the American R&R Beach with its Beachcomber Restaurant serving hamburgers, beer and soft drinks, and next to it was ROK Beach, where the Korean troops congregated. Further on still was an area of laughing and shouting — the picnic area of Aussie Beach. After that came a long barren stretch where a burned-out tank stood like a landmark.

'That tank marks our City Limits,' remarked Colonel Hempling, the US commander of Vung Tau area. 'On the other side Charlie Beach starts.' Soldiers weren't allowed to venture beyond this tank, and it also marked the turning point for speedboats and water-skiers — the limit of the safe waters.

When I arrived at the R&R Beach the following Sunday a strong wind had changed the face of the ocean. The jellyfish had gone and several soldiers were surfing on the steel-blue waves of the South China Sea.

I jumped a wave and a familiar voice drawled, 'Don't you know how to body-surf?'

Green-eyes again!

'Here — let me give you a lesson.'

Shoulders hunched and head down, he went with the wave, which

9

carried him practically to the beach. He swam back and I tried to imitate him but it was a poor attempt and I emerged coughing and spitting water.

He laughed.

'You didn't keep your head down and you must hunch your shoulders to form a hollow under your chest, like this.'

Facing me, he grabbed both my shoulders and forced them forward, making the top of my royal-blue bikini gape alarmingly.

'Yeah. I can see where you would have difficulties.'

I wrenched myself loose and jerked away from his stare.

Then I realised he wasn't being fresh — he was deadly serious. All he was seeing was my anatomical unfitness for body-surfing as he knew it. I burst out laughing. It was my first experience of the mentality of an Australian.

We stayed in the water and talked for a long time. He told me his name was Robert, and I told him mine. He talked about Kalgoorlie, where he grew up, and about Perth, the city he loved; and in return, I told him about the little town on the French-German border where I was born. Nearly two hours passed, during which we exchanged childhood memories while jumping and dodging large waves rolling towards the shore.

Our conversation was abruptly interrupted when someone shouted my name. It was one of my friends calling me from the beach. They had been alarmed at my lengthy absence and were relieved to find I had not drowned.

'Who was the fellow you were with?'

'Just an Aussie, homesick and glad to find a round-eye to talk to, like thousands of boys over here.'

The following Sunday Robert wasn't at Vung Tau Beach.

And I felt oddly, unaccountably disappointed.

# 2

## *A STORY AND A STOREROOM*

When the young private came looking for me I was sitting outside the Danang Press Centre watching sampans glide by on the river, gracefully silhouetted against the setting sun. The view was only slightly marred by the barbed wire fence which protected the compound.

'You Rena Briand?'

I nodded and he explained, 'I heard about you — and I've a friend here who'd like to meet you. He's an Australian missionary doctor and I think you might be able to help him.'

'In what way?'

'I'll take you to him if you don't mind, and he can talk it over with you.'

As he drove me to the home of the World-Wide Evangalisation Crusade, he talked about Dr Stewart Harveson, the man I was to meet. A native of Melbourne, he was treating the people of remote mountain villages in Southern China as far back as the thirties. During World War II he was practising in London and after the war he heard about the high percentage of TB among the Chinese refugees in Hong Kong, so he came out and worked for the next few years there. In the late fifties, he and his wife spent a vacation with friends in Dalat, a resort in the Vietnamese mountains. He was told about the shortage of medical help among the Montagnard tribes, which prompted him to return to Vietnam.

'His wife is getting on. She can't take the rough life in the mountain villages any more,' the private explained. 'She lives here in Danang and Dr Harveson comes down to see her every few weeks. This time he's struck trouble getting transport back to his health centre at Son Ha, and I thought you might be able to pull a few strings for him.'

Dr Harveson, tall, sensitive-featured, with thinning white hair, was amazingly soft-spoken and gentle-mannered for a man who had led such a rugged life. We talked for a long time and he told me about his life among the tribal people, while his wife served coffee and home-made biscuits.

The doctor showed me a couple of dozen cases stacked in one of the rooms.

'That's stuff badly needed at Son Ha — medicine, vitamins, bandages, soap . . . all sorts of things that have been received from various organisations. I've been trying for weeks to find space on a military flight going there but they say there's none available. My friend thought you might succeed where I have failed.'

I promised to do my best, and next morning saw the PIO.

'What's your biggest worry at the moment?' His reception would not have been as cheerful and casual if he'd had any idea of what I had in mind.

I wasn't about to let him know the full story, not all at once. Somehow I had an idea he'd turn thumbs down unless I eased him into it.

'I want to do a story on a missionary doctor at Son Ha. Any chance of arranging transportation up there?'

'Sure — I'll see what I can do.'

Half an hour later he had me scheduled on a flight leaving that afternoon for Quang Ngai and he explained, 'I've been in touch with the PIO there and he's promised to get a chopper for the rest of the way to Son Ha. He wasn't too keen at first: the area is insecure, but there's a milk run* to the Special Forces camp nearby. I told him you were a woman reporter and he said he'd get you on it.'

'Me . . . and the doctor too, I hope.'

'What doctor?'

'I told you. I'm doing the article on Dr Harveson. Naturally I'll need to have him there too!'

'You mean he's *here*, in Danang?'

'Sure, didn't you know that?'

'You didn't say anything about it!'

'Sorry, guess I didn't make myself clear. I suppose I just took it for granted that you knew.'

More phone calls to base ops at the airfield and five minutes later he held his hand over the receiver and said, 'It's OK — they're making space for the doctor — as a favour, just for you!'

'Hey, wait a minute before you hang up. Better tell them I'll need room for about two dozen cases, too.'

'You moving up there permanently? Want us to shift your whole apartment or something?'

'Not those sort of cases. Cases of medicines and supplies.'

*A regular courier.

By then the PIO knew he was being manoeuvred and he hung up after a brief exchange with the person on the other end of the line.

'Sorry 'bout that. They say there's definitely no room. They've already taken supplies off to make room for you and the doctor. Anything else is definitely O-U-T . . . OUT!'

I shrugged and said with resignation, 'Better call them back and tell them to forget the whole thing then. The doc can't go without his medicines and there's no point in my going up without the doc. Too bad — it would have made a swell story for back home.'

I left the PIO to chew that over. I knew how much importance they attached to human-interest stories which helped to build up a good image for the US so, trusting that would have some effect, I wandered over to the bar and ordered a Vodka tonic.

I was only half-way through the drink when the PIO sauntered in and the look of sad defeat on his face told me my try had come off. 'You . . . and the doc . . . and the cases . . . the whole goddam package deal . . .'

I didn't feel one scrap guilty when he threw me a sob-story about what could happen to him if the Brass found out what he'd done.

'The day you guys wake up to the fact that a load of medicine does more for your image than a load of bullets you won't have to risk your skin for nothing any more,' I said.

Strapped tightly into the seat of the C123, Dr Harveson raised his voice above the noisy machine as he told me more of his life in Son Ha.

'I live and eat at the home of a Montagnard family there. I've spent years with them now and I like them very much. But I'm getting old and I can only take the life in limited doses. I've reached the stage where I have to go down to Danang now and again to keep my sanity.'

Despite this statement the doctor was proud of his work and contented with what he had been able to do. In addition to practising medicine he held school every evening for up to sixty children. In perfect command of the local dialect, Hrey, he made illustrated charts from which the children learned to read and write. He also translated books and stories for advanced classes. Some of the teachers and the dispensers he trained at his health centre are now in remote villages in VC territory helping the villagers there.

'When I first came to Son Ha it was very difficult to win their confidence. Even now many of them still make sacrifices to their demons and watch for signs in the smoke before they will agree to take my medicine. Unfortunately some wait too long.'

13

He sighed, then brightened as he said: 'On the credit side many of them are now Christians, and have faith in my treatment. I even had a major victory; I converted one of their sorcerers, after healing him of cholera.'

The reception the doctor received from his charges, especially the children, told me more than any of his words could have.

He had talked about three grown sons of his own. 'One in New Zealand, one doing malarial research in Gambia, one a pilot in New Guinea.' He was a grandfather, and I thought of his words as I saw the small native children swarming about him. 'I often think of my own grandchildren, whom I have never seen, when I am holding one of the little ones here.'

A painfully thin young boy, whose face looked incongrously fat because it was puffy — the common sign of malnutrition — came towards us, and stopped a few feet away, smiling very faintly at the doctor.

There was something different about him — an atmosphere which set him a little apart from the others as he stood there. It was something in his way of walking, I thought. And something, very definitely something about his eyes. There was an odd wariness about them — a tentative reaching-out, with behind that an alertness, a visible readiness to run at a wrong move in his direction: he looked exactly like a half-tamed creature none too sure of his reception, who sidles towards a human, ready to be friendly but equally ready to turn tail and flee. With a sudden shock I realised I was comparing this young boy with an animal.

Dr Harveson had noticed my gaze, and said with a slight touch of pride, 'That little fellow's doing fine, though he's still a bit skinny. We do our best to fatten him up, but he doesn't seem to put on much surplus. I'm going to give him some of the vitamins we brought up with us. Still, he's much better than he was when they brought him in — then he was just skin and bone, and he bit and scratched so much we had to lock him up. He wouldn't eat, and I thought he'd die on our hands. But that's past and done with.'

Slightly shamefaced, I said, 'To tell you the truth, he reminds me of an animal, somehow.'

Dr Harveson gave me a quick look.

'That's rather perceptive of you. I've just realised you don't know his story, of course. A patrol of Special Forces found him roaming in the jungle, up in the highlands, a few months ago. It was a recon. patrol and they were hidden in the bramble, watching for VC movements. They saw something move in the bushes, and spotted him. He was completely naked — they thought he might have been a courier for the VC . . . many quite young children are, you know

. . . so they ambushed and captured him. It took some doing. He bit and scratched and fought like a young tiger. They finally had to tie him up and carry him back. They had an interpreter question him, but he just couldn't get through to the kid. Finally they realised what they had on their hands: his animal-like behaviour, his refusal of the food they offered, the way he lapped water with his cupped hands; the boy had been living wild, on his own, surviving God alone knows how on berries and grasses. They brought him here to see what I could do with him. He improved with time, became less wary, speaks enough to communicate but he doesn't remember anything at all about his origins. He was either lost or kidnapped when he was much younger and miraculously survived up there all on his own.'

When I returned to Danang I wrote up the story of Dr Harveson. Up till then I had sold only photos and captions, but this time I had an exclusive story. There was one snag: I wasn't very familiar with the markets for what I had.

The PIO mentioned an Australian couple, both journalists who had just arrived in Danang during their six weeks' tour of Vietnam. As I had no Australian outlets, and the subject of my story was an Australian, I asked if they were interested in buying the story. I told them it was the first article I had written, and as English was not my native tongue, it would need editing and correction. They seemed interested and asked to see the article and photos. I was disappointed when they returned them to me and said they couldn't use them.

A few days later when I was back in Saigon I received a short note from the Danang PIO, who had sent it to the AP office for me:

Rena — Sorry to send you bad news. That Australian couple re-wrote your story on Harveson and contacted Mrs Harveson. She gave them some of her husband's own photos to go with it since she had no idea of the set-up. Let this be a lesson to you about the kind of cut-throat racket you're in, and don't trust anyone with your material again.

I was so let-down. My first story. And at that time even a few dollars would have meant so much to me. I felt a burning resentment against all journalists at that stage. (Later I was to find that the PIO was over-cynical in his assessment of the profession. I received a tremendous amount of help from established journalists such as Peter Arnett, John Harris and many others who unselfishly sat down and pushed and pulled my clumsy articles into shape.)

Still, all I knew that day in Saigon was bitter disappointment about losing my first story so shabbily.

In that mood I decided a long weekend in Vung Tau would make me feel better so I headed there on Saturday afternoon.

When I first started spending weekends in Vung Tau it was fairly easy to find lodgings. There were always the homes of French friends, or the dispensary of the immense Villa Anna, where the first Australian arrivals stayed, or one of the guest rooms of the former Pacific Hotel which had been converted into a BOQ (quarters for American officers).

The small resort town at the mouth of the Saigon River could be reached in twenty minutes by chopper or by car in less than three hours' drive from the capital, that is, if the VC didn't cause any hold-ups by blowing bridges or erecting roadblocks en route.

With the arrival of the American forces en masse, much of the charm of Vung Tau vanished. Shacks and bars sprang up everywhere to cater to the needs of the soldiers. They announced their trade in cheap, screaming signs. The beach became littered with waste thrown overboard from the enormous number of ships navigating to and from Saigon. As in Saigon itself, formerly attractive buildings were looking seedy, their plaster crumbling, and surrounded by barbed wire concertinaed into unsightly fences. There were sandbag walls everywhere and smelly generators set up on the sidewalks.

After the big build-up started it became impossible to find a vacant room anywhere. Many French and Vietnamese let their villas to the military at inflated prices, and hotels were crowded with permanent residents such as AID officials and surgical teams. The few rooms available were rented by the hour to eager GIs and their bargirl companions — a very profitable affair for the owners.

Several French friends of mine who still maintained residences there were so over-run with relatives and friends bringing their children to the beaches that one could hardly step inside their homes.

I was lucky inasmuch as I had friends — Christa and Ron — who let me sleep on their couch. Ron Brown, dark-haired and skinny, with a friendly smile, was a captain with the First Logistical Command stationed in Vung Tau. He had approached me one afternoon in the bar at the Pacific BOQ, told me how much he missed his wife, and asked if I'd help her to enter Vietnam.

'You see, since the evacuation of dependants I can't get her into the country officially as my wife. But she still has her German passport — and if she could give the name of a non-military person as her contact here she could get a visitor's visa. Would you agree to sign a paper stating she will stay with you?'

I have always had a romantic streak and besides I have an innate dislike of rules and regulations which interfere needlessly with a person's individual freedom. Ron didn't have to talk hard to persuade me to help put something over officialdom.

When Christa arrived I met her at Tan Son Nhut airport. She was attractive, blonde, with huge brown eyes and slim build — and so anxious to be with her husband she almost cried when we found out that the last milkrun to Vung Tau had already left. By then I knew most of the angles, however, and the sergeant in charge of maintenance was persuaded that one of the choppers needed a testflight to Vung Tau.

Within a week of her arrival Christa was working as a secretary with PA&E*, an American firm supporting the First Log, and her employers arranged for her residence permit and gave her a room with shower at their villa near Front Beach.

The Saturday after I had learned of the pirating of my story I arrived at Vung Tau, spent a few hours with Christa and watched a movie at the Pacific.

Next morning I woke at daybreak, quietly slipped into my beach wear, grabbed my bag and tip-toed out of the room without waking Ron and Christa. I wanted to get to the beach earlier than usual because I had a lunch date with my Vietnamese friend Bai and wanted to get my swim over early enough to give me plenty of time to freshen up. We had arranged to meet on the shaded terrace of the Grand Hotel — now a rundown remnant of its former French Colonial splendour.

Bai had been educated in France, and held a prominent position under the Diem regime. Even after coup d'état which overthrew Diem and his followers, Bai managed to retain certain useful connections and influence with the new ministry. I was never quite sure exactly what Bai's position was, but after talking to him over a cup of tea at one of his favourite hang-outs in Tu Do Street, it was a waste of money buying the following day's newspapers: anything worth reading in them Bai had always told me the day before. Small-framed, he was gentle of manner, with intelligent eyes and a fine sense of humour. In his company, I never felt any of the stiffness and awkwardness which often occurred with other Vietnamese of his background, so I was looking forward to a pleasant afternoon with him.

I walked to the corner of the market, about two blocks from the PA&E villa, and waved to one of the little three-wheeled Lambrettas heading in the direction of Back Beach, climbing into the covered carriage behind the driver.

These Lambrettas, which served as taxis, had a small bench on each side — space enough to hold about three broad-beamed Euro-

*Pacific Architects and Engineers.

17

peans or up to six slender Vietnamese. They pick up anyone who hails them en route, and when a passenger wants to get off, he merely signals the driver. The Vietnamese pay a minimal fare, but the drivers make up for this by levying extortion rates when foreigners climb aboard. The American troops didn't quibble at paying up to a dollar for the 'one klick' (km.) ride to Back Beach, but the drivers' demands became excessive until finally Colonel Hempling had the town mayor and police chief enforce a standard 20 piastre fee for the troops. Despite this ruling the drivers always clamoured for more, and got it, too, for many soldiers didn't want to argue.

From Central Market the wide tree-shaded street led for a few blocks past swall villas then turned towards the dirt road leading to Back Beach. Two peasant women got off at the pagoda carrying fruit and flowers in their baskets. For the rest of the trip I had the vehicle to myself, and enjoyed the view of the lotus blossoms in the swampy ponds on either side of the road. As I had anticipated, the driver looked askance at my 20 piastres and sourly demanded more. I was prepared for this, however — I had learned a Vietnamese phrase specially for the occasion. Putting on what my friends called my 'offended expression', I said in Vietnamese, 'Toi nhu My a?' (Do I look American?') He laughed, shrugged his shoulders and said something which I am sure would translate: 'Can't blame a guy for trying!'

That morning there was a slight breeze coming over the ocean, refreshing after the stickiness of the night in town. The beach wasn't crowded yet. A few familiar faces showed and a few familiar voices shouted greetings as I walked towards the inviting water running towards the beach in an easy, flowing ripple.

I have always had a sensual, intimate feeling for the ocean, a special awareness of my body when it was lapped and touched by soft ripples. Sometimes I talk to the waves in quiet murmurs, as though talking to a lover surrounding me with his warmth.

I felt his hands on my hips before I saw him. Then his head emerged and he shook the water from his face. The deep Australian drawl: 'Caught you early this morning!'

'You again!' I exclaimed. 'When you weren't around last Sunday I thought you'd left Vung Tau.'

'So you missed me. Glad to hear that.'

His green eyes shimmered.

'It was my monthly weekend on duty. But I'm due for a long weekend off soon. I thought I'd spend it giving you surfing lessons if you'd let me.'

I had a fleeting thought that I had never seen him out of the water, and as though he was reading my mind he said, 'How would

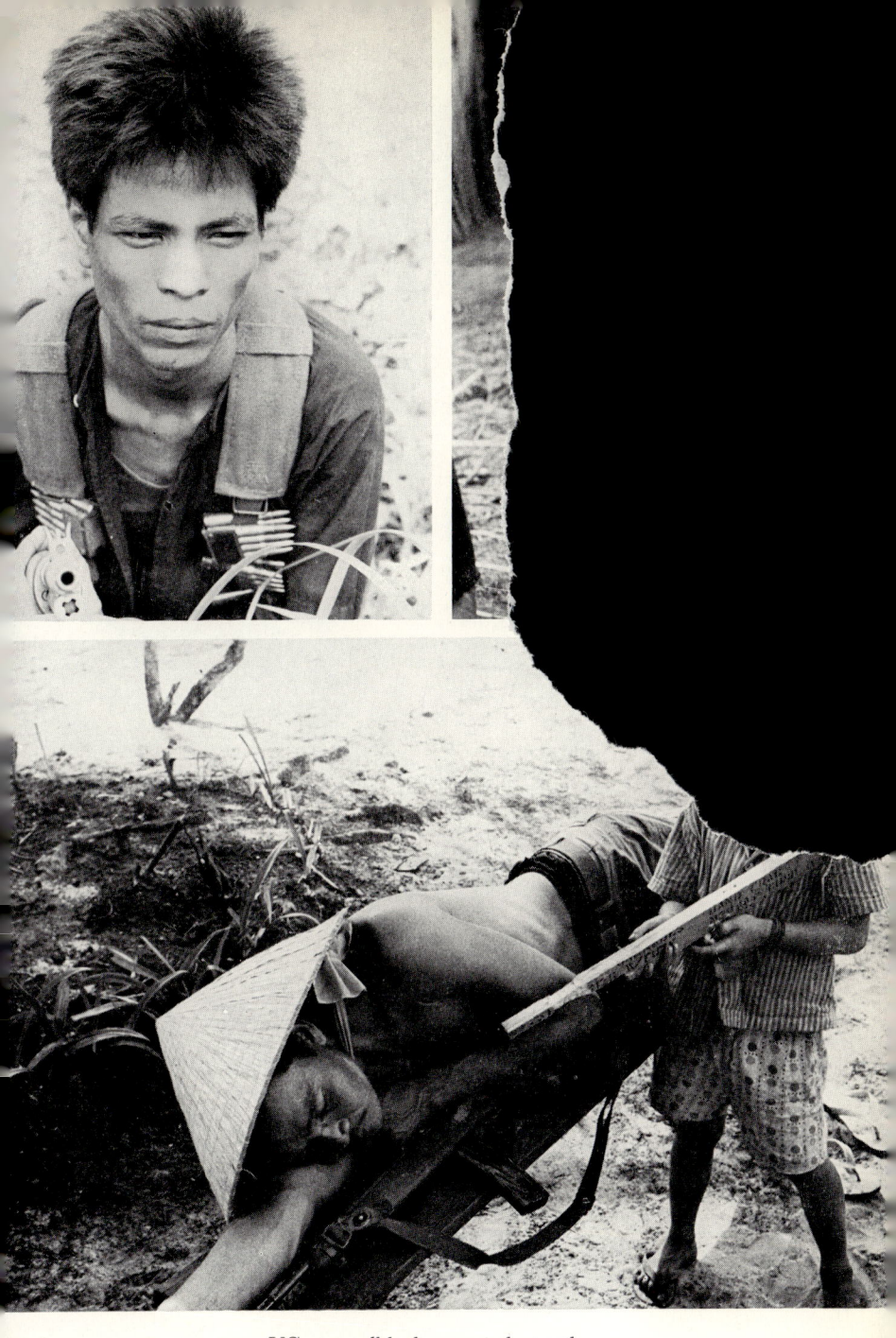

VC at roadblock poses reluctantly.
Girl at refugee camp owns no clothes.
Killing: a way of life.

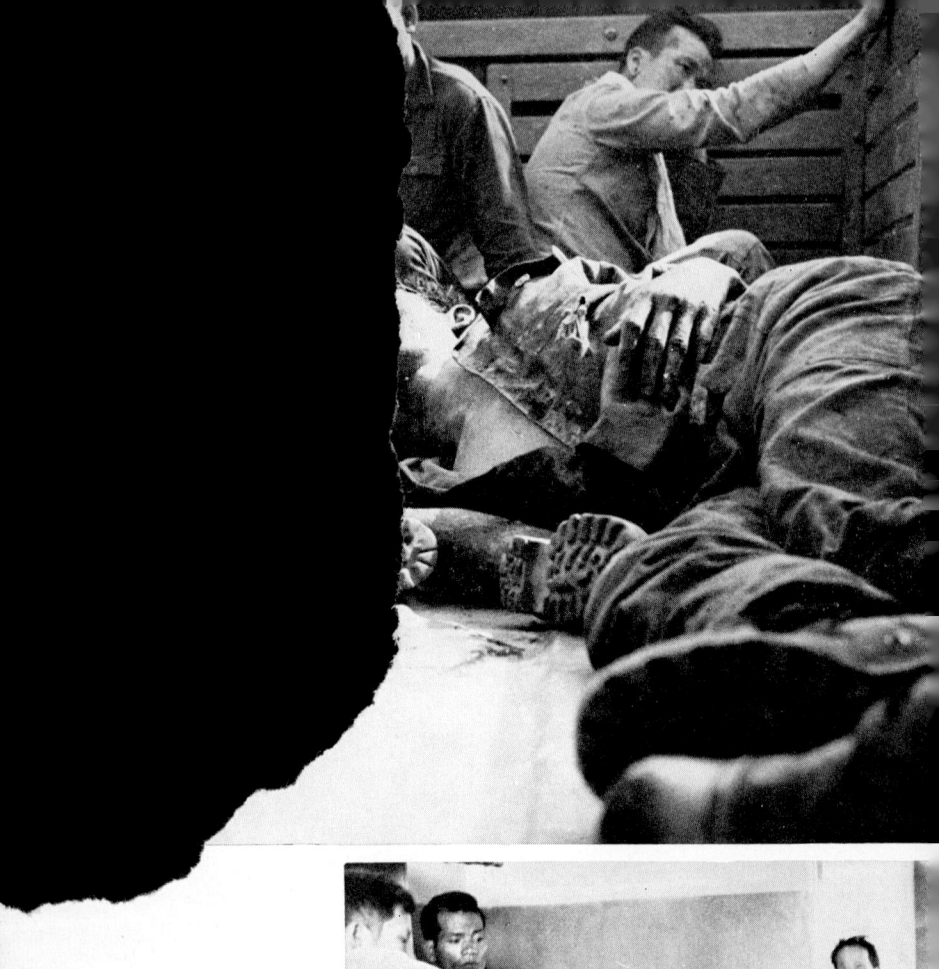

Medevac for wounded
Montagnards: by truck
to the ill-equipped hos-
pital at Gia Nhia.

Why?  (*AP Photos*)

When a bus hits a road mine. . . .

you like to join me for morning tea at the Beachcomber?'

'I didn't think they served tea — only beer and soft drinks!'

He laughed his pleasant throaty laugh.

'A figure of speech . . . pure Aussie,' he explained. 'We say morning tea the way the Yanks say midmorning snack. I really meant a hamburger and a cold beer.'

'That sounds better. I'd love to join you.'

I had to trot to keep up with him along the beach.

Unexpectedly I felt very secure walking in his shadow.

His build, his quiet, confident manner, his calm, slow way of speaking — all radiated such an incredible strength that I was suddenly immensely happy that I was a woman and that I was by his side.

The Beachcomber was a huge rectangular structure with a tin roof on which the monsoon sometimes clattered so loudly it was impossible to hear a spoken word inside. It had a concrete floor, was cheaply furnished with plastic and chrome, and was utterly devoid of atmosphere. By noon it was usually packed with GIs and their Vietnamese girl friends. At the back were the toilets and showers, but these I avoided after the first glimpse. Many of the Vietnamese were young peasant girls unfamiliar with water closets and accustomed to squatting down on the floor.

Robert led me to an empty table, bought a book of chits from the cashier and over giant-size hamburgers and cans of beer he talked about Australia. He told me about his grandfather, a real character, and product of the bush from which he sprang.

"One time he walked seven miles over the shadeless red sandy track to get to a pub for a beer. And when he got there he was so exhausted he fell asleep before the owner could get it poured for him.'

He talked about the two sisters who were married and had children — but he didn't talk about his parents and I didn't pry.

The Beachcomber began to get noisy and crowded. I was the only Causcasian female present and the soldiers started eyeing me.

'Let's go for a walk along the beach where it's quiet.'

He held my hand as we walked silently along the seemingly-endless stretch of sand towards the burnt-out tank. We walked past the Koreans, past a few Australians who shouted greetings to Robert. Again I felt so secure and protected . . . and I wanted desperately to belong to him.

In silence I walked, heavy-limbed with desire, until I heard my own voice whisper, 'I want to feel you inside me . . .' Me . . . who had always been the one who played hard to get . . . and here I was making the first advance. Robert looked at me for a long moment, his eyes warm and grateful, then he said simply, 'Yes I want it very much, too.'

He gripped my hand more firmly and we walked into the scrub-covered dunes until we came to a small pine with a lower branch which nearly touched the ground.

Underneath the branch was a small hollow similar to one where I once found a young deer bedded in the Vosges Mountain near my hometown. Brushing away a few dead twigs Robert laid me down on to the hollow and slowly removed my bikini.

His hands were steady, without the slightest tremble of anxiety or haste and their stroking over my body so utterly reassuring that I was completely calm and relaxed, savouring the moment, knowing that he would take me and use me well.

And he looked at me in silence, his eyes following his gentle caresses over my body and then he looked into my eyes and I felt — as lovers all over the world have felt — that no man and no woman had ever wanted or needed each other so much.

His skin touching mine was so agreeable to me that every cell seemed to melt, embracing as one with his. The ever-so-light odour of his skin was pleasant . . . and I was happy that I could smell his maleness, because if a man's skin is odourless one can never be sure if one really likes him: there is a lack, a loss of identity.

And when he at last took possession of me my entire body unfolded towards him, became part of him, and within seconds the ocean came over the dunes and I was drowning in a marvel of flooding warmth. My brain burst into billions of atoms and so did my entire body under that sea, and then those atoms all floated towards the surface and assembled again, and awareness returned to me.

The first thing I focused on were two green pools filled with tenderness and then I felt the heavy limp weight of his drained body and the gentle touch of his lips on my face and I knew that we were both in love.

I had never been able to abandon myself to such an extent. It was nature's sheer perfection, and perfection comes only when it is mutual.

His lips gently nibbled at my earlobe and he murmured, 'My woman.'

'My man,' I murmured back and we both laughed with sheer joy.

Minutes later I was drifting towards sleep when he gently lifted me up to put my bikini back on .

'Sorry, my love, but we can't stay here like this. If the MPs catch us we're in trouble.'

The MPs — I had forgotten all about them and the Viet Cong and the smell of blood and the sight of broken bodies. All that seemed so distant. The only real things were Robert and me.

We retraced our steps along the blazing sand which itself was alive and part of the entity I belonged to. So, too, was the sea and the plants and everything around. I was vividly, acutely aware of every individual pore and every cell functioning in my body. I felt a deep love for beings and objects I saw.

I was happy, so happy it became close to pain.

The Aussies who watched us pass had knowing expressions on their faces and I remembered the sand on my back but I didn't care. I was so proud to be his woman that I wanted to shout it.

Robert thought of the betraying sand too and at one of the large puddles the ocean had left when the tide retreated he pulled me down into the bath-warm water and washed it off.

Then we both lay in the puddle and played with the little hermit crabs, putting the tiny shells at the water's edge and watching them dash back again into the shallow depth.

I had completely forgotten my lunch date with Bai; like everything else, that had become insignificant. Only Robert mattered.

The next morning in Saigon Bai stormed into the beauty parlour where I was having my hair set. His very efficient spy-system had told him where to find me within minutes of his request for information about my current whereabouts. I stuttered an excuse about breaking our date but he laughed at my sheepish expression and exclaimed, 'Oh lala, what love!'

He waved away my excuses: 'Never mind, never mind! When you didn't turn up I thought you might have fallen asleep on the beach and I went looking for you. And there you were in a puddle with that huge male, quite oblivious to the whole world. I watched you both for a while but you didn't even see me. I felt as guilty as a voyeur.'

It was true. I hadn't seen him the previous afternoon and hadn't spared him a single thought.

Robert and I had supper at Cyrno's and afterwards, at the villa, he met Ron and Christa. I told them about us. They understood; Ron had a spare bed put in a storage room. The barren room had no facilities, but we were offered the use of the villa shower. As the room had no fan or air-conditioning the heat was near-suffocating — but at least we had privacy. We made love with that desperate need for each other which seems to become magnified in a war zone, when danger is all around and death may be expected at any moment.

21

# 3

## *LOOKING BACK*

Later that night as I lay exhausted beside him Robert asked the inevitable question: what had made me come to Vietnam as a freelance photographer?

'I didn't come for that — I was already here . . . as a housewife.'

A frown disturbed his high forehead.

'You are married?'

'Yes,' I said. 'That is, still legally married. My husband left me quite penniless in Saigon some time ago. That's why I became a photographer. I had to work to eat.'

Had I been wise I would have left it at that.

Instead, when Robert asked me where my husband was I told him the entire story.

I met Jean Briand in Montreal where I'd been living since I'd come to Canada at the age of eighteen. The mutual friend who introduced us whispered a warning — 'He's recently returned from Mexico — but please don't ask him too many questions. I think he had to leave because he ran foul of the authorities there,'— which immediately aroused my interest, naturally, and I was delighted when Jean asked me out to dinner that night.

He was tall, with blue-grey eyes and greying temples; he looked amazingly like Robert Taylor and confessed having given his autograph to teenagers on Caleta Beach when I remarked on the resemblance. Even without the hint of an interesting background he was just the sort of man to attract a susceptible female. When we danced I was smugly aware of the envious glances other women gave me.

For several weeks we dated regularly. By then I was so smitten I raised no objection to his suggestion that we live together. He was married, he told me, to a Mexican woman, but he showed me a letter from her asking for a divorce.

'As soon as that's settled if you still want me we can be married,' he assured me.

Jean was thoughtfulness itself in these first halcyon days: small presents, flowers at unexpected moments, coffee and fresh croissants in bed every morning. It was no wonder I became utterly enamoured and clay in his hands to be moulded to his will.

Heedful of our friend's warning that first day, I refrained from asking questions about his former life or his background but from time to time I garnered odd scraps of information which I hoarded. He'd been born in Normandy, left France some fifteen years earlier, spent a year in North Africa, and had lived in Latin America. Sometimes I heard the names of construction and mining firms mentioned — but all were scrappy enough pieces of information picked up at long intervals.

A minor habit of Jean's gave me his main secret. Like so many people he often doodled on a notepad while talking on the phone. One day I found a signature on the pad written over and over again — almost illegible because of the exaggerated lines and strokes. When I studied it more closely a name leaped out: Jacobs. I wondered who this Jacobs fellow was, then suddenly, for no valid reason whatever, I was almost certain it was Jean himself.

To confirm it, I engineered a huge bluff.

Jean had just bought a Corvair and we opened a bottle of champagne to celebrate our new acquisition. 'Let's baptise the car, mon chou,' I suggested. 'What name shall we give it?' Jean shrugged at my silly whim but laughed as I made several absurd suggestions.

His laughter faded and his face froze as I said casually, 'What about Jacob's Coach?'

He was silent but I outwaited him and finally he said, 'Who told you?'

I was jubilant but simply shrugged and said, 'Oh, I've got my connections!'"

'Nobody here knows,' he retorted. Then added, 'Your connections wouldn't be in Washington, by any chance?'

There is an old saying in France which translates — 'Plead the false to get the truth' and I used this technique then.

Convinced that I knew most of his story already, Jean seemed almost relieved to talk about it.

His real name was Bernard Jacobs. He had been a German collaborator during World War II and had been arrested at its end. He escaped after a wild chase over the roofs of Paris. He'd managed to get hold of the passport of a friend, Jean-Henri Briand, substituted his own photograph and reached North Africa. There, ironically, he landed a job in charge of a de-mining outfit of German POWs. When one of the mines exploded he was badly wounded by shrapnel. He would have been entitled to compensation but the investigations

23

and red tape involved were something he couldn't afford. Still weak from his injuries, he boarded a freighter at Tangier and arrived penniless in Brazil.

Dressed as a monk, he found refuge in a monastery and with his personality had little trouble wangling enough money from the good brothers to get him to Venezuela. There he became a disciple of the Mission of the Aquarius and wrote the horoscope for a local magazine.

Jean eventually landed a job with Orinoco mines. One day he returned to his room and found two men waiting there. They identified themselves as American agents and told him they were aware of his false identity. They declared they weren't interested in having him arrested and sent back to France. They had a proposition.

Nothing would happen provided he agreed to co-operate with their organisation as and when the need arose. Jean had no qualms about agreeing to that, and his story from that day on would make James Bond look like a nursemaid.

The organisation naturally knew the value of the man they had found. Jean spoke fluent Spanish without a trace of accent and his French background, good looks and sophisticated manners opened all doors to him. Whenever there was a revolution or coup d'état brewing Jean would be hovering, collecting odds and ends of information.

There were times when his luck ran out, though: in Peru being in the wrong place at the wrong time landed him in jail with a group of revolutionaries. One of his brief 'alliances' came to his rescue then: the wife of a high Government official intervened on his behalf. He had a narrower escape when Duvalier's Tonton Macoutes were after him, and he fled through a Haitian hotel window in his shirt sleeves to find refuge in the Dominican Republic.

His cover screens varied from importing Mexican beer into Haiti to negotiating with a dictator over the sale of a rusty submarine rotting off the coast of Newfoundland.

In Mexico his charmed life appeared to be taking on a fair degree of tarnish and things started going wrong. He was never quite open about what happened but he did mention that his marriage was one of convenience which enabled him to get a permanent residence permit.

The convenience wasn't strong enough to keep him with his new wife for more than a few weeks and he left her, one step ahead of three trigger-happy brothers-in-law.

He headed for Canada, made discreet overtures to Washington but at that time hadn't received any response. He seemed to regard my connections in Washington as a stroke of luck and he never doubted their existence. I was afraid he would walk out on me if I told him the truth.

Jean was still collecting scraps of information from various contacts and told me to place them in the right hands in Washington. I hoped he would forget about the whole business and settle down but I should have realised that was not Jean's way of life. He had been living for so many years on the edge of danger, had surrounded himself for so long with an atmosphere of intrigue and secrecy that it was impossible for him to think straight by then.

There were occasions when playing my own double role became decidedly uncomfortable. Like the time Jean beat up an unfortunate man who was following me. The poor fellow was only hopeful of an interesting pickup, but Jean saw more deadly signs in his interest. Then there was the time he hustled me in the car to the US Embassy and sat outside while I went in to tell them about the plot Jean had heard was brewing in Costa Rica.

I felt a fool.

One day, despite my efforts to encourage him to settle down Jean got tired of waiting for response from Washington and decided to return to Mexico and take up the threads he had left behind there.

His main contact had long since been replaced and Jean was at a loose end.

From then on it was a life of aimless, sometimes hit-and-miss adventure. For me, still as enamoured as ever, it meant trailing three steps behind him all round the globe, carrying suitcases, worrying about his false passport at border crossings, working at odd jobs — teaching French in Acapulco, selling expensive jewellery to casino patrons from a gift-counter in Las Vegas — while Jean found a 'suitable' position.

There was forever this obsession of his for collecting information which he hoped would act as the door-opener to new and important assignments with CIA. It got him into trouble, inevitably, and then I had a new role: pleading, on the verge of tears, with officials so that he would not be prosecuted. For Jean I did things I would never have done to save myself. If I ever wavered, all he had to do was to sneer, 'You say you love me so much but now that you get a chance to prove it you want to back out!' That was enough to bring me to heel. I'd do whatever he wanted.

Eventually, to my relief and delight it did seem as though he finally faced the fact that his chances of returning to the closed shop of the CIA were pretty remote and he suggested settling down in San Francisco. He got a quick Las Vegas divorce and we were married under his real name. Nobody there worried very much about official papers.

I was very happy at that period but I should have known it wouldn't last. Suddenly the CIA seemed interested in Jean again, to his great delight. He was offered a position in Vietnam, officially as purchasing agent for RMK-BRJ, the big American construction company. A few days later he was off from Travis Air Force base. I followed him via Europe where I visited our respective families en route, arriving in Vietnam several weeks after he did.

In Saigon it soon became obvious that I had served my purpose . . . I was no longer needed. Not as a permanent chain. I spent many long, lonely evenings in that strange city while Jean joined his buddies from RMK who were living it up with the local bargirls.

I tried to tell myself that this was just a passing phase — the inevitable result of his being alone for two months in a city like Saigon with its temptations and free-and-easy living. The cronies Jean was associating with made me shudder. Apart from a few adventurous types, RMK was manned by many heavy drikers and people who couldn't get jobs easily elsewhere. Sometimes I suspected the office hiring RMK executives was trying to clean out San Francisco's Mission Street, where all the bums and alcoholics hang out!

This then was the circle in which Jean was moving and I seemed to make him feel guilty. More than once he suggested I return to Canada, offering to send me money every month. But I wasn't prepared to be bought off and hung around hoping against hope that he would change again. The hope lasted until the day I came home and found a note. Jean had moved out and joined two of his cronies in a flat on Duy Tan and I was left with less than three dollars to my name.

After a good cry I bathed my eyes and went to his office, telling him bluntly that I needed money for food and rent.

I got a cold reception.

'I told you to leave the country. I don't want you hanging about here. If you get an exit visa with a non-return clause I'll give you a ticket to any place you want to go plus $2000.00 in cash at the airport. If you insist on staying here you don't get a cent!'

After all our time together Jean obviously didn't know me very well. Nothing he could have said would have been more calculated to make me dig my heels in and stay. I wasn't going to run away whimpering like a dog that had had a pail of water thrown over it. But it was a bitter pill to swallow and after leaving Jean's office, despite the show of defiance put on for his benefit, I headed back to the flat and reached for a bottle.

I survived, but it was a humiliating, hand-out sort of existence and I felt it keenly and bitterly. There was the nagging pain of having lost my husband just when everything seemed so secure. There was the additional humiliation of hearing about his escapades around the bars, and of knowing that the break-up of our marriage was the talk of the French colony.

I drank a lot in those days, often in the company of journalist friends at the Caravelle bar. Bitter about the whole situation, I told anyone who happened to ask casually how I came to be in Saigon the whole unvarnished story — whether he wanted it or not! Jean, his work for the CIA, his false passport . . . I spilled the lot to anyone who would listen.

There was one drawback: it had such an air of unreality, such a text-book similarity to popular paperback novels that many people found it hard to believe. But I knew; and I knew that Jean knew. He had hurt me deeply and I was hurting him back in the only way I could. Then Jean made another false move. He used his influence with the Immigration department to stop my visa being renewed unless he signed his consent. That was a declaration of war!

At that time the Chief of Immigration was Captain De and I had a long talk with him about my problem. He seemed sympathetic and even went so far as to summon Jean to his office while I was there, trying to effect a reconciliation. Jean refused quite viciously and left in a rage. This last insult was too much to bear and I made up my mind to fight back with every means that came to hand till in the end it would be Jean who had to leave the country, not me.

I still had a spare key to Jean's desk at RMK, where he kept his passport, not the one he had used to leave France with, but a Canadian passport he had obtained by using the birth certificate of a Canadian named Jean-Yves Briand.

During Jean's lunch hour I went to his office, opened his desk and took out his papers, going immediately to the British Embassy, who handled Canadian affairs in Vietnam. I told them the entire story and handed over the passport.

The Consul listened quietly, examined the passport then gave it back to me with the comment, 'The passport looks perfectly all right to me, and we have no authority to keep it. We will check with Ottawa and proceed according to the result of their investigation. Meanwhile please return the passport to your husband's desk.'

I had no quarrel with his statement that the passport looked perfectly all right. It was, inasmuch as it had been issued in Ottawa. I thought he had missed the point and said firmly, 'But don't you understand. My husband shouldn't have this passport. His name is *not* Jean Briand. The real Jean Briand is somewhere in Canada, a lumberjack. My husband obtained his birth certificate in order to get this passport.'

27

From his expression it was clear that the Consul didn't believe me. To him, no doubt I was the woman scorned, prepared to make up any fantastic tale just to cause inconvenience and annoyance to her husband.

I had to make a convincing and definite move. In front of his horrified eyes I tore the passport to shreds. 'There,' I said with considerable satisfaction. 'Before you can issue a new one you'll have to make some investigations!'

The Consul ushered me out — he thought he was dealing with someone whose real place was in an asylum!

Two weeks later I got an entirely different reception. They had discovered my story was true, and there was a Mr Miller available with a sudden interest in all I knew about Jean and his activities.

Meanwhile I had talked to RMK's manager, but my friend Lloyce Proctor, secretary to RMK's personnel manager, said a mystery man had visited the office, produced a badge, and told them to cease all investigations concerning Jean.

I was also making daily trips to a fellow at the US Embassy who seemed a little friendlier than the others, and kept bending his ear on the subject of the 'great USA' backing a man who'd leave his wife penniless in Saigon.

To all suggestions about leaving the country I was deaf.

Eventually, because of the stink I had caused and the pressing investigations of the British Embassy there was nothing left for Jean but to leave the country. With a paper in lieu of a passport he reached San Francisco. He wasn't able to stay there — exposed and useless to the CIA who notoriously don't know an agent once he is in trouble, he was deported to France. I knew he would be under an amnesty so would come to no great harm there.

I felt damn good. I, who had been deserted and left penniless in a strange country had won out against him, even though at that time he had the backing of the powerful CIA.

'I'm surprised they let you get away with it,' Robert said. 'From what I've heard of them they don't usually like anyone to tread on their toes, especially for what they regard as petty personal reasons.'

'That's right. But I was in a pretty secure spot at the time. After all, I didn't have false papers, so there wasn't much they could do about me officially. But it was a messy way to part after having shared years with someone. Now I just want to forget about the past.'

# 4
## THE LONE MARINE

Colonel Kelly, commanding officer of the 1st Bn 7th Marines at Chu Lai, looked definitely unhappy.

'It's not that you're not welcome here,' he explained, 'but the camp's still primitive and we don't have facilities for quartering women journalists.'

I calmed him down.

'No sweat, Colonel, I'm used to roughing it and I'll only be here for a couple of days. AP wants some pics for the Christmas editions back in the States. You know, PR shots, Marines in foxholes reading Xmas cards from home, putting up stars on the mortar positions, and all that. Your unit has such a terrific reputation I asked if I could come here. So please find a little corner somewhere for me to sleep in.'

One thing my stay in Vietnam taught me was that flattery can get you most places, especially when you are dealing with the Brass. And the Brass counted if you wanted your stories.

The rank-and-file were a piece of cake: they were always so glad to see a female around that they'd twist themselves into pretzels to please you. The boys with bars and chickens on their shoulders were different: they looked with a jaundiced eye on the prospect of having a woman turned loose amongst thousands of soldiers under battle conditions. They were constantly worried in case something might happen and they'd get the blame. I was never quite sure whether they were more worried about the 'something' happening under enemy attack or from our own side. Fortunately my amateur psychology worked with the Colonel.

'Sergeant Dauwalder,' the soldier beside the desk looked attentive, 'you'll be assigned to Miss Briand as her personal guard during her stay. You'll be entirely responsible for her safety. See that they put a cot up in the legal tent for her.'

The Sergeant didn't look too unhappy about his special assignment; in fact, his voice carried a certain eagerness as he responded and turned on his heel to start work right away.

Just then the Colonel remembered something else.

'Oh, God! We've only got an open-air shower here!'

'Don't worry about that,' I said quickly. 'I can take a bowl of water into the tent with me, and I always carry my "instant bath".' Both men laughed as I triumphantly held aloft a small bottle of Guerlain's Chant D'Aromes.

'Tell the medics to expect an epidemic of flaring nostrils,' said the Colonel dryly.

The Sergeant suggested he might be able to build a small shower stall for me and the Colonel waved permission.

'How about a cold beer while he's getting things organised?'

The Colonel walked towards a large refrigerator and I looked around Battalion Headquarters. It consisted of a huge tent roof over a raised timber floor with mosquito screening on frames forming low walls. There were three desks, several filing cabinets, some green metal trunks, the fridge, an enormous map of the area suspended on a tripod and, in a rear corner, the Colonel's field bed protected by a mosquito net with a small trunk beside it holding a picture of his family.

From the corner a fan whirled the sticky air around creating a movement with an illusion of coolness.

The Colonel brought over a couple of cans and a solitary glass which bore faint traces of toothpaste in the bottom.

'Out of the can will be fine, thanks.' I had to make sure he realised I sought no social trappings.

While we drank I listened to a short briefing about the unit's activities since its arrival in the area some three months earlier. I was warned not to take aerial pictures showing the location of the ammo dump and not to take a swim at the beach, off-limits to troops after a marine had been badly bitten by a sea-snake. I wasn't too keen on the swimming ban.

'Sea-snakes don't worry me. There were quite a few at Vung Tau but they didn't interfere with my swimming. The only guy I ever remember getting bitten there was the lifeguard.'

The Colonel was adamant.

'There's no swimming here. Apart from anything else, the men aren't allowed to and you can guess how they'd feel if I gave you permission. Also, two of our men disappeared while they were taking a stroll along the beach late one afternoon. All we ever found was one dogtag on a broken chain. So don't wander past the perimeter alone, either!'

By the time Sergeant Dauwalder returned about an hour later I had had a pretty comprehensive briefing of the general rules and regulations of the camp.

'Cot and shower stall both erected,' was the Sergeant's report and I was heading off to see the result when the Colonel suddenly remembered something else and grinned as he handed me a key.

'That will open the door to my exclusive one-header,' he explained. 'It's on the left as you go out. Can't have you disturbing the peaceful unity of the four-headers in the mornings.'

The camp itself was situated on top of the dunes which lined the ocean front. Sergeant Rick Dauwalder arranged a round-trip in a chopper so that I could see the general layout. From the air the tents looked disorderly, sitting haphazardly atop the dunes, like a toy camp erected by children. Two missile projectors guarded the area from the highest point, their noses ahead inland. The enormous ammunition dump lay behind the first row of dunes.

The pilot gestured towards it.

'If Charlie ever hits that dump we'll be blasted clear into the middle of the ocean!'

Charming thought. Especially as there were rumours about a regiment of PAVNs* stationed in the area. But then there were rumours about a regiment of PAVNs at every military installation in Vietnam.

I spent the day photographing the Marines preparing for Christmas. At a mortar position a few miles inland a young soldier used red oil paint to write 'Merry Xmas, Charlie' on the barrel of his 81mm. Others had collapsible plastic Christmas trees that relatives had sent, and spent their time decorating these, while one soldier was busy inflating a rubber Santa Claus.

When we returned to the camp I used one of the unit's typewriters to hammer out the captions. I had a few frames left on my film and went down to the beach to shoot them off. The beach was more deserted than usual. Rick was there, doodling on the sand as he sat. Other than that the beach was empty, with only the deep Caterpillar marks of am-tracks giving any indication that it was used. I came quietly behind Rick, sitting with shoulders hunched and head down, and aimed my camera to get him in the corner of the frame, with the vastness of sand and sea beyond.

Half an hour later I gave the film and captions to a Saigon-bound pilot, Base Ops there phoned AP to pick it up at Tan Son Nhut, and within hours the film was developed and the photos radioed to New York.

Four days later, on December 26th, 'The Lone Marine on Chu Lai Beach' made the front page of the Los Angeles Times and several other Stateside papers.

*North Vietnamese Regulars (People's Army of Vietnam).

The quarters that had been fixed up for me in the corner of the legal tent were surprisingly comfortable. The Marines had managed to scrounge me a real field mattress instead of the usual canvas cot. There was a mosquito net and a trunk covered with a green towel, a round shaving mirror in the middle of it.

'What luxury! My own dressing table.'

'That's nothing. Come and see your shower stall,' said the proud Sergeant.

Facing the kitchen tent, it was ingeniously simple yet effective. He'd had the men drive four poles deep into the sand and heavy wrapping paper had been tacked around, with one side slightly overlapped to form an entrance. A humourist had painted 'The Boudoir' on one side in blue paint. Inside were two water canisters with a board across them, a bowl, soap, sponge and the upturned cover from an ammunition box on the ground beside them.

'That's to keep your feet off the sand,' Rick explained. 'You only have to holler when you want a shower and we'll bring you all the water you need.'

I was sticky and dusty enough to start hollering right then, and the service lived up to its promise.

I hung my dusty fatigues over the edge of the paper wall which was just high enough for me to peer over the top. It was surprising how many Marines had business that brought them close to the kitchen . . . with a curious glance in my direction as they went by.

On the way back to my own quarters I passed the open-air shower. Later I was able to inspect it more closely and found it consisted of a pump by the waterhole with a huge perforated hose suspended from two poles. That first evening, however, I thought it more tactful to look the other way as I passed: several men were making use of it at the time.

Next morning I went to the Colonel's tent to check about taking more pics in the area. Major Hackenauer suggested I go with him to deliver Christmas mail and supplies by chopper to Bravo Company, stationed on the peninsula a few miles south on the other side of Tra Bong River. The Colonel vetoed that plan, though I begged to go on the trip. He said Bravo had been surrounded by VC and under almost constant fire during the last few days.

'I'd just as soon see you stay in the camp,' he said. 'But if you insist on going to some of our outposts, you can make a trip a little further south on Highway 1. Sergeant Dauwalder can get a jeep and driver, and he can ride shotgun with you.'

It was just as well I didn't go with the Major: Their chopper was shot down fifteen minutes after take-off, and though the crew escaped unharmed and the 'sick bird' was picked up within half an hour by the Jolly Green Giant* the Colonel's firm stand had saved me a hell of a scare, or worse, since Major Hackenauer later pointed out a bullet hole which had gone right through the middle of a seat.

'That was the only free space: That's the seat you would have been on.'

Rick, the driver and I set off in our jeep after I'd had to settle for what seemed to be the more mundane ride of the two, and we stopped at a couple of outposts on our way south.

En route, the driver slowed down at one point and yelled, 'Cover up, female coming!'

He knew there was a pool in the area safe to swim in, and the soldiers made the most of it. At his shout there was an answering yell from a disbelieving GI, who immediately pirouetted and posed on the bank.

'Sure, sure, buddy. Think my body will appeal to her?'

By then we were close enough for him to see my shoulder-length hair beneath the Aussie jungle hat I wore. He gave an anguished shriek, whirled and dived into the pool. I never did find out if he surfaced again.

Later Rick suggested a jeep ride to Binh Son after lunch.

'Charlie takes a siesta during the midday heat, and the road is in fair condition. I've got a buddy stationed down there. He'd get quite a kick out of having you drop in.'

We travelled further south on the grandiosely-named Highway 1, with the beach retreating on our left and the railway paralleling the road on our right. Rick pointed out the area where the well-known woman journalist Dickey Chapelle had been killed only a few weeks earlier when she had been on patrol with his unit.

'She stepped off to the side to take photos of the patrol and stood smack on top of a booby trap. Sure was no pretty sight, what was left of her.'

I shuddered at the thought.

I had met Dickey in Vung Tau not long before she was killed and liked her immediately and immensely. A veteran of combat reporting, straightforward and outspoken and, under her rough-tough exterior, helpful and kind.

The main trouble in Vietnam was that you lived under constant nervous tension from the minute you stepped outside the relative security of a camp. The worst enemy wasn't an outright attack; you had a chance of warding that off and surviving. Nor was it the ambushes waiting in dense jungle. It was the ingenious booby

*The Sky Crane S64A, with tongs designed to pick up and carry grounded colleagues; also called the 'Praying Mantis'.

traps set up all over the countryside. You could walk through open rice paddies with a view clear across the valley and not another soul in sight, but you always had the underlying knowledge that the next step you took could be your last.

The Viet Cong used imagination in making their booby traps: heavy clay balls spiked with sharp bamboo points suspended from trees, and capable of ripping your skull open if they were tripped; crossbows set up in bushes, angled so that they penetrated at stomach level when triggered off; deadly bamboo vipers attached to a beam above the doorway of a house, or the entrance to a tunnel; pangee sticks poisoned with human excrement, capable of passing through the soles of jungle boots like knives through butter. Some of their explosive devices were primitive enough, but that didn't make them any less effective or deadly.

Though I had to confess a sneaking liking for the exciting tickle a little danger brought, and the tremendous feeling of relief that followed a successful mission, I was always glad to reach the safety of the camp alive. I hoped I'd never end up like Dickey.

At Binh Son the familiar pattern was repeated: more cold beer, more photos, and me lapping up the interest and attention I got from the troops.

Late afternoon we drove back along the highway, joking about Vietnam's definition of a 'good stretch of road'. It was pretty bumpy. Suddenly we heard sniper fire from across the railway line. It didn't sound at very close range but we weren't sticking around to find out whether it was intended for us or not.

Balanced on the back of the open jeep cradling his M-16, Rick yelled, 'Step on it!' The driver needed no urging — the sound of firing had automatically brought his foot down hard on the gas pedal.

Like a monkey, I clutched at any available projection to avoid being thrown out of the tossing vehicle. We raced into camp at top speed trailing a cloud of dust behind us and as we pulled up at the Colonel's tent Rick hurried in to report the incident.

'Looks as though the PAVNs are in the area like we heard,' sighed the Colonel. 'Better double the guards at the perimeter around the ammo dump tonight.' He glanced at the driver. 'Thought there was something wrong when you raced in like that. Just as well or I'd have fined you for speeding if you'd only been showing off.'

I thought he was joking about the speeding fine, but Rick told me that a Marine racing into a nearby camp had been given a ticket by an MP dubious of his report about having been fired on outside the camp zone. My first reaction was that I was being put on: 'A speeding ticket in a battle zone! You've got to be kidding!'

Rick was telling the truth, but he admitted the Marine didn't have to pay any fine: PX Kelly (their name for the Colonel) just tore the ticket up.

I was dusty from the trip, so collected a pair of light slacks, a cotton-knit blouse and a pair of sandals, gathered up soap and towel and headed for The Boudoir. It was almost chow-time and I was famished. Opposite my shower the Marines gathered in line outside the kitchen tent and I could hear the jangle of their mess-kits as they waited.

I soaped and rinsed, soaped again and lifted up one foot to scrub between my dusty toes. What I hadn't taken into account was the fact that the ammo box top was as slippery as a polished ballroom floor, and my over-hasty movements threw me off balance. I grabbed for a hold as I felt myself slipping. But the shower walls were, after all, only made of wrapping paper, fine for resisting a spray of water but not intended to support me.

Like a clown performing at a circus I tore clean through the side of the shower-stall and, stark naked, landed spreadeagled in the sand before the entire gaping chow-line, who didn't miss a curve, I'm positive.

There wasn't a sound as I frantically scrambled for my towel, wrapped it around me and headed for my tent as fast as I could. Behind me there arose a humming sound as every man-jack in the line let his breath go but I didn't dare look back as I dived under the tent flap.

A few minutes later a cautious hand pushed a water canister into my tent and Rick's voice said 'Here . . . this will do to rinse the sand off. I'll bring your clothes over in a moment.'

I dressed, sat on the side of the cot for a few moments, then decided to get it over with and grabbed my mess-kit. There was dead silence as I approached the chow-line and the silence continued as the line parted to let me in. It was just beginning to get oppressive, and somewhat embarrassing, when an anonymous voice said with a touch of nostalgia: 'Say, that was much better than the USO show!'

Those words were just what was needed to release the laughter everyone was politely trying to suppress.

'A floor show with dinner yet!' someone else shouted.

When I could manage to speak I threatened, 'Next time I'm going to charge admission!' and a voice full of regret further down the line said: 'Anytime, anytime. I missed the performance!'

I had my own back some time later. From under the concealing flap of my tent I used a long-range lens to get pictures of some of them under their open-air shower.

The ribbing about my mishap followed me all over Vietnam and the story had already reached Saigon by the time I got back there.

'Hear you gave up photography and went into show biz,' was the first greeting received from a colleague. News like that always travels faster than any official handout.

Colonel Kelly wasn't too happy when I saw him later in the evening. Not over the shower incident. The Marines had repaired it, and there are some things the 'other ranks' are quite adept at keeping from the Brass if they want to. It was my afternoon trip to Binh Son that had him bothered.

'I was worried like hell when I heard you'd gone way down there,' he told me. 'Sniping on the way back proves I had good reason. And to think you were nearly on that chopper today! After Dickey, if another woman gets killed with my outfit I'll never live it down. I expect the VC to take a crack at the ammo dump any day now. I'm asking you to head for Saigon as soon as possible. You're welcome back when the area is more secure, but right now I can't afford to let you stay.'

I didn't really mind leaving. I was anxious to get to Vung Tau for Christmas, the following day. That was easier said than done. There was no transportation going to Saigon that evening and I spent the next day in the searing heat of the airstrip hoping for a ride out.

Finally, towards 1800 hours, Rick and I heard of a Caribou going to Danang and I decided to take it, hoping there would be a flight to Saigon from there. By the time we reached Danang the Flight Sergeant at the hangar told me the last Saigon-bound plane had left and everything else was grounded for Christmas Eve. He provided me with transport to the Press Centre and promised he'd get me on a flight out the next morning.

I was resigned to spending the evening at the Centre along with any fellow journalists who happened to be stranded there too, but when I arrived all was deserted. The guard told me in pidgin French that everyone had gone by chopper to spend Christmas Eve on a carrier which had anchored nearby. I couldn't get access to the radio to contact anyone — the office was locked. The war had stopped for Christmas.

So I sat in the communal room at the Centre, presently joined in my lonely vigil by two young Vietnamese photographers, neither of whom spoke any English or French. They spent the entire evening playing poker machines and listening to rock-and-roll on the jukebox. A skimpy tree stood in the corner with coloured lights flashing, flashing, flashing . . . while I wanted desperately to be in Vung Tau with my man. I felt so utterly lonely.

I thought of other Christmasses . . . at home, and in Canada. Christmas where there was snow, and fireplaces alight and glowing, and warmth and friendliness. The lights on the trees in the stickily-hot Press Centre kept winking and I became so depressed I could have torn them right off. Finally I went to my cot and cried myself to sleep.

I made good connections to Vung Tau next morning and arrived at the beach in time to join the all-ranks picnic in the Aussie dunes. Content in the hot sand with my man next to me I wiped out the memory of the previous evening. I was no longer alone or lonely, not any more.

We talked of many things that Christmas. Robert had a slow way of speaking. He paused often, sometimes groping awkwardly for the right word. Yet whatever he said had impact. I listened to his views on the Vietnam situation and thought how much of what he said made more sense than a lot of the bull expressed by more articulate 'authorities' on the subject.

'If we have to fight here, alongside the South Vietnamese troops then we should be fighting under the same conditions. No special privileges. We should get the same pay in piastres, not a cent more. The difference in pay should be put into an account in Australia or the States, and used only on rotation. The only privileges should be our mess and preventive medicine because we're not conditioned to the climate and diseases here. But that should be all. That way inflation wouldn't be ruining the country's economy and it would stop our soldiers outpricing the bargirls and the taxi drivers so that the locals haven't got a chance. If we didn't have special comforts — refrigerators, cameras and luxuries from the PX, which end up on the black markets anyway, — then everyone would fight like hell to get the war finished so they could get back home. We wouldn't be alienating the sympathies of the people and practically driving them into the arms of the VC, the way we are now.'

How much more reasonable his simple ways sounded than the comments of the Brass I'd listened to.

When he was with his mates, Robert's speech was more rapid and assured — but it was in drawling Aussie and heavily sprinkled with idioms and expressions I wasn't familiar with.

'I'll never understand your lingo! It seems as though I'll have to learn another language if I'm ever going to understand Australians!'

He replied mischievously: 'No sweat. We don't have to talk to get along fine, you and me!'

In mid-January, Sergeant Dauwalder came to Saigon's AP office and brought with him a gold wristwatch as a delayed Christmas present. The whole unit had chipped in to buy it for me at the PX and the enclosed card read: 'To our No. 1 Morale Booster:'

Rick brought something else that interested me almost as much as the watch: clippings of papers from the States, showing my picture of him on the beach. Several women in the States had been so touched by the lonely figure on the sand that they had written letters to him and enclosed the clippings. I was thrilled. After months of freelancing this was the first time I had seen what happened to my pictures when they reached the other end.

But my most treasured gift at that time was a book Robert had sent to Saigon via courier for me, a novel about Australia by Xavier Herbert. As I leafed through *Capricornia,* I realised I wasn't ready to read it yet; the dialogue held a lot of Aussie terms I wasn't familiar with. Though the character descriptions were brilliant and vivid, I hoped Aussies weren't quite as weird and screwball as they appeared on these pages. I just didn't know them then.

With the book came a letter from Robert — a letter which rather astonished me, coming as it did from a man who had such difficulty in expressing himself in words:

> My love,
> Another day, another shower. More water dripping off me all over your letter. I wish it were dripping over you instead. These are not the thoughts that would be passing through my mind if it were so.
> My darling, terrible attempt to explain my view of this war when you were here last time; couldn't concentrate, didn't want to. One night when I'm drunk I'll tell you. I am sure these things can be explained and reasoned better with the help of stimulants. The only thing I succeeded in telling you is very clear to all — we are just a mob of bastards at heart. That's not hard to figure out. And no matter who or what we are and follow, we'll all wind up with our just deserts.
> And yet, darling cherie, I am glad about this stinking war; I am glad they sent me here. It gave me the one thing I wanted so much in life — you. How easily I might have missed you. Thank God for the one thing that makes the entire goddam war worthwhile.
> Miss you Rena, miss every little thing about you. You are such a wonderful bed of womanhood for me to be buried in. You completely drain all the love from me when I take you. You're always so eager to please me, my love. So much love searching for fulfilment from my body —yours the only body that can satisfy all and each part of my love for a woman. So that body must be my body — that woman my woman.
>
> Your man,
> Robert    xxxx

How I treasured that first letter of his. I carried it with me on missions, read and re-read it over and over again until it nearly faded from wear. Many other letters followed, for we had decided to write to each other whenever we were apart. There was always an aircraft going to Vung Tau or coming from there to wherever I was at the time, and we turned the obliging pilots into veritable 'postillions d'amour' for our correspondence.

# 5

## VIVE LA DIFFERENCE!

⌇⌇⌇⌇⌇⌇⌇⌇⌇⌇⌇⌇⌇⌇⌇⌇⌇⌇⌇⌇⌇⌇⌇⌇⌇⌇⌇⌇⌇⌇⌇⌇⌇⌇⌇⌇⌇⌇⌇⌇⌇⌇

I managed to get to Vung Tau on Saturday afternoon. After dinner I went to the Sergeants' Mess and found Robert playing darts with his mates.

'Hullo.' His greeting was casual enough but the brightening of his face betrayed him. He tossed his mess stubs on the bar. 'Here, get yourself a drink and bring a rum 'n coke for me.' I waited patiently until the game finished and he joined me.

We stepped outside on the terrace. A soft tropical wind stirred branches of palm trees which were coated with silver moonlight. Against the inky velvet of the sea shone chains of blinking lights like Christmas tree decorations — the endless line of freighters waiting their turn to bring supplies up the crowded Saigon River.

'You look sad tonight,' Robert said, taking my chin gently between his hands. 'What's wrong?'

I reminded him of an American who had joined the Aussie party in the dunes, 'the friendly one with the round face who talked all the time about his wife and kids back home in Idaho.'

'You mean the chap who sang Waltzing Matilda completely off-key?'

'That's him. He asked me to bring some silk pyjamas for his kids from Saigon. This afternoon I waited over an hour at the Pacific for him then asked one of his friends to take the parcel on his behalf. He shook his head and said, "You're too late — they've already sent his stuff back Stateside. Some bugger of a VC shot him right through the head last Monday when he was flying supplies in the Delta".'

'Too bad." Robert was quiet and sympathetic.

'I walked along Front Beach and had a good cry. I really liked that fellow. I put the pyjamas down near some refugee kids sleeping there. They might as well have them.'

Robert's hand caressed my head.

'That's tough. He was a good bloke.'

I was suddenly bitter.

'Now someone will give his wife a medal and tell his kids all that dulce-et-decorum-est-pro-patria-mori-shit' I spat out.

'Shhhh. Come on, let's have a drink at Cyrno's.'

Half an hour later, over my second Pernod, I was laughing at a GI at the next table who was trying to eat with chopsticks.

Later still, in the sticky heat of the storage room at the PA&E villa, the dead, the dying, the cruelties, the injustices around us didn't matter for a while.

The next morning we were the first guests at the Grand Hotel for breakfast. Robert checked the menu. 'I love mushroom omelettes — but they're not marked here.' He asked the waiter if he could order one. 'No have . . . no have,' was the irritable answer.

'Let me try,' I suggested. 'Monsieur adore les champignons vietnamiens. Regardez donc s'il y en a dans la cuisine!'

'Oui, madame, vais voir, madame.'

The waiter shuffled off.

'Now what was that all about?' Robert asked.

'I told him that you adored Vietnamese mushrooms, and asked him to check with the kitchen if there were any there. I bet you a hundred dollars there will be!'

Sure enough, a short time later Robert was happily eating his mushroom omelette.

'It's amazing the improved service you get around here if you speak French,' he commented between mouthfuls. 'They were at war with them, and yet they're much friendlier towards them than they are to us, their allies. It really gets me.'

'Well, firstly, I said you liked *Vietnamese* mushrooms. It always helps if you flatter people's national pride, especially with an emerging nation. Secondly, don't forget they won the war against the French, and winners seldom bear long grudges against losers. Thirdly, most of the trouble comes from the Americans having too much money, as you've said yourself, and from their weird attitude toward different cultures. Either they try to change other people to their own ways, or they want to preserve them as museum pieces, hampering their natural evolution and regarding them as objects of curiosity. I have some material I collected for an article on the remaining French colony which I was commissioned to do. I'll let you read it — perhaps it will give you some of the answers.'

Talking to members of the French colony had taught me a lot about their unique position in Vietnam. When the French rule ended in 1954, many officials and businessmen returned to France, but a minority remained as teachers, doctors, technicians, restaurateurs, businessmen and planters.

41

I asked some of them why they stayed on after France lost the war and received a variety of reasons. M. Bedue, the huge robust Corsican owner of the Paprika restaurant, nicknamed Fil-de-Fer (Beanstalk), whose Vietnamese wife had just given him a healthy son, said he wouldn't dream of leaving the country, no matter who was in charge. 'I didn't plan ahead like so many others. I had no money tucked away in Europe. At my age, I couldn't face starting all over again with nothing. And I'm doing tremendous business here at the moment. I'd be stupid to give it all up.'

One planter simply said that his wife was Vietnamese and she was happier here than in France.

Guy Picard, the manager of the Givral, told me: 'When the massacres were on after World War II we went through hell. Many of my friends were cut up by the Viet Minh. I even knew of some murdered by Vietnamese wives they'd lived with for years. I didn't trust anyone. I hid under the stairs, cursing myself for not having left in time. And yet I stayed, even during the Indo-China war. Then suddenly it was all over. And, being human, we forgot the horrors and resumed our normal lives. Since they won the war most Vietnamese treat us without rancour. In France I'd have to work hard and I'd be a nobody. Here I take it easy. I earn a living, have a pretty girl friend twenty years younger than me. I'd be a fool to leave.'

Dr Chabeuf, at the Hospital Grall, admitted he sometimes thought of returning to France, 'But with the lack of competent medical aid here, I'd feel like a deserter. I stay because I am needed here.'

Until the big build-up in early 1966 the war had little effect on the daily lives of the French, who followed their usual routine in schools or on plantations. They gave parties that lasted throughout curfew hours and generally managed to ignore the powder barrel on which they sat.

The French, approximately 6,000 in number, were seemingly tolerated by both South Vietnamese and Viet Cong. Many were still driving their cars to Vung Tau or Dalat for weekends whereas US soldiers could travel these roads only in heavily-guarded convoys. The NLF claim they are the government representing the will of the majority and therefore have the right to impose road-taxes. The French pay these taxes and carry an official NLF receipt.

The few incidents involving French residents are usually accidents, or personal grudges against individuals. A typical example of the leeway given to the French in Vietnam is the 'three-price' system that prevails. In Saigon shops asking for an item in English (or accented American) brings one price. Calling for the same item in French means an automatic drop of some 20 per cent. The price to the Vietnamese is, of course, even lower.

I found at least a partial explanation for the Vietnamese tolerance of the French, and their all-too-frequent dislike of the Americans, in the words of Jacques Arnaud, a French-Vietnamese métis.*

'The French were hated for their administrative rule here, it is true. They made the natives work hard on plantations. But, in a way, they treated the Vietnamese with more respect than the Americans do. They didn't try to change our way of life or our basic culture. Wages were low in French times but the price of necessities was correspondingly low, so nobody starved. Politically and economically the American policy here has been an outright disaster. Prices have increased as many as five times over in the space of two years. This European-type meal I am eating costs 350 piastres. The average Vietnamese labourer makes between 75 and 100 piastres daily, before kickbacks. No wonder my people turn to prostitution, blackmarketeering, stealing and begging. They can't make ends meet under present conditions.'

A French merchant visiting Saigon from Phnom Penh was horrified at what he saw.

'Saigon has become a filthy gutter, an open and uncontrolled brothel,' he declared. 'Three years ago I was in Hanoi; it was clean and the people were looking hopefully to the future. The contrast is painful.'

Mme Cyreau, running Le Paris Bar on Tu Do Street had no complaints about the profitable aspect of the Americans' presence but stated she preferred GIs on leave from the field to the regular 'TuDo warriors' who acted as if they owned the place: 'My girls help them spend their dollars and I must admit on the whole they are less rowdy than the Legion was. So you'd probably be surprised if I told you that I'd rather have the Foreign Legion back: I loathe the stupid arrogance of most Americans.'

My French friend Jacqueline, a teacher at a Saigon college, once took me for a trip in her car to Vung Tau in mid-1965. We travelled placidly along the curved road until just before Baria where the Viets had set up a road block. We slowed down and stopped behind a car. A young guerilla fighter talked to the driver, glanced at a paper he proffered, then waved him on.

'I hope I brought my receipt with me.' Jacqueline searched in her purse, gave a sigh of relief when she found the small stamped document.

The young VC advanced towards our car. He wore a black shirt and mud-caked khaki trousers. His boots were the cheap variety of jungle boots available at local markets. The others wore sandals

*Eurasian.

cut from tyres. Jacqueline handed him the receipt. He looked at it, glanced at our swim gear on the back seat then handed the paper back with a polite 'Merci, madame' and waved us on.

'Drive slowly,' I whispered, excitedly absorbing the scene.

Several armed Viet Cong stood along the roadside, waving for oncoming traffic to slow down. A few checked papers handed over by peasants and bicycle riders. We saw one man on a Lambretta throw up his hands in apparent protest.

'He probably hasn't got his receipt with him and objects to paying again,' Jacqueline said. 'Naturally there's one disadvantage in having receipts. The South Vietnamese make trouble for you if they find you have a FNL* paper.'

'If they can't keep the roads secure what do they expect people to do. Get shot for refusing to pay road tax?'

'I always carry my receipt. I've been stopped several times on this road and the one to Dalat but never had any trouble. In fact, they once warned me not to take a certain turn-off from the main highway. I didn't ask why, it was probably mined in anticipation of a convoy. They're pretty strict about enforcing the road-tax, but they never ask for additional payment. I've heard that if they demand more money they are punished by their own cadres. They are very proud, and say they represent the people's government. Nevertheless there's always the danger of falling into the wrong hands: ignorant peasants, or someone who saw his friends chopped down and to whom any white skin is a fair target.'

As we passed the last Viet standing on a tree trunk, he signalled us to stop. He asked if we had a cold beer or something to drink. We hadn't, but I offered him 100 piastres to buy one. I thought this was another form of shakedown.

To my surprise he refused the money and we continued our trip, reaching Vung Tau without further incident.

This hadn't been my first encounter with the Viet Cong. Indirectly, my first contact with them had also been due to Jacqueline. She had some lovely lamp bases made from opium pillows and suggested I might locate some at an old market near Phu Lam, a few kilometres past Cholon. I took a taxi there in the late afternoon, ignorant of the fact that the Viet Cong had blown up a nearby bridge two days before, and that the Friendly Forces withdrew from the area every day at about 1600 hours.

The overstocked market was crowded and I could feel the hostility. Some Vietnamese openly mocked me; one old woman spat right at my feet. I spotted two of the pillows and didn't even bargain about the price, then headed for the nearest side exit.

*Front Nationale de la Liberation.

There I was confronted by a burly looking fellow in black pyjamas, a sub-machine gun in his hands. He gestured me over to the side of the alley and for the next hour I was questioned by him and six of his comrades, all under twenty. One of them spoke fluent French. They were cool, self-assured and quite polite. I guessed they were VC and told them I was just an ordinary French housewife. I complained about how the Americans were making things difficult for all of us, driving the prices up; I complained about having to walk in gutters because they roped off sidewalks in front of their buildings. In short, I didn't give the Viets a chance to get a word in edgeways and eventually they got fed up trying. They checked my bag, and found my membership card for the French Club in Saigon. That seemed to satisfy them so they arranged for a cyclo-may (motorised cyclo) to take me back to the outskirts of Saigon.

When I told Jacqueline about the incident, she said she was less afraid of the Viet Cong than of the South Vietnamese Government.

'At least,' she qualified, 'I'm not exactly afraid of the Government, but I do get pretty annoyed with its officials sometimes. We are sent here to educate their children as they don't have enough competent personnel to do the job themselves. But every time de Gaulle speaks out against the war they come around to pick us up for questioning. Sometimes they hold us for several days. There are times when I feel we should drop the whole project and let them worry about getting their children educated without our help.'

As a general rule, however, the French are tolerated by both sides. The situation of the de Sevigny family is typical. M. de Sevigny, a grey-haired gentleman of the old school, is manager of the Pasteur research plantation, located about half-way between Nha Trang and Cam Ranh. The de Sevignys live in a small villa on the beach road of Nha Trang. Mme de Sevigny, a lovely Chinese with the type of features that become even more beautiful when emphasised by a few wrinkles, suggested to her husband that I might like to visit the plantation. I was interested but a little doubtful. It was in Viet Cong territory and there had been recent fighting in the area.

'Don't worry,' M. de Sevigny assured me, 'the Viet Cong know my car and they won't shoot at it.'

The next morning his chauffeur picked me up.

I was quite willing to believe that the VC knew his car. There couldn't have been another one like it. It was an ancient Citroen, so tired it hung down on one side till it almost touched the road. If we exceeded 15 m.p.h. it coughed and spluttered so much I was afraid it would explode at any moment. Not the ideal getaway car if there was any trouble on the road!

We travelled the bumpy highway southwards, crawling in and

out of holes like a caterpillar while endless lines of trucks passed by or round us. They belonged to RMK and carried rocks from Nha Trang to build Cam Ranh naval base.

M. de Sevigny commented on these trucks: 'There are hundreds of them rotating between Nha Trang and Cam Ranh. The Americans accuse us French of being Viet Cong collaborators because we pay road-taxes to remain unmolested. But these trucks pay taxes too, otherwise they'd never reach their destination. They'd blow them up like ducks in a shooting gallery!'

The sight of the trucks, for me, confirmed the story of an American engineer in Saigon who had told me he was quitting his job out of sheer disgust.

'Because RMK is operating on a cost-plus contract they use any method available to boost expenses,' he explained. 'The more it costs to build that damn naval base at Cam Ranh the more our politicians back home will be making with their stock in RMK. They use the excuse that Cam Ranh has no stone quarries and therefore the rocks have to come from Nha Trang. The truth is that they could simply build a short road to the nearest mountain and start blasting! A short road is easy enough to keep secure. If it was just costing the taxpayer back home more money I wouldn't beef about it so much, that happens all the time. But what really bugs me is that over here they pay off the VC so that the trucks can go through their territory. And this gives Charlie plenty of green dollars to buy bullets to kill our boys with. What a filthy racket this is!'

As M. de Sevigny said, the French are blamed for paying off the VC in order to survive, but not much publicity is given to the fact that private American firms are doing exactly the same thing on a larger scale to protect their money-making interests.

The plantation was a collection of ghostly abandoned mansions, speaking eloquently of vanished elegance. In the main rooms almost all the furniture was gone except for an occasional closet or table too big to be used in an average-sized house. There were labelled jars and bundles of herbs everywhere. The plantation grows herbs used for serums to combat local ills and epidemics. Since this helps the Vietnamese people the Viet Cong don't demand taxes from the Pasteur plantation.

A Vietnamese assistant took us on an inspection tour of the lab. where herbs and a small amount of rubber were being processed. Later we visited the grave of the famous French doctor Yersin who had dedicated his life to combating the tropical diseases and epidemics which ravaged the Vietnamese population. Grateful peasants had built a small shrine at this graveside and fresh flowers and burning incense revealed recent pilgrimages.

'The Vietnamese don't forget people who unselfishly help them,' M. de Sevigny said. 'That's why streets are still named Pasteur, Yersin or Calmette, though their new nationalistic pride made them take down the sign which read Rue du Dr Yersin and replace it with one reading Dong Bac-si Yersin. The change is significant, don't you think?'

We toured the plantation, picking some herbs and fresh green peppercorns to take back with us and we watched several labourers tapping the rubber trees. Towards the edge of the plantation we climbed a small hill and there below us at the jungle's edge was a group of about fifteen men seated on the ground with one standing up talking to them.

They were dressed in a varied assortment of garments but each one carried a weapon.

'Les Viets,' M. de Sevigny murmured. 'Come, we had better leave quietly.'

I cursed myself for having left my 200 mm. lens back at the plantation and had to satisfy myself with a quick shot with my 50 mm. Unfortunately the resulting photo wasn't clear enough for faces to be recognisable but, to me, it was proof of their close presence and the danger the RMK trucks faced unless they had an 'arrangement'.

We returned homewards over the bumpy highway and stopped at a fishing village a few miles before Nha Trang. There we had supper at a French restaurant famous for its seafood.

Several Americans were dining when we walked in and I recognised some from Colonel Kelly's Delta team of the Special Forces camp at Nha Trang airfield.

Colonel Kelly reputedly disliked journalists but we had become friends over a few drinks.

The village was off-limits to the troops after dark and soon after our arrival the men prepared to leave.

'Don't stay here too late, Rena,' one of them warned as they passed my table. 'We don't want to go looking for you in Charlie country tomorrow.'

'No sweat, Charlie and I get along fine,' I kidded back. 'He likes to have his picture taken, too!'

François, the owner, joined us at our table.

'I have the Americans eating here in the daytime,' he confided, 'then a few French come during the evening. I drop the prices for them. After ten o'clock the place belongs to the Viet Cong and the prices come further down . . . for reasons of my health! The Americans overpay, the Viets underpay, and I make a living in the middle. That's life now in Vietnam!'

# 6

## CANVAS COT AND KINGSIZE BED

An Khe is located on a plateau in the Central Vietnamese High-lands and has only two seasons — muddy and dusty. The trail our C130 left as it landed on the red dirt strip showed that this was the latter season.

The radio operator at the strip called for a jeep and offered me a lukewarm Larue beer. 'Ice melts so damn fast,' he said apologetically.

The jeep arrived and we drove through the village, past about a mile of sun-baked fields, skirting clustering shacks Vietnamese had erected on the outskirts of the First Cavalry base camp.

An American wearing fatigues and carrying a large brown case hurried from one shack and entered the next, where two young Vietnamese girls waved to him from the doorway.

'Medic's doing his weekly round with the needle,' my driver grinned.

The shacks, bearing such colourful names as Carousel or Times Square, were pseudo-bars. In reality, they were the district's brothels.

The camp was huge and widespread, each unit having its own self-contained area. It was rather deserted when I arrived, as the First Cav. were on operations in the Bong Son valley. Told I couldn't get transportation to Bong Son until next day, I parked my gear at the grubby press tent, changed from boots into light sandals, grabbed my camera and hitched a ride to the helipad at the other end of the camp.

At the helipad, nicknamed the golf-course by the troops, I noticed a commotion — a man came running from a chopper and as he raced by me I asked, 'What's up?'

'Can't find number two gunner who's supposed to be on stand-by,' he puffed. 'Got to pick up a guy hurt on patrol. Dust-off's busy somewhere else.'

'Can I come along?'

'Sure.' Then he noticed my feet and asked, 'Where are your boots?'

'At the press tent.'

'Well, we can't wait till you get them. Better stay here. If we're shot down and have to make it back through jungle it'd be murder without boots.'

'Charlie manages!' I waved aside his protests and ran back towards the chopper with him, stumbled and broke the strap of my sandal.

At the chopper, the first gunner said, 'Can you shoot? Looks like you'll ride shotgun!'

'Sure. But not a machine gun.'

'Nothing to it. Just point it and hold this trigger back.'

The gun was suspended from a thick cord and he put a belt of ammunition in it, showing me how to reload in case of need. Then he placed a metal plate on my seat to protect my most tender target against bullets from below, zipped me into a flak jacket and put a helmet on my head. From the waist up I looked like any well-dressed GI. Waist downwards were black slacks, with my dirty bare feet sticking out below.

'If the VC snipe us I'll stick my feet out and they'll think "buddy's up there" and stop shooting,' I joked, but I was a bit wary. So far my target practice had been limited to empty beer cans. The thought of being involved in a firefight horrified me.

We clattered westwards over the mountains and about twenty minutes after take-off started to circle, looking for the patrol in the dark-green sea of the jungle. We only located their whereabouts when we spotted the pinkish cloud of a smoke grenade seeping eerily from the foliage. Through radio contact our pilot guided them to the nearest clearing and we circled for another half-hour until they arrived at the spot. We descended rapidly, hovered over the low brush while the wounded man was lifted aboard, and took off immediately. By the time we were airborne again the patrol had disappeared into the jungle. The chopper could have betrayed their whereabouts to possible enemy troops in the area.

The casualty had one boot off, and a nasty gash went straight through his foot, already bright red with inflammation. His face was grey-green with agony. 'Goddam shit-dipped pangee stick,' he muttered between clenched teeth. He forced a smile when I pushed a lit cigarette between his lips, but he clutched at his bent knee with both hands, as if trying to stop the pain from reaching his brain. I felt sorry for him, but I didn't get as upset and shaky as I had in the beginning of my Vietnam field days. I'd had to harden myself to worse sights than this.

It still made by heart ache to see children, and even animals, hurt in the war — because they didn't understand what was happening, and their mute suffering expressed through accusing eyes could still reach me. Grown men should know better than to fight over political differences, therefore I felt deep compassion only if the casualty was someone I knew and liked. This might sound callous, but I had to toughen, or I really would have gone insane doing that job.

We had barely deposited our casualty at the 'golf course' when we received orders to return into the mountain range. We refuelled and took off just as night started creeping over the horizon. The second gunner had joined us in the meantime, so I moved to the middle seat, which was a little better protected against bullets coming from the side.

Night fell rapidly and the mountains clouded over. Without lights or radar, it was a dangerous area to circle in, and I began to wish I had left the chopper when we landed. The gunner on my left handed me a cigarette, and I noticed his hand trembled as he held the lighter. Though my hand was steady, nevertheless I was just as scared as he in that pitchblack dark. The difference was I'd get the reaction after landing. On me, fear had a paralysing effect. Surrounding actions came through in slow-motion, noises were magnified and echoed, my limbs were leaden, my speech thick, but my thoughts very clear. Once the danger had passed, I'd get the shakes, chatter nervously, and whenever possible have a few stiff drinks. We cruised for about two hours that night and returned only when fuel became low. I never really knew why we went on that mission: there were always things they kept from reporters, and it was useless to pry.

I discovered one good way to get information. If the tents were raised on wooden floors against monsoon rains, I'd try to crawl under the briefing tent before the officers assembled for their session. Lying there quietly, I'd find out what really went on in the area. And sometimes I heard more than that — it was often amusing to hear the 'woman reporter' discussed, whether seriously or not depended on the commander's attitude.

The night after my two chopper trips, I emptied two bottles of champagne the boys at the 1st of the 9th had on ice for me at their club, and ended up sitting on the bar singing Lili Marlene, and almost sobbing over the boys' sad tale of the unit's pet donkey, who had been shot when he ventured outside the nearby perimeter one night. I left for Bong Son the following morning with a dilly of a hangover, my tongue tasting like a Ho Chi Minh sandal from a 3-day cadaver.

The camp at Bong Son was erected for the duration of the operation only, and therefore had only the bare essentials — a few tents, shelters against mortar fire, drinking water on trucks; no refrigerators, no luxuries. The only elegant structure was the latrine next to the press tent, completely enclosed with metal sheets and bearing a prominent sign saying, 'Anyone is welcome to use this latrine' and 'Tom Tee-Dee sat here.'

'What's the joke?' I asked Martin Stuart-Fox of UPI.

'The MPs beefed about the press using their hole in the ground, and said we should dig our own. So we built this beauty to bug them,' he said cheerfully.

The PIO, Hitchcock, told me later, 'The MPs could bite their own asses now . . . they had no idea a woman reporter would be here, and they'd love to get you over in their area . . . with any excuse!' He also told me that, unfortunately, they had no small spare tent, so he assigned me a corner cot in the press tent, where about a dozen reporters and PIOs stayed.

That was fine with me. I just told everyone to turn their heads at night when I took my dirty fatigues off before rolling up into my poncho liner. The set-up gave Hitchcock a chance to brag later, 'She was in my tent with nothing on but her panties.' But when he told the story he conveniently forgot to mention that Martin, Al Chang from AP, Winston Churchill, Jr, and quite a few others were also present, and anyone who knew how I was dressed must have peeked!

That first evening an MP came over to tell me that the press bunker wasn't very safe. They had been mortared the night before from a nearby mountain, and he advised that if it happened again I should run to the more secure bunker of the MPs. I told them the press bunker suited me fine. I didn't add that Martin had told me of its additional attraction, that they kept a few bottles of beer cool there, rolling them into a poncho and submerging them in the muddy water left behind from the first monsoon rains.

There were no showers at the camp, and the troops used to drive about 2 km to the nearest river, but the first evening I made do with a steel helmet full of drinking water. I chased everyone out of the press tent, cleaned up, and washed my undies in the water too. I hung my panties on the tent line to dry, and the little black lacy things looked rather absurd among fatigues and heavy socks. Passing GIs photographed the unique clothes-line.

The next morning I left with a patrol, setting out towards a nearby village which was supposedly Viet Cong dominated. We camped on a hill overlooking the area. Planes dropped leaflets over the village, telling the VC to give up, and promising glorious treatment from the government's Chieu Hoi (Open Arms) programme if they surrendered. We waited for results. Apparently the press bunker was the only area still showing signs of the first monsoon rain—here where we waited the ground was cracking from thirst and the hill was overgrown with cactus.

We were thirsty and the water in our canteens reached near-boiling point in the heat. A few soldiers ventured to the bottom of the hill and climbed coconut trees, bringing the fruit back for a more refreshing drink.

Suddenly two black-clad figures emerged from the village and through field glasses we saw they were waving Chieu Hoi leaflets. I was excited and so were the men around me. Two VC giving themselves up — a good catch! They approached, several men descended to meet them and I followed, camera ready. We discovered they were village boys, about twelve years old, who'd come out to see if we'd pay them a few piastres for getting us coconuts.

'They're probably VC, at that,' grumbled one soldier. 'Still, what can you do but pay them for their coconuts?'

Around noon we opened our C rations. The only place to sit down in relative comfort was a huge grave surrounded by a stone wall, set on the hilltop and I headed there with half a dozen GIs. We sat down with our rations and coconuts and I fleetingly wondered what my mother would say if she could see me picnicking on top of a grave.

During the mid-day heat our platoon leader decided to enter the village. He sent an advance guard of several men ahead and the rest of us followed at a distance when they signalled it was safe to do so.

Holding their submachine guns in readiness, the men searched each of the huts, ducking for cover as they ran from one to another. Women, children and old people stood warily in the background anxiously watching every move. Some soldiers muttered derogatory remarks at them and received hostile glances in return, but the villagers were more pleasant to me, the female, and readily posed with their babies in their arms.

We found nothing of interest in the village — no men, no weapons. And yet the wary attitude of the villagers told me something was up. I had a feeling their men weren't far away, possibly in a complicated, ingenious network of tunnels just below us, its entrance well-concealed by a bush, or perhaps leading off one of the thick-walled mud-bunkers the peasants used for storing rice. Anyway, the old men present couldn't be responsible for all those babies.

Before nightfall several Chinooks landed outside the hamlet and evacuated us to Bong Son Base. Now the village men could return: the night belonged to the Viet Cong.

The following day was the end of the operation and the camp broke up again. Anything that the convoy didn't take back to An Khe was burned — empty ammunition boxes and many other things.

'Why don't you leave the wood for the villagers to use?' I asked.

'Leave it for the VC? Not on your life!' was the retort.

This didn't make sense to me. I could understand that nothing in the way of war material or anything usable for that purpose could be left. But they were burning items of vital importance to the peasants while AID and Psy-War were simultaneously spending millions bringing in things to win these peasants over by providing them with the self-same necessities. But then — there were many things in Vietnam that didn't make sense.

Though Martin tried to talk me into hitchhiking from Bong Son to Qui Nhon with him, I hurried back to Saigon. It was Robert's long weekend off and he would arrive on Friday evening. Chi Hai had bought me a chicken, mushrooms and fruit from the market and I cooked coq au vin, decorated the apartment with flowers and waited.

This would be the first time we'd be together in normal surroundings in complete privacy. Compared to the storage room at Vung Tau the simple flat seemed like a real home, with its brown couch and matching armchairs, an enormous built-in closet beside the room divider which hid a king-sized bed.

In the closet a bulb was perpetually alight to keep the humidity from rotting its contents.

A dining table filled one corner and a door lead to a tiny kitchenette, a shower and a toilet.

It was already late and through my rear window I could hear the sounds of the karate instructor in the black market hall below. There was always some noise or entertainment at nightfall, including the wailing of Chinese opera over loudspeakers, usually calculated to make me flee beyond earshot.

I heard Robert's knock.

He looked so good in his freshly pressed uniform, which smelled of soap when he cradled me against his chest.

I thought he'd never let me go.

'Cheri, my coq au vin is burning.' I tried to wriggle loose.

'Let it burn — whatever it is!'

He picked me up and carried me to the bed.

'A good big bed. It looks so comfortable I might be tempted to fall asleep in it tonight. If I do, be sure to wake me . . . often.'

He kissed me again.

The coq au vin wasn't burnt but it was slightly overcooked by the time I rescued it.

'The first hot shower I've had since I came here,' Robert yelled from the bathroom. 'I'd forgotten what it felt like!'

I followed him in and soaped him from head to toe.

'What service! I must come here more often!'

'If you like establishment, siree, please bring much-much friend!'

I imitated the sing-song of the bargirls and he grabbed me and pulled me against his soapy chest.

He cut me short by pulling me down on the bathroom mat and, wet and soapy as we both were by then, making violent love to me.

'When I'm through with you you won't be able to serve anyone else!'

Much later he carried me over to the bed and caressed me, guilty about having used me so brutally — but I smiled contentedly knowing that it was actually I who had made him serve me: I who had reached satisfaction so many more times than he; who knew the complete fulfilment only women can reach, for which men will always keep searching and therefore wandering. And I knew that neither of us, if we chose a thousand different partners each, would ever again come as close to completeness as we had this first weekend in Saigon.

When at last we got around to eating dinner Robert once again asked me to be his wife. This time I simply said yes. I would try to get a divorce in Vietnam and if that wasn't possible would go to Las Vegas. We decided to check the technicalities with the Australian Embassy.

'I don't want you tied to any man but me for the rest of your life,' Robert said.

Then he told me that he'd been dating someone in Australia for four years before he came to Vietnam. Now he would have to write and tell her not to wait for him.

'In that case,' I said, 'let's wait till we get to Australia. You might want to go back to her when you return.'

My scruples dwindled when he told me the woman was married, had two children, a kind husband, and was much older than Robert. I certainly did not feel I was taking him away from a girl who would be heart-broken because of my actions.

'I never felt so much like a man until I met you,' he assured me.

From the way he talked about her once the ice was broken I realised that this woman had been like a mother to him and had been a substitute for the motherly affection he had lacked as a child.

At the same time I was a little worried. I knew I could never mother a man and I didn't want to, because in my book mothering equated smothering his manhood. But I thought this separation from her, this war, would surely mean he had now outgrown his need for her.

Never once did I doubt his deep love for me. But I also knew that sometimes need is stronger than love, so I kept worrying a little until I had enough champagne to forget my fears and be his woman again in that big bed.

And this time I really served him alone because I had been physically fulfilled. This time my pleasure was mental, derived from serving my man, also a deep satisfaction.

The next morning Robert was still asleep when I quietly disentangled myself and went to make coffee. Steaming cup in hand, I woke him with a soft kiss.

'Good morning my love, my wife,' he said.

We drank our coffee in bed, and while Robert showered I cooked his favourite mushroom omelette.

We sat down to breakfast — with champagne.

'Now that's a great idea for breakfast,' Robert said admiringly as he lifted his glass. 'Let's do it often when we get back to Australia. We've got some damn good champagne down there, not too expensive either. No matter how poor we are, even if we have to go barefoot, we'll have champagne every Sunday morning for the rest of our lives.'

'Darling cheri, if all married couples had champagne every Sunday morning, there'd be no more divorces in the world,' I said.

Around ten o'clock Chi Hai quietly let herself into the apartment and shushed by us with a shy 'Bonjour', scarcely glancing in our direction.

She disappeared into the kitchen and started clattering around with the dishes, calling, 'Madame, café encore?'

I walked out and said, 'Oui, Chi Hai. Monsieur prend lait et sucre . . . hai duong!' We always conversed in a mixture of pidgin French and Vietnamese.

'Oui, madame.' She impulsively grabbed my arm, pointing in Robert's direction and nodding towards the bed. With deep satisfaction she announced, 'Madame found her man. Good. Very good!'

I was amazed. How on earth had she known? She was used to finding men in my place. They came at all hours, even for breakfast, whenever they happened to be passing through and needed a place to stay. How had she known that Robert was different — that he was not just a casual acquaintance, like the others?

I went back to Robert and told him what she had said.

'She barely glanced at us when she walked in. Yet she knew you weren't like the others. I can't get over it!'

'Easy,' said Robert. 'She knew because of the Cheshire-cat smile on your face!'

Chi Hai brought our coffee, eyes cast down, in the Vietnamese tradition which considers it impolite to stare at employers or 'superiors'.

When she had gone out again I said to Robert, 'I am sure the neighbourhood thought I had a pretty profitable sideline going. Many men drop in and we get so busy talking that curfew is often on us before we realise it. I've had Vietnamese friends, soldiers, diplomats . . . only last week an attaché from the Australian Embassy spent the night on my couch. The sudden military build-up has made rooms unavailable at any price. I've often put up freelance journalists or GIs with a few days' leave from camp and nowhere to stay. A few weeks ago I saw half a dozen Marines outside the Rex late one evening. I knew one from a unit I had visited in Chu Lai and he told me they were trying to decide whether they'd sleep on top of the Freedom sign or underneath it. They couldn't get a bed. All six of them came back with me and we put up air-mattresses and pillows on the floor. You should have seen Chi Hai's face when she discovered that invasion! But they gave her money to do their laundry and buy food from the market, so she was happy. They stayed for three days and we had a ball. After all, I have slept beside Marines out in the field, all buddies together, so why shouldn't they do it here in town? I've run into the odd spot of bother, of course. There's always one or two who take an invitation to stay as an invitation to crawl into bed with me, but I can handle them.'

'Does that mean I can bring my mates home after a drinking spree in Aussie?'

'Sure — you'll all sleep on the floor, though!'

Talking about this reminded me of a British author who once camped at my place. He was quite drunk, and at about 2 a.m. persisted in attempting to crawl into my bed. Eventually I lost patience, took my gun from under the pillow and marched him downstairs. I woke the startled janitor, who tremblingly unlocked the door. I warned my ex-visitor that he had better spend the rest of the night sitting among the refugees or he was liable to get shot because of the curfew.

The next day my French landlord, alarmed by the janitor, demanded an explanation. After my recital, he wrung his hands and said despairingly, 'But, madame — please do not shoot anyone inside the house. The beautiful blue tiles . . . I cannot replace them!'

I promised that if I ever planned to shoot someone, I would wait till he was safely out in the street!

After breakfast we went to the Australian Embassy on the seventh floor of the Caravelle Hotel.

Mr McCabe, one of the attachés, was a friend of mine and he received us warmly. He listened to our problem and advised that he doubted I could get a local divorce, but that a Las Vegas one would suffice.

We lunched at the poolside at the Cercle Sportif, the former exclusive French club where Jean and I had been members since our arrival. A few high-ranking American officers had been granted membership to help ensure that fees covered club expenses. As a sergeant, Robert couldn't have joined, but I took a wicked pleasure in watching Cabot Lodge take his noon-time swim with all the brass sitting importantly around the pool while I had my three-striper guest beside me.

Later, armed with champagne, wine and small tins of delicacies from the PX we returned to the apartment and stayed there, making love again while a Chinese opera wailed outside.

We stayed in all day Sunday with me cooking meals in between discussions on names we would give our children.

'Ulysses. That's what our first boy is going to be!'

I thought he was kidding.

'The poor kid,' I spluttered. 'He'd have to become a general at least to live up to a name like that!'

That wasn't all — apparently our first girl was to be named Alcheringa. A real tongue-twister, that one. 'It's an Australian aboriginal name meaning dreamtime: their equivalent of Paradise.'

After repeating it a few times I liked the name better than his choice for a boy but pointed out she'd have trouble learning to spell it and she'd probably be called 'Al' for short.

Robert had some substitute names in mind. Nothing mundane about them — Jason and Mercedes for example — and it was obvious I was going to have little say in this matter.

'Never mind. You'll have the pleasure of producing them,' Robert said grandly. 'And you can decorate our house anyway you like. You'll spend more time in it than I will.' But he spoiled this concession by adding: 'As long as you don't pick something I really can't stand!' There wasn't an atom of doubt about who was going to be boss in our Alcheringaland of the future. And I wouldn't have had it any other way.

One thing I stubbornly resisted. Robert wanted me to leave Vietnam soon, go to Las Vegas for my divorce, then on to Australia to wait for him. I had an inner fear that I might lose him if I left him alone too long so I insisted on staying in Vietnam as long as possible.

It was, I suppose, inevitable that Robert would be impatient to get started with a family of his own as soon as possible and I agreed. I loved him and wanted to have his child even if something happened to prevent our marriage. In a war zone there is always a lurking fear: you soon learn that the 'something' doesn't always happen to the other guy. And I desperately wanted a strong, healthy baby, a miniature Robert.

We made love many times, with an unsatiable longing for each other, till the moment I walked unsteadily across the steel matting of the 3rd corp ATCO airstrip to talk an American flight officer into giving Robert a lift to Vung Tau. He had missed the last Aussie courier back.

Parting was terrible that time — the worst it had ever been. I couldn't bear to face the empty apartment we had shared so I went to Jacqueline and spent the night at her place.

# 7
## THE MONTAGNARDS

Through Dr Harveson I had become very interested in the Montagnard tribes and in the weeks that followed I visited several mountain villages, observing their way of life and coming to love and admire these simple, honest people.

Communication with them was comparatively easy — there was at least one man in each community who had served under the French regime in some capacity or other, and was reasonably fluent in that language. In fact, since their dialects are not related to the Vietnamese language, it wasn't unusual to hear a Montagnard and a Vietnamese communicate in French, their only common tongue.

I once even acted as interpreter to a Montagnard who spoke some French and a Vietnamese who only spoke English, two natives of the same Asian country needing a European to be able to communicate!

Of a lower cultural level, sturdier build and darker complexion than the people of the lowlands, the Montagnards are referred to, quite unjustly, as the Moi — 'the savages'. As their name indicates, they live in the inhospitable, jungle-covered highlands, and generally come to townships only to barter for goods at the markets since money, as such, is non-existent among the tribes. They meet Government taxes by delivering goods such as hides or cinnamon bark to the province capital. They consider the payment of these taxes as tribute to foreign rulers — for just as the Vietnamese were colonised by Imperial China for over a thousand years, the mountain tribes had to bow to the Vietnamese for centuries. Their longing for freedom and autonomy from a regime that has always treated them with contempt is expressed through various independence movements, like the FULRO movement which made recent headlines.

Both Saigon and Washington are belatedly waking up to the importance of Montagnard support in relation to the outcome of the Vietnam war since they are the main inhabitants of the vast, near-impenetrable mountain region. While Saigon and Washington have been blind to their importance Hanoi, on the other hand, has trained

59

thousands of these tribesmen for their cause, promising them autonomous areas in the event of victory, and giving them free basic education.

Most of the Montagnard villages are simple, but I did visit one impressive settlement — Tra Bong, home of the Kor (or Kol) tribe, located in a valley high in the mountains. I went there by chopper from Quang Ngai with Colonel John Sadler on his weekly trip to a Special Forces camp stationed there. Below, the Tra Bong River was our only guide to the valley. It showed a trail that led through the pass between two high mountains. With the monsoon clouds making visibility poor, the pilot had difficulty seeing it and at times had to fly so low our undercarriage was dangerously close to the tree tops.

'The VC usually take potshots at us when we chopper through the pass,' Colonel Sadler warned me. 'Especially when we have to go as low as this. But don't worry. They're lousy shots around here. They haven't hit us yet!'

'Do you get shot at every trip?'

'No, only every other trip. Most of the VC farm a little in their fields during the day and do their guerilla work at night so they catch up on a few hours sleep at this time of the day. We hope.'

I'd had some warning beforehand of what the trip was like.

'We stay as high as the clouds allow,' Colonel Sadler had said before our departure. 'We only circle downwards when we're right above the camp. The whole valley is surrounded by VC. They attacked a few weeks ago. Over sixty people were dead on our side, including villagers. Two Australians attached to Special Forces were killed.'

He also told me the VC executed several village elders, supposedly because they had been reported as being friendly towards the Special Forces men. They kidnapped some of the young village boys too. And as if that wasn't enough, half of the village was wiped out by a landslide shortly afterwards. This slide destroyed part of the settlement, the bridge over the river which connected the village, the airstrip, and also killed most of the livestock in the area.

'We got a rebound from that,' the Colonel said ruefully. 'One of the relief organisations heard about it and shipped a cow to Quang Ngai. We hadn't the faintest idea how we were going to get the damn animal up here. You can't fit a cow into a Huey, the road's impassable, and you can't land a plane in Tra Bong since the slide.

'Finally some guy had a bright idea. We got the Vietnamese to crate her then we put the crate with a parachute on the static line and pushed the whole damn thing out on rollers from the back of a Caribou while we circled overhead. I wasn't on the trip that brought her up but I sure wish I had been. It must have been really something to see! The pilot told me the villagers had been notified that a cow was coming so they were all lined up down there like a reception committee. The guys who built the crate couldn't have done too good a job — it was so poorly made that it split wide open when it landed and the cow scrambled out and took off down the valley like a bat out of hell. The whole damn village took off after her, running like mad, men, women and kids. They knew that if she got as far as the valley exit she'd run right smack into the VC and that's the last they'd see of her. Now you watch out for that cow when we land. . . .'

The valley was misty with monsoon, unreal as a ghostly movie set as we circled down.

I could spot the vague outlines of the Special Forces camp, the solid, fortified building of the village chief placed between two arms of the river, the huts and longhouses scattered over the valley, a waterfall descending the steep mountain side, all covered in a grey film. As we circled lower we could see a few goats, a buffalo, and a solitary cow grazing below.

'That's the cow. Keep your eye on her.'

Figures streamed from the huts and looked up towards our clattering chopper in the sky above them. Suddenly the cow stopped grazing and lifted her head. Our last turn brought us hovering directly above her — and as though shot from a pistol she took off for her life down the valley . . . with the watching figures suddenly sprinting into action after her as fast as their legs could carry them.

'It happens every goddam time,' the pilot roared over the head-set. 'She sure is allergic to aircraft since that flight of hers!'

On touchdown we were greeted by the village chief, Captain Nguyen Dinh Trung, a slender wiry little man with a worried expression. He was startled to see a woman arriving with the soldiers. As he led us to his house which also served as his headquarters, passing Montagnards stopped to stare at me.

'The only foreign women who live in this valley are missionaries,' Captain Trung explained. 'A young attractive girl in combat outfit seems rather strange to us.'

At his house we ate a delicious meal cooked by his Chinese wife and listened to the problems of the community. Cinnamon was the main industry of the village and VC activities were limiting harvesting in the surrounding areas. There were also problems involved in getting cinnamon and lumber to Quang Ngai.

'In Quang Ngai they desperately need lumber for construction,' the Captain told us. 'The Vietnamese army will supply guards so that the people can go out and cut the wood but what are we to do with it when we get it? The road to Quang Ngai has been repeatedly bombed and it is also mined. It will be a long time before it can be repaired and safe to use. Since the landslide the Tra Bong River has found a new bed and in some places it is now too shallow to float the logs and cinnamon bark. If the monsoon will be kind this year we might try to use the river as transport again.'

But the monsoon was on the side of the Viet Cong. It had stopped raining by the time we finished lunch, and the valley shimmered with freshness and bright colour.

Tra Bong was one of the most beautiful places I have ever seen. Farmers planted fragile shoots in their terraced ricefields on the slopes of the majestic mountains. A few grazing buffaloes and goats were scattered over the area, the chopper-shy cow by now having joined them. A tiny white chapel stood on a hill. The whole scene was a picture of infinite peace and it was difficult to believe that only a few months previously this valley had been a hollow of death, ravaged by the fighting which took so many lives.

A 'Green Beret' who accompanied me pointed to a high peak at the western end of the valley — twin waterfalls drizzling down its side made it look like a beaky, running nose. 'Up there the VC have a regimental headquarters. All around us, they own the region. It's a real deathtrap, this valley.'

His words didn't seem real. It looked so peaceful, rather like an artist's impression of Paradise in an old Bible.

And yet I suddenly had that eerie feeling of being watched by a thousand eyes.

'There are about ten thousand people living in the area, mainly Montagnards,' he continued. 'They call themselves the Kor but the Vietnamese can't pronounce the "r" so they call them the Kol. I guess about half the people are on our side, maybe more since the VC attack. But they are too frightened. When we have another attack I hope their anger over the killings is stronger than their fear or we might be in real trouble.'

'You seem certain there will be a next attack,' I said.

'As certain as an Amen in church.'

How calmly he took for granted the prospect of death coming at any moment.

On our trip we met several Montagnards walking alongside the paths. Some men still wore G-strings, others Western style clothing. The women dressed in handwoven wrap-around skirts and carried sleepy-eyed babies in shawls draped around their shoulders. Many wore beads, blue predominating. Some women were bare-breasted.

'Friend of mine stationed in Qui Nhon hadn't been told about the Montagnard women,' the Sergeant said. 'The first time he drove along the road he saw a pretty, strapping young girl walking towards the market with her full breasts jutting into the air he drove his jeep right into the ditch.'

Neat houses with heavy grass-thatched roofs and floors of dirt made concrete-hard by the stamping of countless feet showed the increasing fashion for individual family dwellings. Further on, the settlements still consisted of traditional longhouses built on stilts. Longhouses have no windows, but light filters through walls of loosely-woven bamboo. The floors are of more sturdy bamboo weaving, but walking on them takes getting used to, as there is always a slight movement. It seemed as though we would crash through the floor.

We sat in the large communal front room which also serves as sleeping quarters for the men and boys. They sleep on the floor or on mats which are rolled up during the daytime. The rear part of the longhouse is divided into individual kitchens, one for each family, and the women and small children spend the night in this section.

'During my stay at a village near Son Ha, my hosts rotated me to a different kitchen each night, and in my honour the husband was banned from his nightly visit,' I commented to the Sergeant. 'Hospitality like that and we call them savages!'

'Yeah, it's a damn shame how these people are treated. They're really fine folks in my mind.'

We inspected tools ranged alongside the wall of the room. They were primitive but solid, and beautifully fashioned in their simplicity.

The Sergeant reached for a crossbow. 'Can you span it?'

'The small ones they use for fishing in streams I can manage,' I replied. 'Not the larger ones. You should see the enormous one the chief gave me when I was made a member of the Rhade tribe. It's one they use for hunting tigers and boars, and I couldn't budge it an inch!'

I valued that crossbow for this was something that a millionaire could have coveted without ever owning: he would be turned down with a shrug if the chief didn't like him, no matter how many dollars he offered. After living in a materialistic, greedy society it was refreshing to meet people who saw value only in the goods they themselves made.

Our hosts served us rice wine in a hollow bamboo container and gladly accepted the cigarettes the Sergeant handed back in return. It was late in the afternoon and already the mountain air was chilly as we continued our journey.

The Sergeant showed me a school which they had built. 'Only problem is we can't get teachers to come here and educate the

63

youngsters. Hardly any of the Montagnards speak Vietnamese. I'll take you over to visit the missionaries who are working on an alphabet for the Kol dialect.'

The two missionaries were women, a Canadian and an American. They had lived in Tra Bong for over two years and the Montagnards called them Madee and Madong. They were trying to bring Christianity into the valley while acting as teachers and compiling a written language of the dialect.

Madong, the Canadian, talked to me about the landslide.

'Luckily no one was hurt; the Montagnards had miraculously anticipated the disaster.' She told me a village elder had come to rouse them, saying mysteriously: 'The mountain is going to visit the valley tonight' and asking them to come with him to one of the longhouses situated higher on the hill.

'We didn't quite understand what he meant. But we trusted him so we did as he asked.' It was just as well. Their house was one of the buildings buried under the landslide when it tore down the side of the mountain. 'The elder even remembered our little cat and returned to the house to save him for us.'

The Sergeant asked if I would like to visit the longhouse at the other side of the valley.

'How will we get across the Tra Bong River now that the bridge has been destroyed?'

'No sweat,' he assured me. 'I know a shallow spot where we can cross.'

Unfortunately he over-estimated his knowledge. We missed his 'shallow spot' and landed in deep water. Holding my camera safely above my head I reached the shore soaking wet. My notebook drifted downstream somewhere. 'I hope Charlie finds it,' I said. 'I'd like to think of some unlucky VC interpreter poring over it. Half the time I have to rely on guesswork myself to find out what I've scribbled!'

A few friendly Montagnards helped pull the jeep on to dry land and we continued our journey. The mountain air was chilly, Tra Bong River had been frigid and by the time we reached the longhouses I was trembling with cold. Immediately they saw us the natives served hot soup, rice wine and for me they provided a wrap-around skirt so that my soaking fatigues could be dried at the fire smouldering in the middle of the communal room. I changed in a kitchen and emerged with the skirt wrapped sarong-fashion under my armpits. As I hunched over the warmth of the fire the Sergeant raised his camera — and back to Saigon floated the rumour that I had 'gone native' and was living with the mountain tribes, wearing nothing but a wrap-around skirt.

The story was even written up in an article in the *National Observer* by Wesley Pruden, Jr:

She works hard as a freelance photographer and she has taught herself to be really quite good. She goes out where the fighting is oftener than a lot of the men. She is a particular favourite of the Montagnards, the primitive tribesmen in the central Vietnamese highlands who don't usually get along very well with anyone.

The Montagnards like her because she, like the soldiers of the Special Forces, takes up the simple Montagnard life without complaining. She has drunk goat's blood with them, and the chief in one of the villages gave her a set of gold bracelets as a token of the tribe's esteem the last time she went up to Pleiku.

She also brought back a remarkable set of colour slides which perhaps explains part of her popularity with the Montagnards.

She willingly wore the Montagnard women's dress while among them, and this is a simple costume that begins at the waist and ends demurely below the knees.

She looks better in it than most Montagnard women.

However those who believed the last part of the story didn't realise that, for a thin-skinned Westerner, Tra Bong was much too cold to be running around like that!

The Montagnard villages close to the Cambodian and Laotian borders were usually smaller settlements than Tra Bong and consisted on the average of four longhouses. The villagers prided themselves on their skill in taming a herd of elephants for village use. They lived mainly on the results of their hunting, wild fruit and greens. There was little or no agriculture.

The men of the Special Forces were Americans and Australians, sturdy, masculine types in whose midst it was impossible to feel anything but secure. The origins included Mexicans, Germans, Slavs and many of them had colourful backgrounds, like a chap called Felix. Of Hungarian origin, he had fought against the Nazis when he was a mere boy, escaping after participating in the 1956 Hungarian uprising and joining the Australian forces after his arrival in Sydney.

Most Special Forces men I met were tough, ruthless killers when they suspected collaboration with the enemy, yet they were kindness itself when treating children, and patience personified when trying to educate the villagers in hygiene, sanitation and so forth.

They told me how easy it usually is to win the loyalties of the Montagnards: 'Simply treat them as they should be treated . . . as human beings.' But the contempt shown by the Vietnamese counteracted what they were trying to accomplish. 'Trying to win the Mon-

65

tagnards' sympathies for Americans is useless . . . They will have to be taught a feeling of belonging, of loyalty to the South Vietnamese government — or all our attempts are in vain.'

Paradoxically, the South Vietnamese Government doesn't look too kindly on Special Forces winning the co-operation of the Montagnards because they know this doesn't necessarily mean the tribal people will obey the rulings of Saigon. So the orders were that aid given by the Special Forces to improve the living standards of the Montagnards was to be presented as being done under the guidance and orders of the South Vietnamese Government.

'Montagnards don't really want to fight,' one Green Beret commented, 'but they have been pushed around so much by the Vietnamese that quite a few would be only too glad for an open season to be declared on Vietnamese. And they wouldn't be over-particular about whether they pointed the gun at VC or ARVNs.'

At one camp a Montagnard couple arrived carrying a young boy on a stretcher made from bamboo strung between two poles, his body perforated in several places by shrapnel, probably the victim of a booby trap. The couple put the stretcher down and waited, solemn-faced and silent, while someone went to fetch the medic. They were dignified and quiet, with none of the anxious wailing or complaining so often displayed by people bringing a relative in for treatment. I had the feeling that if they had been waved away they would have picked up the stretcher again just as quietly and walked off without a gesture of begging or protest.

'If they must call these people savages, they should never omit the adjective "noble",' I said to a young American standing next to me.

The interpreter told them after the medic's examination of the boy that he would be all right, but would have to stay at the camp for a few days' treatment. Still there was little outward show of emotion as they agreed, walking away as upright and erect as they had come, with only their shining eyes betraying their joy at the good news they had been given.

'They'll be back bringing us presents, whatever they can possibly spare of their tools and materials,' the American said. 'They always do and we must accept them, even though they need the articles more than we do. Montagnards are too proud to accept charity. One consolation — we'll have won another family over who'll be willing to protect us with their lives.'

This I knew was true. If you are accepted as a friend there are no people more loyal than the Montagnards. Once I heard shooting near a village I was visiting and I went outside the longhouse, somewhat worried as I listened to the sounds. One of the elders moved

A tale of war.

After ambush near Tuy Hoa, refugees stream through clearing. (*AP Photo*)

'Sad . . . but it could be me.'

Small dots between dead branches are VC crossing the valley.
Tuy Hoa Valley is burning.

Old prisoner with leg wound in Tuy Hoa Valley. (*AP Photo*)
This woman thought the Americans had 'freed' the area from Koreans.
A window sill is 'home' for this emaciated refugee in Saigon.

near me and said gently, 'No be afraid. We protect you. You our friend.' The Montagnards of that village would have been bewildered had you spoken to them either of democracy or communism but they knew how to stand by a friend.

Though they are tough, dedicated, courageous fighters once won over for a cause, the Montagnards I met were basically peaceful.

'All we want to do is live our simple lives in peace,' one village chief told me. 'That has become impossible! The Government makes us fight, often with outdated weapons too few in number. The Viet Cong harass our villages and sometimes abduct our young boys to train them as guerilla fighters. If we refuse to co-operate the village elders are killed, to set an example. If this is the civilisation they are trying to bring to us, we'd sooner be without it.'

What he said was backed up by a WO of the Special Forces who told me, 'The South Vietnamese often use the Montagnards as guinea pigs. They send them, poorly armed, into VC territory to draw fire, so that the enemy's position is betrayed. Because of the Montagnard's simplicity, the Vietnamese regard their lives as less important than that of a dog. Yet they call the Montagnards the "savages".'

During my stay among them, ironically enough I found the Montagnards less 'savage' than many so-called civilised people I encountered. They are dignified, they never raise their voices, not even to reprimand their children. Noisy and rowdy behaviour is considered a sign of utmost stupidity. A Montagnard friend who had been educated by a French priest asked us, 'Why do some Westerners think that to become honorary tribal members they must act like savages from overseas?'

As a general rule I found I was able to take most tribal customs in my stride even when they differed somewhat from the mores to which I had become accustomed.

There was one, though, that certainly startled me when I first noticed it. A young Montagnard woman was cuddling her small boy who was crying and when his whimpering continued she took him out of the shawl she had wrapped around him, caressed him, and took his little penis in her mouth. I observed it on other occasions and it dawned on me that it was a normal custom for them. In our civilisation the baby gets the pacifier . . . in the Montagnard world it's the mother. I must say it was very effective and never failed to change little boys' tears into laughter. 'Even at that age . . .' I thought.

Another time I watched the women plant rice in one of the terraced fields on the hillside and bent down to help, I was soon signalled to stop, and quite a commotion arose. I asked one of the men to tell me why the women didn't want my help and he listened to their protests then explained: 'You make holes too deep they say. Women fear you disturb spirits who live below. I don't believe in spirits but women do and won't disturb ground more than necessary.'

Their dealing with crime is equally as simple and effective as other customs. The offender is banished from the longhouses and has to contribute sacrifices and food before he regains admission to his quarters. There is no such thing as an habitual criminal in these regions: a repetitious offender is simply killed!

The only time I ever saw the Montagnards noisy and even cruel was during their yearly buffalo sacrifice. During this they drink huge amounts of rice wine from enormous gourds, using thin hollow bamboos as straws. Once they become drunk they believe their 'spirits' have fled into the woods where they cannot observe their behaviour for the day.

The butchering of the unfortunate bullock is done slowly while he is tied to a pole in the middle of the settlement. Some tribes drink the blood while the animal is still alive. This was a real test for me — I was nauseated, feeling the warm, sticky liquid on my face and lips after the chief had smeared symbols with blood all over my forehead and cheeks. I could not withdraw without risk of offending my friends so had to ignore the taut spots on my skin caused by the drying blood which stiffened in blotchy patches as we ate pig roasted on a spear, rice cooked in hollowed-out bamboo with coconut juice, and saute dog with bamboo sprouts.

Monkey and dog were things I had to become accustomed to eating while living with the Montagnards for they are staple items of their diet. Together with the small pigs of the highlands (the best-tasting pork I ever ate), the dogs roamed the villages unhindered until they were considered fat enough for the pot. I had been told about their rather gruesome custom of 'natural tenderising' (slowly beating the animal to death) but I never observed this practice though it is possible they refrained from it during my presence.

Actually, I found nothing offensive or unpleasant about the taste of dog but there was one time I couldn't continue my meal. I had become quite attached to one of the village dogs, a sausage-like, sandy-haired little fellow who used to hang about while I was eating, waiting for me to throw him some scraps. I nicknamed him Freddie the Freeloader because of his begging eyes which I found hard to resist, and I was half-inclined to consider taking him back to Saigon with me.

One evening during supper I suddenly realised there was no Freeloader waiting for scraps but, unsuspecting, I called 'Here, Freddie . . . Freddie . . .' Then the furtive grins told their own tale.

I set my bowl down, muttering 'You Moi bastards' under my breath. To be fair, however, I have to admit that though they realised I was upset they quite honestly failed to see any connection or any reason for my taking Freddie's disappearance as I did.

Though at that stage I was quite prepared to dismiss the whole of the Montagnard tribes as heartless savages, a small incident two days later changed my opinion again. One of the men returned from the market town, the basket on his back loaded with traded goods, and one hand tightly clutched by a small girl about six years old. The whole village crowded about them and there was an animated discussion, then one of the women disappeared into her longhouse and came back with a few grains of rice in her hand. In the midst of a burst of excited chatter and laughter she put the grains of rice on top of the small girl's head then led her away.

I wasn't sure of the significance of her action so sought out one of the men who spoke French reasonably well. To him, the story was simple enough.

'Papa, Maman dead,' he explained. 'Woman put rice on head now girl is hers.' What a lovely gesture to signify the adoption of a child, I thought. A few grains of rice — a symbol that from then on the feeding and care of this orphan child would be her responsibility.

# 8

## *STARCH AND SILK*

ఇంఇంఇంఇంఇంఇంఇంఇంఇంఇంఇంఇంఇంఇంఇంఇంఇంఇంఇంఇంఇంఇంఇంఇంఇం

Apart from a few feathery clouds drifting aimlessly across the vast blue, the sky over Vietnam was amazingly clear the day I went to Hue. Joe Mish, an Air America pilot, took me as far as Danang where he was collecting some VIP from USAID. I sat in the co-pilot seat next to him. 'Nice countryside — without the usual haze,' he commented.

Vietnam seen from the air is a landscape of contrasts. The picturesque ruggedness of blackish-green mountain ranges is interrupted by valleys of lush rice paddies, patches of banana trees and clusters of palms surrounding quaint villages whose thatched roofs peek through the vegetation. Along the coastline are vast stretches of pure, brilliantly glistening sand broken by odd rock formations, with here and there the intriguing architecture of a pagoda or mysterious decaying Cham ruins. Fishermen in their graceful boats surge offshore, nets float on stakes in the river beds, buffalo graze in the meadow.

Forever changing, forever beautiful.

Yet on closer inspection the landscape is marred by gutted, coal-black remains of 'pacified' villages or craters that bomb and artillery shells have torn into the wounded earth. And for every crater hole there are many small mounds, carefully rounded and looking like pockmarks in the ground: the simple earth hills which are the graves of the poor.

At Danang, Colonel Poudre, easy-going and proud of his French name, offered to take me personally to Hue in his little 'bird-dog'.* Under the wings two rockets were attached on each side and as we were gliding over the mountains north of Danang, while I was observing the area through my 200 mm. lens he shouted over the intercom, 'Hang on — I'll show you how we shoot these things off.'

As he spoke the plane plunged into a dive towards the mountainside below. I let go my Nikon, fortunately it was on a strap around my neck, and grabbed two handsful of plane. My stomach lifted,

*01-E, a Cessna.

and I could hardly catch enough breath to scream through the headset: 'No — please no. Don't. STOP IT!'

The plane curved and returned to its normal altitude.

'No need to be scared. I only wanted to show you how the rockets are shot off. Take it easy.'

'Please don't! I hate diving in a plane. Besides, if you shoot rockets into the jungle you could hit someone!'

'That's Charlie Country. If we're lucky enough to hit a target so much the better!'

But I mentioned my Montagnard friends, who also live and hunt in these jungles, and the animals which populate them. 'It's not only Charlie Country and I couldn't bear to think of a living thing down there suffering senselessly, just so that I can have a demonstration of rocket-firing.'

'I guess you're right,' he agreed. 'Up here we tend to forget about such things. Below us is only our territory or that of the enemy.'

South of Hue we flew low over the royal Nguyen graves. Solemnly they stood on the hills, guarded only by leprous-looking weathered stone sculptures.

Colonel Poudre circled a few times over Hue itself so that I could get some aerial shots. This was Vietnam as I had imagined it before I came to Saigon: the colourfully ornamented roof of the Imperial Palace in the citadel, enclosed by a gigantic stone wall growing out of the surrounding moat, the perfect square of the market place, sleepy-looking houses, neat wide streets lined with palms, the Y-shaped University, an impressive cathedral, sampans rocking at the edge of the River of Perfume. Yes, this was what I had dreamed of, before I met reality.

We landed on a short, rough airstrip and a jeep ride brought us to MACV compound where I was to meet the commander, Colonel Boulder. The guard told us that the Colonel was still at the Vietnamese headquarters with General Chuan. As Colonel Poudre had urgent business to attend to and wanted to return to Danang before dark he handed me over to Major Thompson, a handsome friendly Negro with kind eyes and an intelligent face. I took an immediate liking to him.

We walked towards a small villa within the compound.

'Colonel Boulder has his private quarters in there,' Major Thompson explained, 'but there are two rooms reserved for guests. We had a couple of journalists from *Time-Life* here a few weeks ago but we don't often get correspondents. Nothing much happens in this area. Hue is as peaceful as Switzerland on Christmas Eve.'

'Suits me,' I said promptly. 'I'm more interested in background material anyway. I'm a "namba won" chicken — that's me!'

71

He laughed. 'You and many others!'

My bags were deposited in the guest room and after showing me where the bathroom was he left saying 'Dinner's in about an hour back at the main building. See you then.'

He had opened the faded brocade drapes and switched on the ceiling fan before he left. The furniture was solid and dark and gave the room a gloomy look. I took my two Banlon dresses from my bag, hung them in the closet and took out my high-heeled sandals. I arranged my cosmetics on the dresser, took off my fatigues and lay on the bed, letting the fan cool my damp skin while I smoked a cigarette.

A door opened and closed down the hallway and I assumed the Colonel had returned.

When I finished my cigarette I slipped into a Vietnamese house-coat, a gift from the Chu Lai Marines, grabbed my towel and headed for the bathroom. I lingered long under the refreshing stream of water then reached for my towel, to find it streaked with oil all down one side: I slipped back into my housecoat and went down the corridor to knock on the Colonel's door.

For a moment there was no answer then I heard a brusque, 'Who is it?'

'Colonel, I am Rena Briand, the journalist staying in your guest room. I don't have a clean towel. I wonder if you could help me out.'

There was another moment of silence, the sound of a drawer opening and closing, then a green army towel came snaking out through the partly-opened door. I had a glimpse of someone short, balding and sour-looking.

In the dining room Major Thompson led me to a corner table and we were halfway through our meal before Colonel Boulder appeared and sat down at the table on my right. Major Thompson immediately rose and introduced us but the Colonel muttered his acknowledgments almost without raising his eyes from his plate.

He was definitely unfriendly and a few moments later proved it when he shattered the silence with an abrupt, 'Major Thompson, have you checked her credentials?'

Somewhat taken aback, Major Thompson ventured, 'Sir, Colonel Poudre, whom I know personally, delivered Miss Briand to me. I hardly thought it necessary.'

'Negligent of you, Major. Do it now.'

'Now sir?'

'Right now!'

I left the table and came back with my MACV press card, handing it to the embarrassed Major. He glanced at it then walked stiffly over to the Colonel's table.

The Colonel waved it away: 'No need for me to see it if it's in order.'

The atmosphere for the rest of the meal was hardly congenial and after dinner Colonel Boulder called Major Thompson out of the dining room. A few moments later the Major returned and said: 'I'm sorry but the Colonel doesn't want you to stay at the compound. I've arranged for a room at the USAID house and will get transport for you.'

'Will I have time for a drink at the bar first before I'm thrown out?'

'Better not. He's really upset by your presence. He is terribly religious, and said you disturbed him during his meditation when you knocked on his door this evening.'

I probably looked as incredulous as I felt.

'You're not serious!'

'Sure am.' But the Major laughed too.

He introduced me to Major Butler, a fine-looking soldier, who drove me to my new quarters, where a pale-faced member of the USAID staff received us with a miserable expression.

In my room Major Butler opened a couple of cans of cold beer he had brought along and explained 'the trouble with Boulder'.

'They're crazy, putting someone like him as commander to advise the Vietnamese troops. I won't go into detail but I'll introduce you to General Chuan and you can find out for yourself. I'll tell you this much: Chuan thinks Boulder is cracked! And he has reason to. But let's forget about him for now. I'll take you out for a nice French supper.'

Butler was an entertaining host and over our meal we talked on many subjects. After we'd finished he said, 'I've arranged to take you back to the compound for a drink with the boys at the bar, but we'll have to wait till the guard sees that Boulder's asleep. I don't know where we can go in the meantime. The only two places open are the boy-meets-girl sort of place — I could hardly take you there.'

'Why not. Do I look as stuffy as Boulder?'

'Well, if you're game. . . .'

The bar we entered was so dimly lit I could barely see. Velvet paintings on the walls, tiny coloured lights, a few tables and chairs. The surprise of my entrance stopped conversation abruptly. A couple of Vietnamese girls slid from the laps of GIs who looked the other way in embarrassment. There were about twelve girls present, with Madame seated at a table near the bar, where she could keep an eye on the action. A tall attractive girl slowly moved towards our table, staring at me.

'Mai-Lieu,' Major Butler said, 'meet my friend Rena. She would like a vodka tonic and bring me a Ba Muoi Ba.'*

Mai-Lieu returned with our drinks and I said, 'Ask her to join us, if she wants to.'

'I speak English,' she said quickly, 'I like talk to you.'

She brought a bottle of orangeade for herself and sat down. The other girls abandoned their GI friends to crowd around our table, obviously discussing me animatedly in Vietnamese.

'What's the verdict?' I asked Mai-Lieu laughingly and when I saw she didn't understand, 'What are they saying about me?'

'They much-much surprise you come here. They say you pretty, much nice smile. They say you friend Major Butler, Major Butler good friend, you good friend too.'

'Tell them I would like to be their friend.'

Mai-Lieu spoke in rapid Vietnamese and laughter followed as the girls gained confidence. They fingered the material of my flowered shift, touched my hair, the skin of my arms, all the time chattering madly.

Mai-Lieu learned I spoke French so we conversed fluently in that language from then on.

Madame joined the circle, an amused smile on her lips. She invited me to lunch the following day with her and her girls. I accepted with pleasure, adding — 'I adore Vietnamese meals.' Past experience had shown me the wisdom of this, as people had often tried to please me by cooking the unfamiliar European food, the result being tough buffalo steaks and greasy, stale potatoes. I'd forced down many a culinary disaster that way.

Madame, the businesswoman, chased the girls back to their duties and we continued talking for about an hour with Mai-Lieu.

The Major explained she was a favourite with the Americans, a very friendly and intelligent girl, someone they could really talk to. Many of the men were quite willing to pay just for her company at their table.

When we left Mai-Lieu arranged to pick me up at eleven the next morning at the USAID house. She thought I might not find my way back to the bar in daylight.

We entered the compound without difficulty — I ducked down in the jeep just to make sure. I had a marvellous time with the gang at the bar who thoroughly enjoyed putting one over their commander.

On the way back I made Major Butler stop at a street-vendor's soup carriage and bought a huge bowl of soup, paying for the bowl and china spoon so that I could take it to my room.

'Ugh — look at that bowl!' the Major said. 'Don't you ever get

*A local beer called 33.

74

sick from eating that stuff?'

'Never,' I laughed as I wolfed down the hot broth.

Actually, it was quite a pretty bowl with a blue dragon on it, as I found out in Saigon later, after Chi Hai had scrubbed its grey film off.

Mai-Lieu appeared in a cyclo just after eleven next morning. We both squeezed into the seat and returned to the bar where she insisted on paying the driver.

The meal had been set out in Madame's main room next to the bar — a room crowded with faded French armchairs and a sofa and jammed full of knick-knacks of various origins.

Five of the girls lived in. The others stayed in town and only came to work at night. We all sat round the enormous circular table set with rice-bowls, to eat the delicious Vietnamese food two maids kept bringing from the kitchen.

There was Cha Gio, tiny rolls with seafood and vermicelli, mushrooms and herbs finely blended, wrapped in leaf-thin rounds of rice-dough, sizzling hot as they came out of the oil. Rolled up into a salad leaf together with fresh mint they were my favourite Vietnamese dish. Fish steamed with ginger and greens was so tender it melted in the mouth. Then came Chao Tom, shrimp rolled around sugar cane and broiled: Cua, salt-and-pepper fried crab; Bo Bay Mon, beef in seven dishes, each prepared with its own delicious sauce; and Com Tay Can, rice steamed with a mixture of chicken, pork and mushrooms, all cooked in an earthenware pot. I helped myself generously to Nuoc Mam, a smelly sauce made from fish fermented in sea-water, and Madame and her girls giggled, obviously pleased with my evident enjoyment of their food.

With Mai-Lieu's help I found out a good deal about the lives of the girls. And they found out about mine.

Mai-Lieu pointed to a girl with rather a voluptuous figure for a Vietnamese. 'Suzy,' she informed me, 'is in love with you,' and everyone laughed.

Suzy walked over to my chair, leaned down and cupped my breasts with both hands. Mai-Lieu translated the comment: 'They are real,' she said with a note of satisfaction in her voice.

After the meal we went to the small courtyard which led off the bar. There were several children playing there and each of the girls proudly indicated which offspring was hers. Others said they had children with their families nearby.

Each girl had a tiny room leading off the dingy courtyard, the space mainly taken up by an enormous double bed. Mai-Lieu's room furnishings consisted of a shabby dresser with a spotted mirror, against which were fastened picture postcards, a tiny cabinet crammed with dresses and ao-dais, a chair and a small table fan helplessly trying to combat the sticky heat. The walls were covered with magazine clippings of actors, mainly Western ones.

We sat on her bed and drank orangeade, watching her two children playing outside the door. Mai-Lieu was slim, but solidly built. Most of the Vietnamese are bow-legged, but she had nice straight legs. Jet black hair reached her waist; her face was roundish, but with high cheekbones and her skin was lily-white.

'You look more Japanese than Vietnamese,' I commented, and she told me she was half-Japanese, the result of a pack-rape during the Occupation in World War II.

She had been abandoned and placed in an orphanage where she learned French from the Sisters. Later she married a Vietnamese who was killed in the Army while she was pregnant with their second child. His family was of no help as they resented her because of her Japanese blood.

Work other than the sort she was doing would have meant that her two children lived at subsistence level. Now, because she could pay for it, they had everything they needed: the best of food and medical care if it became necessary. To her it was a matter of practical economics: you worked in the field which gave the best return.

'Do you invest your earnings so that you will have something later?' I asked.

She shrugged philosophically.

'No chance. I wish I could. We girls, we are easy prey for officials. If I owned anything they'd find a reason for taking it away. I bought some gold jewellery, which I have safely hidden, but that's all I can do. Nobody would give me a half-decent job. Anyway you need connections for that. If only I could leave the country things might be better but it is impossible to get a passport. The only chance for girls like us is to marry a foreigner. Then we can leave. But how many have that luck? How many men would marry a prostitute?'

She spoke without a trace of drama or self-pity; it was merely a clinically-detached statement of facts.

That afternoon we visited the Imperial City, built by the Emperor Gia Long at the beginning of the nineteenth century.

The overgrown walls shimmered grey-green in the sunlight, and the surrounding moat was a heaven of pink and white waterlilies. The city had grown into the space between the inner and outer walls and where once only a few favourites could tread, chickens and pigs now mingled among laughing mobs of playing children.

We entered the second wall through one of the four gates and were in what was formerly the 'Forbidden City', reserved for the Emperor and his immediate entourage only.

The courtyard was in a state of disrepair and bore traces of shell-craters which had been roughly patched over.

'The Japanese,' explained Mai-Lieu and added jokingly, 'maybe my father!'

The caretaker took us into the Throne Room from which the Nguyen Dynasty had reigned. The canopied gold throne with its two blue dragons in the background was much too ornate for my taste. I concentrated on the artifacts and antiques which interested me more. Beautifully designed vases, among them a set of Ming; delicate screens, ornamentally carved tables and trunks; exquisite bowls of all shapes and sizes.

The room was so quiet and overpowering we hardly dared whisper, and I had the eerie feeling that its former occupants still hovered threateningly over us in ghostly forms — I felt relieved when we were back in the sunlight with the dirty children running about us, laughing and shouting.

We headed back through the calm, serene town on cyclos, with Mai-Lieu nodding to people she knew, smiling her friendly smile and receiving smiles in return. She was a popular girl and I was amused to intercept the startled looks which followed recognition of the fact that I was her companion — the surprise shown by the Americans who knew Mai-Lieu was especially noticeable.

We laughed a lot that afternoon . . . Mai-Lieu has a great sense of humour.

'Let's go to the Cercle,' she suggested, 'and watch the disgusted look on the waiter's face. He is an old-timer — used to serve there in the days when it was a very posh club for French only. Now the poor snob feels it is far below his dignity to serve the likes of us — but not many people here can afford to go and eat there so they can't very well refuse us admission.'

The club was terribly run-down, with only the barest traces left of its former comforts. The original furniture had been replaced by inexpensive substitutes, the panels gaped off the walls (a rat actually ran behind a panel while we sat there) and rain had streaked the crumbling plaster. The windows overlooking the River of Perfume were covered with a grey film.

We were the only guests at that time, and the waiter Mai-Lieu had spoken of shuffled in, looking fed-up as she had anticipated. He spotted me, and despite his attempt to conceal his reaction it was clear enough that he was wondering what the world was coming to if a French lady came to the club in the company of a prostitute.

Mai-Lieu and I grinned at each other contentedly. We had become real friends by then. Because of this I knew I could be frank and ask the questions I wanted to without fear of giving offence.

'What are the men like you go to bed with?' I asked bluntly. 'How do they treat you?'

'Generally, not too bad. Many will talk about their country, and how much they miss it, and how good life is there. Most of them say that's where I ought to go. They don't say *how*! They tell me about their homes and show me photos of their wives and children and talk about what sort of cars they have back home or the ones they're planning to get when they return. Then we go to bed and I'm just there, that's all. Often they ask me if I love them a little bit. Americans always want to be loved. So I tell each one that he is my favourite and make a fuss if he hasn't been there for a week or so: it makes them happy. When it's all over, they usually go very fast. They act awkward and guilty. Some are more loving and grateful than others and bring me presents from the PX. Some just want to stay with me. I have one who comes every Friday and he only looks at me and touches me, and never does anything else. Gives me $20.00 and just spends the night, lying there. It could be that he is afraid of catching something, though he knows that the medic comes twice a week with needles. Still perhaps he's afraid of disease. I am afraid of that, too.'

And she told me that the Viet Minh in French times, and now the Viet Cong, had beautiful dedicated girls who voluntarily became infected with venereal disease then went to work in bars where they could be sure of meeting many officers. In this way they spread the disease and demoralised the enemy.

'Sometimes I wish I had such a disease, when I meet the mean ones. They come, insult me and treat me with contempt, or want to do things that aren't normal. When I refuse they hit me. They're often so drunk and they make me feel cheap. One even kicked my little boy when he came in to see why I was crying. He tried to pull the man away, and he kicked him. Those are the times when I hate Americans. But, before that, I once had a rich Chinese merchant and he was like that too; now that I have Western men, the Chinese don't want to have anything to do with me. I think they are jealous of Western men who are usually bigger built. The Chinese merchant never made love where he was supposed to, only the other way. I hated him. We girls tell each other about these men, and we refuse to go with them. But, the first time, you never know what they are like. I often wish my husband was alive, then I wouldn't have to worry about anything. He was bossy — but he was good to us, and he gave most of his money to me. He was so fond of his little boy — he wanted me to have a child every year.'

We spent that evening at the bar again and Madame made me a present of a hideous, gaudy shawl. The girls came to chat in between customers and only the GIs were embarrassed about me watching the action. The girls were lucky they didn't lose out on business because I was there — what saved the situation, I'm sure, was the fact that the toilet was in the back court, and once the boys went there, out of sight of where I sat, they didn't feel so guilty about going to the rooms.

Later on Mai-Lieu visited me twice in Saigon. She stayed at my flat and I introduced her as a friend from Hue. One of my acquaintances became quite rapt in her — and she frankly told him she was a bargirl. This didn't upset him — on the contrary, he was quite delighted and fully prepared to lay out a substantial sum of money for her favours.

Mai-Lieu was offended.

'I am on vacation,' she said firmly, 'and I would never work while I am here as Lena's guest' (she had the usual Eastern difficulty with the letter 'r', and never did get my name right).

The morning after my bar-visit I had an interview with General Chuan. Sturdy, with a broad nose and full lips, the General had the type of smile that flashed all over his face; even the corners of his eyes folded into laughing wrinkles. He talked about his tour in St Cyr, and of the American equivalent, Fort Leavenworth, how much he had liked France and how awful he thought American food was: 'Quite uncivilised!' He talked about the Untakeable Valley, about 50 miles west of Hue and just south of the DMZ, which his troops had captured a few months earlier.

I told him about my plight with Colonel Boulder and he wasn't surprised to hear it.

'I could get along fine with his predecessor — but this man, what an imbecile! I cannot imagine why the Americans sent him here as advisor. It'd be a joke — except that it isn't at all funny. Amongst other idiosyncracies, he seems to regard himself as some sort of missionary. Once he declined an invitation to dinner because it was a Buddhist festival. I am a dedicated Buddhist but I also respect the beliefs of others. When a Catholic friend of mine was killed I went to the Mass for him. I stood up whenever others did and sat when they sat — I was showing my respect. In the same way I wish others to respect my beliefs. But not Boulder. What a political blunder to send him here as commander of MACV!'

General Chuan arranged for me to have a jeep and a Vietnamese driver for the remainder of my stay in Hue and his hospitality made up for Boulder's lack of it. Chuan proposed a trip north to Ben Hai bridge at the 17th parallel.

'We can do it in a non-military vehicle and I will wear civilian clothes. You must keep it an absolute secret, however, otherwise they might ambush us.'

The simple long-drawn span of the bridge which crossed Ben Hai river was awesome. Before reaching it, the high monotonous squawk of a Vietnamese sing-song could be heard. As we neared, it took on a deafening loudness. At the southern end of the bridge a huge loudspeaker boomed propaganda to the other side. A few minutes later it was matched by an equal racket from the other end of the bridge, with the southern 'broadcast' being arrested abruptly in mid-phrase.

'They used to have both booming continuously all the time,' Chuan shouted in my ear. 'It was absolutely nerve-wracking. Now they have an unwritten agreement, and each one plays for about half-an-hour in turn.'

The bridge bore traces of damage on the southern side.

'American planes coming back from missions over North Vietnam tried to hit the northern side to destroy the speakers. Instead they hit our side,' Chuan explained and shook his head, giving a laugh. 'You can imagine the glee of the northerners and the sarcastic statements that came over their loudspeakers after that incident!'

There were two flags, each as big as a house, waving at us from opposite ends of the bridge: North and South Vietnamese flags suspended from enormous masts.

We took a few steps on to the bridge, stayed just long enough to shoot a few pictures, then fled before our tortured eardrums burst.

On the trip back Chuan spoke of how much he wished for a peaceful reunion in Vietnam.

Months later I met Colonel Butler, newly promoted, in Saigon. He said Chuan was a prisoner of Ky's Government because he had been unable to control the students during the Buddhist uprisings in Hue. Butler feared for the life of Chuan, whom he liked, and said he had been speaking on his behalf for intervention by the United States' authorities. To date his pleas had fallen on deaf ears.

I felt badly as I had found Chuan the most sincere highly-placed Vietnamese officer I had met. I never did find out what eventually happened to him.

# 9

## *FRIENDLY ENEMIES*

Saturday night, and Robert and I strolled along Front Beach, with
Robert in shorts and shower clogs, me in a navy cotton blouse and
black tights, with my inevitable elephant-skin bag slung over my
shoulder. It was pitch black, cloudy and sticky and the beach was
fairly crowded, the usual refugees camping under the palms, and
villagers occupying the benches. I was suddenly aware of being
followed, glanced over my shoulder, and saw a group of seven Vietnamese Rangers right on our heels. I was about to say something
to Robert when they suddenly surrounded us, as swift as a pack of
nimble-footed wolves.

'Why you here Vietnam?' one addressed Robert in pidgin English. 'Why you take our women?'

Robert stood in front of them, arms outstretched and fists
clenched. Seeing a knife flash in the background, I stepped back
and tore my purse off my shoulder, searching for my automatic,
frantically cursing my habit of cramming so much junk into my bag.

Robert's head swung round. 'You stay right here,' he yelled, and
I called back, 'I'm getting my gun.'

Robert swung back towards the menacing men.

'Sorry, Sir, mistake, mistake.' One of the Vietnamese spoke urgently, then gestured and spoke rapidly to his companions. I understood the words 'Australian' 'his woman' and 'foreigner', and again
he repeated to us, 'Sorry, so sorry, mistake . . .'

The entire mob vanished as quickly as it had appeared, and we
were left standing alone, me with my gun clutched in my hand. I still
held it, trembling from shock, as we walked back towards the
PA&E villa.

'When you pulled away from me I thought you were going to
run down the beach — where I couldn't protect you. I'd have
handled them all right, but I couldn't help if you'd run and some
of them had followed you.'

'Darling, how little you know me,' I sighed. 'I only stepped back to make sure I wouldn't hit you if I fired. I'd never run and leave you to face trouble alone. Don't you know that if you were taken prisoner by the VC I would walk up the Ho Chi Minh trail barefoot to get you out? And I'd either succeed, or not return myself.'

'Yes, I should have known,' he said shamefacedly and added: 'If anything had happened to us the Aussies would have had a field day. The last time a Ranger shot an Aussie in a bar several Rangers disappeared over the next few days — nobody ever found a trace of them. If something happens to a Yank there are official complaints and official investigations, until everything runs into the sand. In Nha Trang two GIs and bargirls on the beach were attacked by about twenty Rangers. The Yanks ran — and the next morning the mutilated bodies of the girls were found. Aussies do their own retaliation and the Rangers know it.' He added, 'Funny they could tell I was an "Uc-dai-loi" before I had time to say a word to them . . .'

'You spoke to me, and with your drawl, you couldn't be mistaken for anything else!' I laughed. 'Their ears are trained to catch sound and cadence, not words. Their own language is a series of tonal monosyllables, with some words having five different meanings, according to pronunciation. They can easily pick Yanks from Aussies. Even though they mightn't understand a word you can't fool them on the accent.'

At the Villa bar I told everybody how bravely Robert had faced the pack of Rangers, which made him furious, because he's rather shy and modest.

'Yeah,' said a GI, 'the craziest thing is that we never have trouble with the VC here in Vung Tau — but there's always fighting between the South Vietnamese and us, and we're supposed to be allies!'

I interrupted, 'All the fighting here isn't between you and ARVNs. I was in the middle of a fire fight between Rangers and White Mice* a few months ago, in front of the market. We'd just driven onto the square when bullets came from all directions, and we jumped off and crawled under the jeep. The shooting lasted about five minutes with one Ranger killed, several minor casualties on both sides, and one of the White Mice sustaining a nasty head wound.'

'Colonel Hempling said the whole thing started when a policeman refused to pay at a restaurant,' Ron explained. 'The owner's son, a Ranger, drew his gun. Because a Ranger was killed, the others were out for revenge — you couldn't see a White Mouse on the streets for the next week or so.'

Everyone laughed.

*Civilian police, in white uniforms.

At a jungle mortar position.
Montagnard women accompany their men into battle. Hours later, this
convoy was nearly wiped out west of Minh Long.

Mai-Lieu: 'My father? A pack of Japanese soldiers.'
Suzy in the dingy hallway of Madame's brothel.

Refugees saving their meagre goods (*AP Photo*)
Women carry heavy loads.
General Chuan, later jailed by Ky's Government.

VC prisoner tries to protect his head while dragged by South Vietnamese Rangers. Victim in foreground shows the result of this horrible death.

(*AP Photo*)

Prisoners are blindfolded with Australian sweat cloths.

'They're big heroes, the White Mice — until someone else carries a weapon, too.'

On the other hand, it was a well-known fact that the VC came to Vung Tau on R&R, but they never caused any trouble in the area.

It wasn't unusual for VC to walk by the American Beach. Unarmed, they couldn't be distinguished from civilians. They would always glance curiously at the assembled Yanks, but never sit down and join the crowds. They would walk to the food stalls at Vietnamese beach, to eat or drink and return.

'How the hell can you tell a native is a VC?' asked a newcomer to PA&E.

'You can't around here,' the GI replied.

I told him that my friend Bai had said it was very easy to recognise who's who.

' "Rule of thumb",' Bai said dryly, 'is very simple. Look into their eyes. If you see arrogance you're looking at someone connected with the Southern regime. If you see pride, he's a member or fighting man with NLF. The rest of our people have the vacant stare of despair.'

Everyone was quiet, reflecting on that statement, until Christa said to me, 'Tell them about the guy with the sign walking by the R&R beach.'

This was an incident which happened a few weeks before I met Robert. I was sitting by the water's edge when I saw three figures coming from the direction of the burnt-out tank. They were dressed in black pyjamas, which meant they could be peasants, PFs or VC. As they passed me I eyed them curiously, then suddenly spotted a small plastic sign pinned on to one pyjama top: 'QUAN—DOI GIAI PHONG MIEN NAM.'

I could hardly believe my eyes as I read the inscription. I raced up the beach to some American friends.

'John, John . . . listen — the nerve of those guys!' I yelled at a young Lieutenant. 'One of those three who just walked by had the NLF slogan pinned to his pyjama top!'

My friends stared incredulously after the figures disappearing towards Black Rock. They decided to watch until the three returned. It was close to two hours later before I spotted them.

'The tallest of the three, the one walking by the water,' I whispered.

'I'll go over and ask him to give it to me as a souvenir,' John said. But the sign had disappeared.

'You were seeing things!' John murmured.

I knew better and glared at the offending VC, furious because I had been made to look foolish. He glanced at me, saw my frown, then suddenly flashed a big grin in my direction. He knew! My American friends saw his comprehending grin — and no longer claimed I had invented the tale.

'It certainly is a screwy war,' Robert said. 'We share the same beaches then we go back into the jungle and kill each other!'

Another added: 'I'll bet that any slant-eye who gives you a friendly smile here is a VC. Maybe that's also a way of distinguishing them.'

'Let's go to Back Beach for evening strolls and swims from now on,' Ron suggested. 'It's off-limits, but we can drive without lights from the village edge and hide the jeep in the dunes. At least it's calm out there and we really have nothing to fear from the Viet Cong — it's much more secure than Front Beach, over-run by "Friendly Forces"!'

Robert was tired; so we bid everyone goodnight and retired to the storage room. I surprised him with an expert massage — I had taken lessons from a Vietnamese woman in Saigon who taught young girls the art of keeping their husbands happy — the Oriental way. While he relaxed under my treatment I kept purring into his ear what a hero he was, while he threatened to spank me if I didn't stop talking about it. Nibbling his earlobe, I continued to tease him until he turned me over his knee, despite my mock protests.

I was still laughing when he started making love to me. Then everything became very quiet in that storage room.

On Sunday afternoon the RAAF No. 9 squadron had an all-ranks party at Aussie beach with plenty of steaks and a trailer-full of Australian beer packed in ice, and I was having a busy time cooking steaks over the charcoal when one of Robert's mates came and stood alongside me. He chatted casually for a while but I sensed there was something he wanted to say and couldn't find the right opening.

'Stop prowling like a cat around a bowl of hot milk,' I said eventually. 'What's on your mind?'

He was a bit taken aback but seized the opportunity I had offered him.

'It's really none of my business . . .' (why do so many unpleasant or unwanted conversations start that way?) — '. . . Bob has been my mate for fifteen years and he'd probably clobber me if he heard me talking like this . . .' he took a deep breath and plunged on '. . . but the whole unit has got to know you and we like you, Rena. We wouldn't want you to get hurt. Like I said, I've known Bob a long, long, time and I know for certain he's just not the marrying kind. We'd hate like hell to see you hurt — because, in a way, you're just like a mate to us, too.'

I felt a fleeting shadow of foreboding and also a feeling of tenderness for the friend who spoke. I knew he meant well and I also knew what it had probably cost him to talk as he did.

But there was one thing he didn't know and that was how deeply my feeling for Robert went.

'I know you mean well,' I said slowly, and could sense his relief and then his slight surprise as I continued, 'but you see, I'm not making a marriage certificate one of the conditions of loving Robert. I am happy just being with him!'

The steaks were cooked to the Aussies' taste . . . which meant burnt black, so I slipped them off the barbecue and piled them on paper plates. Mine was as I liked it — rare and bloody and they shuddered as I bit into it.

Robert's friend joined in the jokes that followed and the banter — 'Watch out, it's still kicking!' — 'You cannibal!'

I don't know if Robert had any idea how his friends felt about our relationship but suddenly he stood up, pulled me up next to him and with his arm around my shoulder, shouted for a bit of silence.

Then he made his announcement — 'I just want to tell you blokes that Rena's field days are numbered. I'm going to take her back to Aussie and make a housewife out of her. Then with her co-operation I'm going to do something about the under-population of West Australia!'

There was an outburst of clapping and whistling and his friends swarmed around with handshakes and good wishes.

Robert's mate was amongst them and as he shook my hand I whispered, 'See — never jump to conclusions. The big trees often fall the hardest!'

'Good luck to you,' he said — but his eyes said something different, and I could only hope that his eyes were wrong.

# 10

## HOUSE OF THE TOP BANANA

AP received a telegram from the *Montgomery Advertiser* and Ed White scowled as he read it.

'They think we have nothing else to do but chase Alabama boys?' he said grouchily.

The paper had asked for a month's supply of daily photographs, accompanied with a three to five hundred word caption, of soldiers from Alabama, to publicise a blood-collecting drive for Vietnam.

'Not a chance. Not with the time limit they've set!'

I followed him into his office.

'Give me a week, just a week. I'll have them for you.'

He hesitated, then said laconically: 'It's yours — *if* you can do it. But I wouldn't count on it.'

During the hectic days that followed I knew he was right. And if I'd had time to stop and think about it I'm sure I would have given up. But I was too busy rushing from camp to camp by helicopter, sending word in advance to the PIO that I needed every available Alabama boy rounded up.

I interviewed and photographed them at whatever job they were on: repairing aircraft, taking off on patrol, loading artillery. In six days I had twenty-eight pictures and stories, and not the faintest idea where to find the two more that were needed. I felt as though I had drained Saigon and its environs of Alabama-born boys.

I headed back to the AP office with my collection. A man wandered into the office — tall, blonde and arrogant as he sized me up. I didn't take kindly to his manner, but when he casually interrupted our conversation to say, 'I'm in charge of USAID in Quang Duc province, and at MACV compound in Gia Nhia there's an Alabama soldier who's a favourite with the camp's pet honey bear,' I would have forgiven him anything for that bit of information.

And he put himself right at the top of my personal totem-pole when he added, 'I'm going back with the supply plane tomorrow morning if you'd like a lift.'

If I'd like a lift!

That evening I wrote a letter to Robert telling him I was off to the mountains and wasn't sure when I'd have transportation back, so he wouldn't be worried if I wasn't around the following weekend.

I was at the Air America depot bright and early the following morning and spotted the C130 loaded to the hilt with sacks of rice. We were only three passengers — George Gaspard, the USAID man (whose nickname was Speedie), his interpreter Y Klong, and myself. Y Klong was a well-educated Montagnard who spoke several tribal dialects as well as fluent French and Vietnamese, and had a fair command of English.

The crew member in charge of loading glanced at me then did little for my ego by calling to his men, 'Take three of the rice bags off.' As each bag weighed 100 pounds I wasn't flattered by the insinuation!

The airstrip at Gia Nhia itself was too short for us to land there; the strip we used was 8 km from the province capital, a bright-red gash in the middle of green jungle. It looked more like a poor country road, and was in insecure territory, at that. When we arrived the pilot circled, reluctant to land as the arrangement had been that Vietnamese troops were to signal that it was safe — a necessary precaution in an area where control could switch sides overnight.

No one was in sight when we made our first circle, then we saw an old truck arrive, with armed passengers dressed in an assortment of clothing.

'They could be VC,' said a worried pilot. 'We might be wiser to head back for Saigon.'

He mentioned that once before when he brought rice to a similar airstrip in Kontum province a truckload of PFs* had unloaded the plane and taken off, waving a friendly goodbye. Later the village chief complained that the promised rice hadn't arrived and they realised the PFs had actually been VC.

'They look alike, dress alike, sometimes even are the very same people, collecting their few pennies PF pay from the government and getting a bit more from the VC for actually being on their side,' the pilot explained. 'We've even had VC posing as PFs hitching rides in our planes; and some of the "friendly" PFs waving to passing convoys are busy counting their strength. The VC never attack unless they are pretty certain of victory, or the goal they're seeking is worth any losses. This is a screwy war. The way that lot were unloading our plane so cheerfully, I would never have picked them for VC.'

After a brief consultation in the air, weariness won the argument. The pilots were tired of the bumpy ride, so they took a chance. It

*Popular Forces; villagers trained to defend their areas.

87

was a bumpy landing, too, but fortunately for us the awaiting personnel were Montagnard PFs who saw us safely through the jungle to Gia Nhia. Quang Duc is the second largest province of South Vietnam, situated at the Cambodian border, its population mainly Montagnard.

Our ride from the airstrip to the province capital, a mere village, was through beautiful rugged mountain area of dense jungle, with huge trees and tangled undergrowth of ferns and liana so intertwined that it was difficult to imagine anyone penetrating it.

We travelled fast. Territory like that was ideal for an ambush, as past experience has shown only too often.

At MACV compound I found a bonus: two Alabama soldiers instead of one. I interviewed them and sent films and captions to Saigon via chopper.

The honey bear Speedie had mentioned was called 'Uncle Sam' and was quite a character. Not very big, but strong and with enormous claws and teeth. The soldiers often teased him and he retaliated with a quick nip at a pair of passing heels. The Vietnamese cook was terrified of him and always gave him a wide berth. Uncle Sam was still very young and as we became friends he started following me about, making little pleading noises until I let him take my hand. He would roll onto his back and suck my fingers, making slurping noises. 'He finally found a mother,' a soldier joked. When the bar opened at five o'clock Uncle Sam was always at the door, waiting. Sitting on a bar stool, he'd lap up all the beer he could scrounge, then crawl away to sleep it off in a drainpipe, waking up next morning with such a hangover that no one dared go near him until he'd had his milk and bread for breakfast.

One time he came crying, scratching himself and whimpering. He rolled over to show me his belly, covered with ants — apparently he'd been digging and had struck a nest.

MACV compound was on a hill with a tremendous view across the jungle-covered valley, at the end of which rose an enormous even-shaped mountain.

'What's the name of that mountain?' I asked a WO.

'We call it VC mountain. They have a radio station somewhere on top of it,' he said dryly.

Round the perimeter of the camp was concertinaed wire, hung at intervals with empty beer cans — not an attempt at decoration but a very practical warning system: if anyone interfered with the wire the cans gave off a noisy clang.

At an open flat space at the camp's edge was a huge wooden arrow, mounted on a turnstile arrangement, with empty tins nailed along its length.

'The flaming arrow . . . literally flaming,' my guide explained. 'If we call for an airstrike at night we fill the cans with gasoline and set them alight. The arrow is pointed in the direction the trouble's coming from so that the plane can locate it.'

The village itself was situated on a nearby mountainside, with steep roads leading from the river bed. Here ARVN headquarters and the province chief's well-protected house were located.

I had innocently accepted George Gaspard's invitation to stay at the USAID house. USAID Outpost would have been a more accurate description! It was placed two hills away from MACV, right past the village and beyond sight of the province chief's house. In fact, a little further out than the last military post of the Vietnamese and right on the edge of the jungle — Charlie Country.

It was built like a blockhouse of pioneering days: one large rectangle and, since the mountain air is very chilly at night, a natural stone fireplace. Partitions came half-way to the roof, making semi-walls for three bedrooms alongside the main living room section, and mosquito screening was nailed against tough tree-trunks which formed the frames of openings serving as windows. Grenades were ranged along the length of the beams. There was a single strand of barbed wire around the outside lawn. God only knows what purpose it was supposed to serve. This, then, was to be 'home' during my stay in the area.

The province chief, Colonel Man, a jovial man in his mid-thirties, invited Speedie to bring me over for lunch. He had a tall, sallow-skinned American staying with him as a guest. Officially he was the agricultural or economics advisor (I forget the actual title under which he was introduced) but since my days with Jean I had developed a sixth sense about some of these 'advisors' and I was so sure he was a CIA agent he might as well have had an insignia embroidered on his shirt-sleeves.

After lunch we sat in the lounge drinking a digestif and I casually mentioned that I'd feel much safer at the USAID house if I had brought my gun from Saigon.

'I can help you out,' said the American, who jumped up and trotted off down the corridor to his room.

I followed slowly, green chartreuse in hand. Through his open door I saw him bend over a huge metal trunk that he pulled from under the bed. The trunk was three-quarters filled with bundles of brand-new 500 piastre notes — thousands of dollars' worth, and the rest of the trunk held pistols and revolvers of various sizes. He selected a .25 Browning automatic and handed it to me.

I couldn't resist a comment. 'If you can't buy your way out, you shoot your way out. That how it is?'

He gave me an odd smile as he closed the lid and turned the key in the lock, but made no reply to the remark. I was more than ever convinced that he was a 'spook' but refrained from any further comment and simply thanked him for the automatic.

'Don't mention it — and I mean that literally,' was his pointed reply.

I made good, though unorthodox, use of the gun the following day. Speedie had been somewhat glum and I noticed his frequent trips to the outhouse.

'Not feeling too good?' I asked and he said mournfully: 'Everyone else around here gets Ho Chi Minh's curse — and I have to get constipation instead!'

Next time he headed for the outhouse I sneaked up behind and fired a round into the ground. Pants half-mast he raced outside then stopped as he saw me running away, laughing. A short time later he came into the house and said, 'For Chrissake, what were you up to?'

'Thought I might scare it out of you!'

'You were dead on target!'

Outside his establishment were two big water tanks, elevated on a wooden structure with pipes leading inside to a small kitchen and a shower room. The Montagnards used to fill the tanks each day and the warmth of the sun was sufficient to make the water an agreeable temperature by evening whereby we had the luxury of a warm shower before dinner.

The maid cooked delicious meals and served them on the large table in the main room. A couple of benches and two armchairs made up the rest of the furnishings in the room. Rather primitive, but with a good deal of charm.

The maid did not live in but two Filipino USAID boys stayed at the house.

We had a slight disturbance on my third night — there was some trouble in the area so a lieutenant from MACV came across and evacuated us — a precautionary measure as a few weeks earlier members of FULRO* had taken over the USAID house and planted their flag on the roof. They had not harmed anyone but MACV was not taking chances while I was there.

The following day I left on a short patrol with Colonel Man's ARVNs. For several miles the trucks followed a rough trail leading across rivers and through jungle so overgrown in places that no matter how we ducked to protect ourselves the branches whipped our faces and arms. When we continued on foot hacking a way through the jungle the going was so rough I was glad we turned

*The Montagnard Independence Movement.

back after about an hour. I'm sure we hadn't covered a quarter of a mile and I still can't see the purpose of the patrol; whatever they were looking for could have been right under our noses and yet invisible. So dense was the growth I couldn't even photograph the man directly in front of or behind me. It was like being caught in a huge green surf, with arms and legs perpetually struggling against the powerful element.

Back at MACV in Gia Nhia I collapsed in a chair at the compound bar and only came back to life when someone handed me a letter from Robert, brought by a courier from Saigon.

My darling-cherie,

Seven p.m. Had dinner, a shower and wished to God I could have you. I wonder where you will be sleeping tonight, my love, and hope that you are safe.

The first monsoon yesterday. Would have loved to make love to you under it. Pity — a rainstorm gone to waste. We were out with Medevac in pouring rain, and in the dark — which made it worse. Called out at 11.30 p.m.

My woman, nothing can change my love for you and my need for you. You are my first and only, now or later, *wife*.

I love you with an intensity that I did not think possible. My body's cries are painful but not as terrible as the other longing I have for you and the only way I can express that other longing is through my body.

As I lie here writing to you this hand that guides the pen can feel the touch of you, your entire body where it had roamed and lingered and loved. When you read this, when and wherever, it will again retrace its wanderings so firmly etched in my mind — the vision, the touch, the smell, the taste of you.

I am sure you will make a loving mother for our little Ulysses and Alcheringa. A beautiful loving mother of whom their father is very proud.

I shall give you the most elegant champagne breakfast when we are re-united. You, champagne, you, an omelette, you, more champagne . . . that's what I call a well-balanced breakfast.

I want to conquer you and you shall be my slave, but I shall also love you very gently and quietly drown you in my love.

I miss you, my woman — please come back to me safely.

Your man,
Robert.

After reading his letter several times that night, I fell happily asleep with the pages under my pillow, next to my automatic.

The following morning I took a stroll along the jungle's edge with Colonel Man's mistress, a tiny, pretty girl from Saigon who had the temperament of quicksilver and could never keep still. She was very amusing, chatting away and telling entire volumes, using hands and eyes to make up for her limited English.

When a group of black-pyjama clad men appeared at the jungle's edge, carrying arms and eyeing us curiously, we turned swiftly back to the USAID house.

After lunch and a siesta I went to MACV compound to study a map of the area. A radio message came in — a convoy of Montagnard PFs had left Gia Nhia en route to Ban Me Thuot and had been ambushed. They had passed Pang Sim, a tribal village and a short distance further on the first truck in the convoy hit a mine. The Montagnards jumped from the trucks and hit the ditches but these had also been mined and the Viet Cong had them under cross-fire. They reported many dead and wounded and asked for a rescue operation. I grabbed camera and film, radioed AP in Saigon to tell them about the incident, mentioning that I was going out with the rescue. Horst was on the line. 'You crazy or something, thinking you can go out with a rescue convoy?' he yelled at me. 'They're the ones they really lay on the ambushes for — don't be so damn stupid!'

But I stuck to my guns. Apart from the fact that I wanted to be in on the story I had another reason: the rather cynical attitude several of the officers had displayed at MACV compound, especially one, a Hawaiian of Japanese ancestry. The trouble was I had never yet been in real action. On the several patrols I had accompanied nothing much had happened and, in fact, had reached a point where the troops declared I brought them good luck! Apart from twice being in choppers that were hit (once we only saw two bullet holes after landing and had no idea we'd been hit since sounds were muffled by noisy rotors) I had always arrived on the scene after the action was over. I had no idea at that stage what it felt like to sit in bushes, like a mouse in a trap, watching VC come across a valley. It was easy to willingly confront an action before I experienced the creeping fear and the anticipation that lasts and lasts for what seems an eternity.

I hunted for someone at the compound to give me permission to accompany the rescue convoy. The American Colonel passed the buck. 'You'll have to ask Colonel Man. He's in charge of the Vietnamese military.' Colonel Man was far from encouraging but when he saw I was determined to go he took a more fatalistic attitude. 'If she's keen on committing suicide, who am I stop her?' was the impression he gave.

I was still sitting at ARVN headquarters some two hours later and we looked no closer to organising a rescue convoy. When I wondered aloud why it was taking so long a CO VAN MY (American advisor) said casually, 'No one's too keen to get out there into that mess.'

I should have known the reason for the delay: the ambushed were Montagnards and the Vietnamese were in no hurry to risk their lives for them. I felt pretty awful when the truth finally dawned on me. They claim to be fighting this war for mankind's freedom and equality, but while a wounded American would get immediate evacuation and attention his Montagnard 'brother' could lie there for hours with his guts spilling out on the grass. I kept pounding at them and asking them when we would be starting. I firmly believe that finally, reluctantly, they set off mainly because they did not want to 'lose face'.

By the time we left it was late in the day and a couple of miles outside Gia Nhia we met a truckload of wounded on their way back. They told us those left behind were all dead and the bodies taken to Pang Sim, so there was no point in our going on. I switched to the truck carrying the wounded and went with them to the hospital, a barrack containing a few dingy rooms housing cots without sheets. A huge old table covered with a blood-stained grass mat served as an operating table and the young Vietnamese doctor in charge seemed to have little idea of what he was supposed to be doing.

Serious head injury cases were left lying on stretchers unattended while he was treating minor flesh wounds.

The situation was chaotic.

I took a few photographs of the wounded being unloaded but every pair of hands was needed to help so I set aside my camera and tried to remember what I had learned at a nursing course I'd attended some years earlier. When the Montagnards realised I was willing to help they made things somewhat awkward by lining up to show me their wounds in preference to being treated by the Vietnamese doctor.

The worst cases died under our hands — and there was nothing we could do. One soldier had a ghastly gaping head wound. Another had his hand torn to bits, leaving just a stump, and his body was perforated by shrapnel. There seemed to be no facilities for blood transfusions or anything but the most elementary treatment; there was little medicine and few instruments.

All the doctors and nurses seemed to do was clean the wounds with spirits and dab them with mercurochrome.

'Don't you have antibiotics?' I asked the French-speaking doctor. 'Oui, oui,' he smiled in reply — but I never saw him give injections.

I looked at the dirt-encrusted, wounded limbs; I knew that Montagnards wouldn't have the benefit of immunisation.

'These men need tetanus injections, urgently,' I told the doctor, who continued smiling and assuring me everything would be all right.

93

I spotted the Colonel who had arrived in time to be photographed helping unload the wounded.

'Why don't the US medics come and help?' I asked him and he mumbled something about them being too busy.

'That's a fine war,' I said. 'You guys are all supposed to be fighting the common enemy together and you haven't even got the bloody courtesy or humanity to help these poor bastards here.'

He assured me that Medevac choppers were on their way to take the worst cases to the better-equipped hospital at Ban Me Thuot, which was more help than the Montagnards would usually get. That was true enough, but it was ghastly to know that at least two of the cases needed help right then or it would be too late. I stood by helplessly as they died.

Next day Colonel Man took me to Pang Sim, the village from which several of the Montagnards had come, where the chief presented me with wrap-around skirts, handwoven and very colourful, a gourd and a tribal bracelet. I was given the honour of a ride on their treasured elephants.

The dead had been brought back, which did a lot to mitigate the distress of the villagers. Unless the dead are buried within the grounds they believe their spirits must wander forever, which is why Montagnards often risk their lives to recover the bodies of slain friends.

The compliment I cherished most of all was the changed attitude of the Hawaiian officer who had antagonised me earlier. He had assisted at the hospital, handing me bandages, bottles of merchurochrome and finding a few instruments for me to use. After the wounded had been evacuated he gave me a lift back to MACV compound and offered to get me something to eat. I told him I had no appetite — what I really needed was a good stiff drink.

He headed straight for the compound bar and gave the Mess Sergeant the shock of his life by collecting a double vodka and bringing it back to me.

'That guy never waited on anyone in his life. He never even walked in here before, because he doesn't drink!' was the Sergeant's comment later.

After I'd had the welcome pick-up, the officer drove me back to the USAID house to clean up and as he let me out he leaned over and stretched out his hand with a simple, 'Let me shake your hand to show my appreciation.' That one act meant more than a long and flowery speech could ever have conveyed.

Though there had been a lack of medicine at the hospital at Gia Nhia I had seen stacks of boxes of supplies at the USAID warehouse and I asked Speedie why they were not being distributed.

'If they need medicine they'll come and ask for it,' he said bluntly, so when I saw the Vietnamese doctor I asked him why he did not get supplies from USAID.

He told me it was because he did not speak English and was therefore unable to communicate with Speedie. This was ridiculous. Speedie had his own interpreter and it was his duty to see that enough medicine and supplies were available to the hospital.

There were many things about Speedie I admired: his courage in living on an 'outpost' and his efforts to get the local orphanage and school built for Montagnard children. (Raymond Burr, the well-known actor, donated a large sum of money to this project.) Speedie showed great ingenuity in procuring the necessary material, one way or another. Nevertheless these good points didn't alter the fact that I thought he was falling down on his job of outfitting the hospital and I had no compunction about tackling him on the subject.

One of his main faults was that he spent too much time on what were, to him, more important projects. Like the pretty half-Montagnard girl who couldn't even say 'Hello' in English . . . but was on the USAID payroll as a secretary. When a man is away from home in a place like Vietnam lapses can be excused but not when they are carried so far that duty is neglected.

I did a tour with Speedie of a Montagnard village called Kim Duc and there I saw a woman with a tiny skeleton of a baby at her dried-out breast. I was horrified to learn that the baby was about a year old. He was so tiny and skinny this didn't seem possible. Once again I challenged Speedie.

'You have all that powdered milk at USAID warehouse being eaten by mice and rats — why isn't it given to someone like her?'

With a shrug, Speedie said, 'They wouldn't know how to use it. They'd just throw it away.'

My blood was up and I wasn't going to let things slide as easily as that. The following morning I hunted up a baby bottle at the Gia Nhia market and returned to the village with some powdered milk. Another hunt produced a battered aluminium pot, none too clean, and I poured some water in it and set it over a small fire burning outside the longhouse. It took about thirty minutes to boil the water then I had to let it cool to dissolve the milk. All this time Speedie was pacing up and down, bored stiff and anxious to get back to Gia Nhia. The only nipple I had been able to get was of cheap quality rubber and it was difficult to perforate but eventually I succeeded.

When I tried to give the bottle to the baby he was too weak to suck on the small hole so I had to enlarge it. Speedie kept nagging at me to hurry up but I was cross and stubborn. I had been willing

95

to return to the village alone but he had insisted on accompanying me — so now he could jolly well wait. I finally managed to get the baby to take some milk but Speedie was not at all appreciative of my efforts.

'You're supposed to be a photographer. Why don't you stick to your job and stop meddling with something that's neither your business nor mine. I have orders not to do too much for the Montagnards. The Vietnamese are supposed to deal with the handouts because Saigon authorities don't want the credit to go to us.'

I wasn't in the least mollified by that glib explanation.

'That's all very well in theory,' I blazed back at him. 'But like your goddam psy-war* it simply doesn't work in practice. The Montagnard aren't likely to forget overnight that the Vietnamese have always regarded them with contempt. And if you give the stuff to the Vietnamese to distribute you know as well as I do that most of it will end up on the black market. The day a Vietnamese will voluntarily hand over something to a Montagnard for nothing is one neither you nor I is likely to see. And you know it. And finally — no one gives me any orders to say I can't help someone in need. So blast your orders from Saigon — or Washington either, if it comes to that!'

A village woman, who probably thought I was a doctor, came up to show me a badly infected wound on her leg. It was a cut, green with pus. I asked Speedie for the use of his first-aid kit but he refused and told me that the Vietnamese medical team looked after any treatments that were necessary, and they would not appreciate it if I interfered.

Through Y Klong I asked when the team was due again in Kim Duc and found out that the team had *never* visited the village. Speedie still refused to give me his first-aid kit so we drove back to Gia Nhia without speaking.

Y Klong was sympathetic.

'The people appreciate Mr Gaspard's help in such things as building the orphanage, but they sense his basic indifference to their everyday problems. He insults them by always refusing drink or food in the village, saying it would make him sick. And he chases our girls and displays such arrogant mannerisms.' He sighed and said slowly: 'He does not understand that to these villagers treating a woman's leg here in Kim Duc is much more important than building an orphanage at Gia Nhia.'

I was angry with Speedie and left for Saigon the next day.

*Psychological warfare.

# I I

## *SAIGON BARS*

It was only Wednesday and I had to wait three more days until I could join Robert in Vung Tau. I was free to go there but he had to work hard during the week so I decided to see him on weekends only.

I went to the Caravelle for a drink. Until tourist trade to the war zone had become fashionable, the Jerome and Juliette bar at the Caravelle sometimes resembled a private club for correspondents, who congregated there in the afternoon and again after the 'Five O'Clock Follies' which was our name for the official news release at MACV.

When I walked in that day everyone treated me with awe. The story of my trip to Gia Nhia had gone before me and, like all stories, had gathered a build-up en route. By the time my friends heard it I had crawled out under fire and rescued everyone of the wounded Montagnards single-handed. This I could do without for there is nothing worse than being a No. 1 chicken and finding yourself with the reputation of a heroine to live up to! But that was Saigon — a hotbed of gossip. And a woman reporter was always meat and drink for the gossipers.

Various sources brought back to me some of the 'facts' from discussions held about me in my absence: I was a lesbian; I was a push-over for any guy; I was an agent (for whom was not quite clear — but for someone, obviously); I was nothing but a dumb crazy broad; I was a phony; I was a nice girl having a tough time; I was a nut running around with the Montagnards wearing nothing but a wrap-around skirt and so on.

The stories didn't bother me. In fact I derived a bit of amusement from some of them and even took a wicked delight in starting one myself to see how far it would go.

In 'strict confidence' I told someone about a helicopter pilot who took me for a tour in a H13 (a little two-seater glass bubble), landed in VC territory and demanded a 'price' for my safe return — a sophisticated version of the girl offered the choice of a car ride or a walk home! Oddly enough, no one seemed to find it incredible that a girl and a GI would have a roll in the grass in VC country and the tale went the rounds. By the time I heard it back, in Bangkok, from a British journalist who was unaware of the identity of the mythical 'woman in the case', it had been beautifully enlarged and embroidered. I let him tell it to the end before spoiling it for him by admitting I had invented the whole story in the first place!

I used to call the Caravelle Bar my 'office'.

As a 'stringer', AP provided me with film, which I returned exposed, complete with captions. Horst would cut out the negatives they bought and put the rest in my AP locker. The 'locker negs' I kept on file to peddle to other correspondents. Often something on hand would serve to illustrate a story they had. I also took photos which weren't needed at the time, for example, of every bridge and important structure I passed. There was a good chance the VC would blow it up sooner or later, then I'd be able to supply 'before' and 'after' pictures.

I did rather a flourishing trade at the bar, especially with short-time correspondents who weren't too keen on setting foot outside Saigon, but preferred to get their news from MACV or for the price of a few drinks for a GI who had just returned from action. A typical query would be: 'Hey, Rena, I'm writing up "Chieu Hoi". Got any pics of turncoats?' I'd promise to bring them in the following day.

One 'Caravelle Correspondent' used to dress up in his khaki fatigues, decorated with dozens of shoulder patches and complete with strapped-on pistol . . . all for a dangerous patrol to the PX! An Air Force Colonel regarded him with amused tolerance and confided, 'I'm keeping my Purple Heart ready — for an on-the-spot award in case he steps on a nail!

A rule-of-thumb assessment for recognising the short-time reporters was to check their clothes. They would come back from Bien Hoa in mud-caked, smelly fatigues and sit around the Caravelle in them for at least three days. The hard-core regulars were only too glad to reach a shower and clean clothes.

Still, even with the posturing there was drama aplenty in that L-shaped bar with the horrid Dali-esque murals, and the white plastic cushions covering the benches along the wall. Coups were plotted there, top secrets revealed, news stories toned down or coloured.

Through windows crossed with masking-tape against the possibility of an explosion one had a splendid view over Saigon, and could observe riots and demonstrations, the flares of the nearby war —all with a feeling of remoteness.

I remember seeing a few tourists running to watch something happening on the square below.

'What's up?' someone called.

A blasé correspondent turned and said casually, 'Nothing much. Just another monk trying to burn himself, but the White Mice took his gasoline can away.'

Another night someone came in shouting that a bomb had been discovered in the elevator shaft of a military hotel. We broke speed records getting there, to find the hastily evacuated GIs and their companions standing at a safe distance away, clad in whatever attire they had grabbed when the alarm was given. There was a stir in the crowd as the squad came out of the hotel with the disarmed 'bomb' — a twenty pound cheese that a Vietnamese employee had hidden in the shaft, waiting until he'd have a chance to sneak it out of the building.

It wasn't only correspondents who bought my pics at the bar. Businessmen and tourists wanted them to take home and show their families because they were much more impressive than newspaper clippings. One attaché always bought photos of Hueys landing under difficult conditions: 'In case we ever need to do it. Good for training to see how far these choppers will go.' One day he handed me a small package over a drink. 'A little present. Don't open it till you get home.'

As curious as the next woman I made an excuse to go to the ladies' room a little later, and opened the package. It contained a very small, very precise, very expensive camera. I stuffed it into my purse. Back at the table, I saw he guessed I had opened it.

'Have you ever been inside a Mohawk?'

'Yes, in An Khe. But it's against rules, and they didn't let me take my camera.'

'You noticed the side-view radar? My Government intends to buy some from the US at a pretty high price. We're not sure how well they work. We'd pay $2000 for some good photos of it.'

Catching my breath, I said firmly: 'That's a lot of money, but no thanks, I don't want to get mixed up in espionage of *any* kind. I'll give you a piece of information for free, though. If all the radars are as lousy as the one in the plane I was in, forget it!'

I offered to return the camera, but he waved it aside.

'Keep it. I said it was a present. It might come in handy if you ever change your mind.'

I never did, but every time I sat with the Attaché, I noticed curious glances from the 'duty-spook' of the day. (CIA agents were very easily recognisable because of their pointed ears and studied indifference!)

We took most Caravelle Bar stories with a grain of salt and yet, on investigation and after making allowances for a spate of local colour, many proved to be true; in Vietnam amazing events were a daily happening.

'This buddy of mine got tanked up last Christmas in Phu Bai,' a Marine told me on one occasion. 'He bet a case of whisky he could drive his jeep to Danang and back. We didn't think he'd do it but when he wasn't around later we got worried. The CO phoned Danang but no sign of him there. At three in the morning we got a call: the last outpost past Danang saw a GI driving south on Highway 1. The road was in the hands of the VC and so bombed out it was considered impassable for anything except tanks. We felt pretty badly about it at breakfast time, guilty about ribbing him and saying he was only shooting his big mouth off. Later that morning we heard he had arrived in Chu Lai and asked how far he still had to go to Danang. They arrested him, but at first nobody believed he had come from Phu Bai. A Chinook brought him back, jeep and all. He was in the soup but, oh boy, what a guardian angel that guy must have!'

I heard the incident confirmed later in Chu Lai.

And there was no doubt also that a certain Colonel's story was true, though somewhat off-beat; he was much too unhappy for it to be an invention. His trouble was a goat. The chief of the Delta village where he was stationed had given him the goat as a token of esteem. The goat had promptly fallen in love with the Colonel's warm, steadily-humming, grease-covered generator. He would nuzzle affectionately up to it and then nuzzle as affectionately against the Colonel or any visitor he had. The Colonel couldn't get rid of the beast, for fear of offending the chief. 'Would you believe,' he brooded into his glass, 'I go to West Point, come 34th in my class, there's a war on . . . and what do I turn out to be? Nursemaid to a goat with a crush on a generator!'

Then there was the platoon leader stationed near Bien Hoa, who used to lead his patrol to a local girlie-house instead of into the field. From the roof of the 'edifice' he would radio colourful reports back to base and he got away with it until the day he informed HQ that 'all was quiet' in the area he was supposed to recon. He had no way of knowing that the VC had ambushed a patrol nearby and at that very moment B52s were unloading their deadly cargo practically 'on his head'. To his great dismay Command discovered exactly what he had been reconning.

I heard another tale from two different sources, though the Brass in Danang denied any knowledge of it, naturally enough.

'This guy from our unit got roaring drunk one night, went to the village, raped three women—they were old, betel-chewing types, would you believe—then walked into the pagoda, pissed on the Buddha and passed out. It's not the business about the women — give them 50 bucks and they forget the whole thing. It's the pagoda incident — they're roaring mad about the insult to Buddha, and that's something we won't be able to buy off with cash!'

I agreed. I could just picture an Asian walking into a church in a Puritanical mid-western village of the US, and doing the same to a statue of Christ!

I wasn't too happy about the outcome of one business transaction effected in my 'office'. The NBC suddenly expressed interest in an interview I had taped with a British missionary some time before and offered me cash on the spot for it. I didn't ask what had made them change their mind. I'd thought all along it was a good story. John Haywood, a young missionary at the Danang WEC centre had built a leprosarium a few miles south of the city. He and his Swiss wife, Simone, who was a nurse and carrying their first child, had taken care of about sixty lepers until constant fights between the Marines and the VC forced their evacuation. Neither side would intentionally shell the leprosarium so the lepers remained in the care of a kind and courageous Vietnamese dispenser Haywood had trained. The road was mined, but once a week the assistant would transport the worst cases a few miles up the beach where Haywood would administer treatment. I'd interviewed him on tape and taken some photos, but when I tried to sell the story in Saigon no one was interested.

'Dedicated people taking care of lepers are old hat,' a colleague said. 'Why don't you get something spicy, like the lowdown on the newly appointed recreation officer in Nha Trang, whose sole job is to provide the camp with blue movies from Hong Kong?'

When I returned to the Caravelle I found out why there was a sudden interest in the young missionary. That morning he had tried to reach Hue by road, after vainly seeking space on a military flight. He'd wanted to pick up livestock and medical supplies at Hue, but he never reached his destination. The VC had stopped his car, pulled him out and shot him in cold blood. So now he was 'news'.

I thought of Simone with the baby due in a fortnight and felt angry and sick. I had a copy of the tape made and sent it to her. Three weeks later I received a letter: The baby was a girl, and Simone said she'd treasure the tape so that her daughter could hear the voice of her father who didn't live to see her.

Aside from being a hangout for the Press, the Caravelle Bar had one more claim to fame: it was the only bar in Vietnam where local girls weren't allowed to solicit. All the others had plenty of bargirls and it was entertaining to watch the action between girls and GIs.

A typical such bar was the Melody, next to the UPI offices in Ngo Duc Ke. Madame had about a dozen girls in this dingy, smoke-filled place. The moment a man sat down at one of the tables they would crowd around him asking, 'You buy me Saigon Tea?' The weak tea served in tiny glasses cost more than a whisky and the girl would get half the price as her bonus. At one time the cost of Saigon Tea soared to such exaggerated heights (over two dollars per glass) that the soldiers went on strike for a fortnight. 'Operation STIF' (Saigon Tea is Fini) was the code name for the protest action, and after losing all their business, the bars dropped the prices to a more reasonable level.

A few of the girls were entertaining and pretty enough to work strictly as table companions; some had their steady men after hours, but most were available for anyone. Prostitutes were generally recognisable by their trade-mark: sheer ao-dais or see-through blouses with black brassieres underneath. (As Vietnamese women are very small-busted foam rubber bosoms sold, stacked like oranges, at the markets and the local doctors did a flourishing trade with silicone injections.)

The girls are artists at charming their clients. Those with steady boy friends will do anything for their man, even providing him with a 'change' to prevent him 'butterflying' on his own, but they will fight viciously to hang on to their income. An American officer who broke off relations with a bargirl returned to his flat to find everything in pieces, from broken dishes to cut-up uniforms and papers, even his mattress was slashed to ribbons.

Most men feel flattered by this possessiveness, ignoring the fact that it is dictated by sheer necessity for survival. Many also fail to realise that the sweet little girl with the innocent face may be earning his dollars for bullets to kill him.

Americans wouldn't accept the fact that many girls were dedicated to the Viet Cong cause, some of their own accord, others forced to co-operate because there was a mother or a little brother to be considered — and something could 'happen' to them. I felt like punching sense into a drunken GI when he babbled to a girl at the Melody: 'Come on baby, we'll do the town together tonight, you and me. Tomorrow morning six o'clock, I go chopper . . . hill number so-and-so . . . near Baria . . . only eight Americans left on hill, fifteen hundred VC at bottom. But you watch me . . . rattattatt . . .' Small wonder the Viet Cong shot down so many choppers if their time of arrival and destination was so readily revealed in a downtown bar.

Apart from its girls, the Melody bar also offered added attractions which made the place near-legendary. Like the evening when a blind-drunk Aussie did a striptease to win a bet with his mates, to the delight of the onlooking Madame and her swarm of obliging girls. As the Aussie took off his underpants he tripped, and an American laughed aloud. That was enough to start a real Donnybrook, Aussies versus Yanks. The MPs arrived within minutes, but in the meantime an enterprising street urchin had taken advantage of the commotion snatched up the Aussie's clothes and made off with them. The amateur entertainer was led away draped in a mate's shirt.

A Special Forces guy in the Melody bar was telling a recent draftee about a tough spot he had been in: 'We went out on recon, five of us. It was the fourth day, the day we were going to call for a chopper to pick us up when we spotted the PAVNs. We hid in the thick bushes, waiting for them to pass so we could radio their movements back to the unit. Do you know what the buggers did? They camped right around us. We were 'frozen' . . . couldn't move. There were hundreds of them. We didn't have a chance of getting out. For two days we lay there — no smoking, no rations left. And all the time we could smell the chow they were cooking. Our water was running out. We were so dehydrated we couldn't even piss . . .'

'Gee,' said the impressed listener, 'you sure were lucky to get out alive. If they'd stayed there a week, you'd have died of starvation!'

'Not that quick, buddy. In the jungle there's plenty of food crawling by your nose, and you can't be choosy in a situation like that.'

His listener looked doubtful: 'Come on, you Green Berets like to shoot us a line!' The sturdy Special Forces man didn't say anything but his eyes searched the room while general discussion turned to the belles of the bar. A few minutes later he found what he was looking for. He jumped up and grabbed one of the cockroaches that inevitably run around such places. Giving the young private a good look at it, he held it up by the head, legs scrabbling wildly, then shoved it right into his mouth. He bit the body off, chewed it slowly, swallowed, and threw the head on the table. Then he drained his beer and ordered another. The point had been made.

# 12

## *DIAGRAMS ON SAND*

Saturday afternoon I went to the helipad about 4 p.m., but it was one of those days when choppers were buzzing off in all directions — except Vung Tau. I wasn't too keen on taking a fixed-wing courier. My last experience with 3rd corps ATCO had landed me in a Caribou loaded to the hilt with nauseating, smelly propane gas bottles, and several Rangers returning from the field who smelled even worse. The plane itself had engine trouble, the radar was on the blink, we took off after dark and landed in Vung Tau strip on sheet-metal matting in such bad conditions that one of our tyres blew.

Also, three weeks previously, I had been in a C130 coming from Nha Trang when we hit a turbulent monsoonal storm. Pitch-black clouds, the plane bucking so badly that some of our ammunition load broke loose, sweat-drenched pilots certain that the wings would tear loose at any moment, and frantic efforts to find a hole in the weather. Their manoeuvring took us in a twisted path, till the pilot considered it was safe to lose altitude because we would be past Dalat, and beyond the peak. But as we dropped underneath the clouds, the side of the mountain was directly in front of us, with the peak disappearing into the clouds. The pilot frantically pulled the lever to gain height, and we soared up and back into the pea-soup, not knowing whether we were going to clear the mountain or hit it. By the time we landed safely at Tan Son Nhut, my knees were jelly.

Recalling these trips I waited for a chopper till about 8 o'clock then trotted over to my last resort: Maintenance.

'You know it's against regulations,' was the usual grumble, and it took the usual five minutes to talk them into taking a test ride.

It was quite an experience. We hadn't known the area between Saigon and Vung Tau was under heavy artillery fire that night until suddenly we were in the middle of it. Flares shot up all around us and their falling light made the shadows below move like ghostly armies gliding over the ground. It was frightening. The pilot was worried that the artillery fire might hit us, and he cursed me for having talked him into the trip.

Because he wasn't supposed to be airborne, he couldn't ask for artillery location. I had a brainwave: once when I was in a chopper with the Aussies they wanted to surprise base with a woman's voice, and I remembered the code they had given me to call. I now asked my pilot the code name for his radio contact, then said, 'Alamo, this is Kangaroo patrol . . .' I repeated the call, gave our route to 'Victor Tango', and asked for the artillery location. We received the information, as well as a few pungent comments, such as 'What are you crazy Aussies doing in the area, anyway?'

We curved according to instructions and landed in Vung Tau safely. The pilot decided to spend the night there: he wasn't about to try the trip again that night.

I found Robert at the tent lines.

'Darling, I'm so glad to see you . . .' he said. 'When it was so late, I thought you weren't coming this weekend and I felt terrible. Last weekend without you was sheer murder . . . as though I was in a giant cage, trapped away from you.'

I explained the cause of the delay on our way to the villa, and he scolded me about my silly fears of fixed-wing planes.

'You'd have been much safer in regular couriers than coming here through artillery fire in a chopper!'

In our storage room, he put his arms around me. 'Nothing will ever prise them open again, darling,' he said, and hugged me so hard I feared my ribs would crack. Then he made love to me very gently, very deliberately, very slowly . . . a sign of how much he had missed me.

Afterwards he again held me tight — and this time what he said sounded like a speech he had carefully prepared.

'Cherie, I love you and want you as my wife as soon as possible, to live with me in Australia. But I do wish you'd leave Vietnam and wait elsewhere, perhaps in Bangkok. I know this solution would be difficult for both of us, our need for each other is so desperate. But a few months is not an eternity, and I would be relieved, knowing you were safe.'

'But I am safe here, as safe as anyone else. And I couldn't leave you now,' I protested.

'Rena, you know how much I hate the thought of being without you, but I also hate the thought of our love being a series of crummy rooms and crowded, bawdy clubs . . . with thousands of Yanks around you — that's Vietnam.'

'So that's it — it's the fellows around me that bother you. Don't you know that there's only *you*. Nobody else is anything more than a mate to me?'

'Yes, love, I believe you, but let's start our new life together in a country where all things are in our favour. There is so much I want to give to you, do for you, take from you. Please understand me — I want you to leave because I need you, and because this poisonous atmosphere could harm us. This is something I don't want to happen, and I'll do anything possible to see that no harm befalls us afterwards.'

But I stubbornly persisted that I would remain in Vietnam until it was time for him to return to Australia. I didn't want to be lonely again, somewhere else. I didn't feel there was any real danger to me — 'They'd never let me go where they expect real trouble in the field' — and in any case, I was worried I might lose Robert if I left him alone for too long. The memory of what had happened to my marriage during my absence was too fresh in my mind to be ignored.

Robert finally realised he couldn't budge me from my decision, and gave up. But he was peeved that his domination over me had boundaries, and showed his resentment by falling asleep with his back turned towards me. I snuggled up against him a little later, and his huge arm landed on me as he turned in his sleep, murmuring 'I love you so much, darling . . . sweetheart . . .'

Sunday morning followed our usual pattern — we had breakfast at the Grand Hotel. The waiter had become familiar with our routine and the moment he spotted us walking in he went to the kitchen for two large cups of Cafe Martin and two mushroom omelettes.

'How was your week?' I asked.

'Hectic!' Robert said. 'While you were in the highlands our squadron was engaged in a large operation with the Army and US forces about 30 miles from here. It's the first time we've penetrated that area. We have been flying pretty steadily — I've been along on the initial troop penetrations dropping SAS* recon patrols. So far the action has been limited. Hope it stays that way.

'Yesterday I went on gunnery practice about two and a half miles off Back Beach. We had just dropped the targets when we spotted a Vietnamese girl floating dead in the water. She was very young, poor girl.'

'How did she die?'

He shrugged. 'Just drowned, I guess.'

*Special Air Service.

Our conversation seemed to continue on the lines of tragedy, and we became quite depressed.

Then Robert said firmly, 'That's quite enough of that sort of thing. Let's change the subject. Tell me something funny.'

I though for a moment then said, 'O.K. I'll tell you about the young Marine who thought he was cracking up when he saw me.'

'Come on now. You're not that hard on the eyes!'

I recalled the exceptionally sticky night at a Marine camp, when after tossing and turning on my cot I went to the beach about 3 a.m., wearing my bikini and carrying a towel. I walked through the moonlit dunes, had a brief swim along the shore, then returned to my tent feeling considerably refreshed.

I was just dozing off when a voice jerked me awake. It was the medic: 'I've got a guy who thinks he's going nuts and I've got no hope of convincing him he isn't. Please come so that he can see for himself.'

A group of Marines had returned from a three-day patrol earlier in the evening. One of them promptly flaked out on his cot without hearing there was a woman reporter in the camp. He'd woken up just in time to see me walk past his open tent-flap in the moonlight.

He dived off his cot and ran barefoot to the dispensary to shake the medic awake, stammering: 'You gotta give me something! I'm cracking up . . . I just saw a woman . . . a white woman . . . walk past my tent with nothing on but a towel!'

Soothing words and a sedative didn't help. But that sure was a relieved young man when I walked into the dispensary.

Robert laughed with me over the incident.

'I know just how he felt,' he said generously. 'The first time I saw you on the beach, it was just like Christmas. I wanted to get to know you right away, wrap you up and carry you off and marry you.'

'That's absurd!' I scolded. 'You didn't know what I was like as a person — how could you think like that when you hadn't even spoken to me?'

'I don't know . . . there was something warm about you, and something little and lost. Straight away I wanted to take care of you. And I will, when you come back to Aussie with me.'

Speaking of Australia reminded him of something and his hand went to his pockets to pull out a folded picture-card.

'My sister sent this over — it's got views of Perth to show you where we'll be living.'

It looked lovely. A neat city with lots of green parks and trees, a serene blue river winding through it, uncluttered by docks or freighters, and a marvellous sandy beach.

I looked at the pictures closely until Robert asked, anxiously, 'You do like it?'

'Oh, yes. I was just looking at the beach part, trying to pick out on which spot we'll make love on every anniversary of our first meeting here!'

'Just to make sure we don't make any mistakes, we'll try several places,' Robert joked. 'And end up in jail, most likely!'

'As long as they put us in the same cell, I won't mind.'

All afternoon on the beach we talked about Australia and planned our future home. Rustic living room furniture, huge shelves with space for my books, Eskimo sculptures and Mexican artifacts, an old fashioned kitchen where dishes weren't hidden in cupboards, a mysterious bedroom decorated with my Oriental acquisitions (Robert insisted on wall-to-wall mattress) . . . these were the world-shaking problems we dealt with that day.

Robert listened patiently as I described my Navajo Indian rug, old Spanish trunks, an Aztec scultpure I had found in a laguna, Siamese temple paintings so old the acid of the paint had perforated the canvas in spots (later an Australian neighbour eyed them curiously and commented 'Interesting tea-towels you have!') — a pencil drawing by Jean Cocteau. I felt exhilarated conjuring up our future surroundings.

In the sand we drew plans for our house and he drew layouts of cricket grounds to help me understand the game. The war and its misery was forgotten and we walked away holding hands, exuberant about our life ahead, while behind us the evening tide crept in and erased our diagrams.

# 13

## *THE BURNING VALLEY*

On a plane scheduled for Cam Ranh we were diverted in mid-flight to Phan Rang. The plane carried wounded soldiers for evacuation to Clark AFB in the Philippines. A pitiful sight with young men lying resignedly on stretchers, some without limbs, others with tubes sticking out from arms, nose, stomach — bare shadows clinging to life, a cargo of misery.

Phan Rang, the base camp of the 101st Airborne Division (the Screaming Eagles) was practically deserted. When I located the PIO he told me most of the unit was on operation in Tuy Hoa Valley and no aircraft would be available for a day or two.

Actually I didn't mind the delay as the valley was quiet and peaceful, a lovely spot in which to relax for a short time. High mountains hovered in the background, Cham temples stood on small hills, strange rock formations resembling huge pebbles stacked by giants were ranged along the turquoise seashore.

I was given a guard, a jeep, and was free to go sightseeing. At the temple hills my guard explained that the Viet Cong knew Americans liked to visit these ruins, so there was danger of lethal traps. We waited till an old Cham woman plodded along a track and climbed after her. I felt a little guilty about using a 'human mine detector' but reasoned she would visit the temple in any case whether we followed her or not.

The graceful acorn-shaped structures bore traces of restoration, undoubtedly dating from French times. The old woman lit incense in front of a crumbling sculpture of the sacred cow.

We spent the afternoon on the brilliant white sand beach and watched soldiers playing volleyball. During the evening I danced with every available member of the club tent.

Next day, with still little chance of transport to Cam Ranh I chatted with the PIO about the units operations in Tuy Hoa Valley.

'Tuy Hoa is the third largest rice basket of Vietnam,' he explained. 'The VC have had control for some years and have collected enough rice to support a large force of men. The Korean 2nd Marine brigade helped the ARVNs secure the harvest but desperate VC attacks gave proof of the region's importance to them, so our 1st Brigade was called in for additional support. The rice is now brought to warehouses in Tuy Hoa and the villagers are given a Government receipt. They can draw against their stock according to their needs.'

'You're sure that they can get enough rice back to live on?' I queried.

'Well, that's what the Government promised, anyway,' he said frankly. 'They'd better keep that promise, though — there's not much sense in taking the valley without winning the people.'

He had aroused my interest in the operation and I caught the next available plane to Tuy Hoa.

While with the 101st ABN, I learned how much a unit depends on its leaders. Brigadier-General Williard Pearson, in command, had none of the stiffness and superior attitude I'd come to associate with many military men of his rank. He was dignified, simple, yet friendly and easy to get along with.

'The VC cannot live off the mountains, nor can they bring sufficient food down the Ho Chi Minh trail to survive. That is why they have fought so desperately to control this valley. Every day our forces suffer casualties in the area, but I'm hoping we'll succeed in keeping the VC from harvesting the rice . . . and harvest a good crop of VC at the same time,' he added.

He explained that refugees arriving from outlying hamlets provided a perfect cover for infiltration and therefore must be screened, with suspects being brought in for questioning.

General Pearson talked about the situation openly and realistically with none of the aloofness I had encountered so often. His various units reflected this attitude right down through the ranks. The men were generally helpful to refugees and I never witnessed any rowdiness or disrespect towards civilians. There was a comradely attitude, what the Australians called 'mateship', between the white and many coloured soldiers; never did I sense the gap that was so obvious in many other units. A year later I read an article headed 'Are Negroes getting a fair shake in Vietnam?' 'Yes' said Sergeant Brown, 'No' said Corporal Fischer. To me the difference in opinion wasn't surprising when I read that the former was with the 101st ABN and the latter with the 1st Cavalry.

My first day out I spent with the 2-327 Infantry Battalion, whose executive officer, Major Charles Dyke, arranged for a short patrol through the area. He accompanied us, cradling his sub-machine gun. My face was badly sunburnt from Phan Rang Beach so I had put thick white salve on my nose and cheeks, wore big sunglasses and my Aussie jungle hat. The peasants who passed us, carrying loads of rice baskets, were so startled they almost dropped their burdens.

'They probably think I've brought a witch along to cast a spell on their harvest,' the Major joked. I laughed and said, 'I'm glad the rice-paddies aren't sodden. I couldn't stand the reflection of the water on my face today.'

'Yeah. I hate walking through paddies when they are swampy, at planting time,' one of the men said.

'So do I,' I agreed. 'Near Danang we once walked across freshly irrigated paddies. Walked? We had to run, to keep our feet from being sucked into the pasty mud. I could hardly move for days after that.'

We reached the main dyke leading through the rice-fields — inevitably known as 'Major Dyke's Dyke' to the troops.

'This is as far as we can go,' the Major said. 'The other side is still controlled by the VC and we could run into snipers.'

I surveyed the area dotted with black pyjama-clad figures wearing conical straw hats. The rice fields shimmered bright yellow in the tropical sun. Both sides of the dyke looked alike. So did the peasants working there. It was difficult to believe that on this side of the dyke they were garnering rice for the Tuy Hoa storehouse, while on the other side the same activity was for the benefit of the Viet Cong. Both sides worked more or less forcibly, our side having to put their rice into Government safekeeping whether they wanted to or not, and the ones across the way feeling the same pressure from the VC. I was still shaking my head over it when we returned to our tents.

The next morning I went to a unit stationed in a nearby hamlet. Sniper fire from there had led to the discovery that the village was a veritable VC stronghold: spiderholes and trenches in every innocent-looking garden, and shelters made of mud with walls four feet thick, solid enough to make them practically bomb-proof.

It had been deserted when the troops finally moved in but now refugees were coming from further down the valley. To rescue their goods they carried loads three times their own weight. The ones with bicycles never ceased to amaze me. They managed to accommodate more on a bike than we could fit in a pick-up truck. Mattresses, household goods hanging from both sides, enormous trunks balanced on the steering handles. Small wonder they say the Viet Minh won Dien Bien Phu with 100,000 French bicycles on which they carried their discreetly camouflaged artillery, section by section, up the hillsides. Some peasants were floating pieces of furniture downstream, edging them along with large bamboo poles.

The unit camped in and around the deserted houses and watched the stream of refugees with a wary eye. The heat was oppressive and we were glad to find a few bottles of warm Larue beer in a cupboard. We searched the bunkers and entrances to tunnels underneath the village, which we were to blow up. Investigating this stronghold was a dangerous task but apparently its occupants had left in too much of a hurry to set up their usual booby traps.

Before nightfall we abandoned the hamlet to the refugees who might easily have turned into a competent, well-armed guerilla unit at dusk.

Back at Brigade headquarters, situated alongside Tuy Hoa airstrip, PIO Lieutenant Appel suggested I join C Company of the 502nd next morning. Charlie Company was ready to move on to a new location and I took pics while they were loading up the convoy. One of my photos caused quite a stir. A GI's well-worn pair of combat boots, with soles practically hanging loose, and laces mended in knots, caught my eye. They told a mute story of long, rough patrols.

But Major Schroeder heard of my camera subject. Almost wringing his hands he said, 'Can you imagine the stink it would cause back Stateside if they saw that picture? Mothers' clubs up and down the country would protest about their boys running around Vietnam in footgear like that, with all the money that's spent over here!' I promised not to pass the photo on for publication.

Later a grateful GI said, 'Gee, would you believe a new pair of boots from supply today!'

I followed Charlie Company to their new location southwards along the ocean front and within half an hour of our arrival a tent was erected for me. I was relaxing on my cot when a chopper brought in a frail-looking Vietnamese who was bleeding from a bullet wound in his leg. His eyes were bandaged. He must have been at least 80 years old: his white hair was a few baby-fine wisps, his back bent from years of hard labour, his body emaciated from a lifetime of malnutrition.

He was trembling with fear — he had probably heard of a sport practiced by ARVNs and also some American units: pushing Viet Cong prisoners out of choppers while airborne. 'We pinned Ky's calling card on their pyjama tops and out they went,' an officer had bragged at An Khe.

The soldiers bringing him back explained they were snipered at from a hamlet, returned the fire and saw two young VC run into a house. They closed in slowly, keeping up their fire, until they pushed their way through the front entrance. All they found was this old man lying on the floor. The two VC had beat it out the back and were long gone, headed for the hills. The old man was to be handed over to the South Vietnamese for questioning. I knew what that meant, and felt sorry for him, VC or not.

'He might just have been in a house the VC picked on to get away,' I said, lit a cigarette and pushed it between the old fellow's lips. 'Let the medic treat his leg, at least, before you hand him over.'

A coloured GI picked up the featherlight frame and carried him to the medic's tent, and his wound was disinfected and bandaged. I was glad the unit was so humane about it: I had previously seen prisoners kicked around badly.

The next morning a chopper came to take me to Bravo Company about 30 kilometres south-west of Tuy Hoa. Under the command of Captain Tom Taylor, the handsome son of General Maxwell Taylor, the unit had rotated to a hamlet the ROKs had taken two days earlier. When Bravo arrived they found most houses had been burned to the ground. Rice storage bunkers were still smouldering, and dead stock littered the area. They discovered a weapons cache the ROKs had overlooked, hidden beneath a partly burnt-out stable.

In the rice bunker of one house was an old Vietnamese women. She was terrified when made to leave her shelter and shaking as she jabbered in Vietnamese. Tom sent for an interpreter from Brigade HQ who came in on one of the supply choppers to question her. The result proved how little peasants in remote areas understood what was going on in Vietnam. The old woman was under the impression that the ROKs had been the enemy and that the Americans had come to free the village from them. Her version served to strengthen the suspicions Tom had. 'The ROKs claimed they killed 83 VC here. There were probably about three men in the whole place and the rest of their victims were VC women, VC children, VC animals and VC fowls. I guess they didn't want to leave any living being in case they were VC — or likely to become VC.'

When I arrived the old woman was happy and relieved to see another female. She kept stroking my cheek, clutching my arm and smiling up at me. Then she busied herself washing the troops' clothing, getting water from the well and bustling about. We gave her a fruit-cake from our C-ration tins, and she looked it over then cautiously began pushing portions into her toothless mouth.

The hamlet had been mortared recently and I was astounded at the nonchalant way Tom Taylor strolled through the area, wearing only a pair of fatigue pants and shower clogs, and quite unarmed as we explored the surrounding fields.

Several men were posted in small groups; at one corner of the perimeter three GIs played cards under a poncho stretched between the trees: near a burnt-out building a GI rotated a 'liberated' VC chicken over a small fire. A Negro was cleaning his rifle when we came across him. Accustomed to exclamations of surprise from soldiers who saw me in unexpected places, such as 'It's a mirage!', I had to laugh at this soldier's reaction. He just stared and stared, his eyes getting wider and wider, his mouth dropping open. Then he vanished into the bushes without having uttered a single word.

The terrible stench of dead animals lying in the sun became intolerable. The bodies were bloated, like immense balloons, and the men decided to douse them in kerosene and set them alight. One cow exploded and the stench of charred remains was almost as bad as the smell it had replaced.

And this of all times I had forgotten to bring with me my ubiquitous bottle of 'instant bath', being able to freshen up only with water from a steel helmet.

The next unit I went with was A Company of the same battalion and with them I had one of the most frightening experiences of my life. The day was quiet and calm, and we were pushing towards the mountain range at the end of the valley. The outline of the mountains loomed darkly against the cloudless sky as they left on what seemed to be no more than a routine patrol. A private commented, almost prophetically, that it was nearly *too* quiet: 'No water buffalo around, no birds singing, no peasants working the fields. It's kinda creepy.'

The patrol pushed on through deserted hamlets and fields, carefully watching for mines and booby traps. Every upturned leaf, every discolouration of grass or ground, every tiny stick of wood was suspect and the men carefully avoided stepping on anything that looked even slightly out of line.

In enemy territory death lies ready to spring from any angle so they walked Indian-file, jumping over or by-passing anything suspicious, grotesquely performing a *danse macabre* across the open countryside.

The few hamlets en route were approached with great caution. An advance guard of the patrol entered first, dodging and running soundlessly, seeking shelter behind bushes, tree-clusters, dykes or the mud walls of buildings. Only after these men had searched every hut would they signal the covering force to follow. I had always admired the advance guard or lead men of a patrol, confronting death so calmly, knowing they'd be the obvious target if the enemy was waiting, protecting their buddies to the rear, who would have ample warning and therefore a better chance of survival.

At noontime the patrol camped to eat their C-rations and have a short rest. They were now at the edge of the open rice-paddies, getting closer to the mountain range, and from then on the dry grassland was interspersed with clusters of bushes and banana trees. The area seemed deserted; the atmosphere was heavy with silent, leaden heat, the only enemy in sight was the sun, sending its merciless rays down on the sweat-soaked men and the baking earth.

On a clearing surrounded by bushes on four sides the ground was covered with hoof marks, showing that cattle had been in the area recently. When the advance guard was in the middle of this clearing the bushes came alive, cascades of bullets streaming from every one. It was a U-shaped ambush, with Viet Cong in front and on both sides.

Men dropped to the ground. Those hit emitted cries of agony while clutching their wounds. Others fired back furiously. Ignoring the blazing bullets, two men ran from the bushes and dragged a wounded soldier back to shelter.

It took some time for the ambushed patrol to realise their fire was not being returned. Their attackers had fled swiftly and silently and it was all quiet again, except for the occasional groan from a wounded soldier. It had been a typical Viet Cong hit-and-run attack: several rounds fired into the ambushed patrol, then an immediate retreat towards the mountainside, in such a hurry this time that they had left three of their dead behind.

The whole action was over in a few minutes — and the patrol counted seven wounded and one dead. Minutes later Medevac arrived in answer to the radio's urgent call.

I stepped into the clearing to photograph the wounded being loaded aboard, and the platoon leader spotted me and yelled to the pilot: 'You've got to take her with you. You can't leave her out here!' I was awfully scared and wanted to go straight back with them but I also wanted to get some photos of the dead Viet Cong I could see lying on the other side of the bushes.

There was little time for discussion or argument — the chopper had to take off again as quickly as possible. The Viet Cong are keen on target practice at choppers, Medevac or not.

'I want to stay. I've got a living to make and want to take some photos!'

One of the gunners tore off his flak jacket and threw it to me as the chopper lifted into the air.

'Here, lady, wear this. You'll need it more than I do and you've got more guts than I have!'

More guts? My stomach felt so low I thought I was walking on my guts at that very moment!

We moved out carefully, wary of sniper fire, and searched the VC bodies for weapons and any papers which might clue us on their activities.

One of the dead Viet Cong, a young chap, had a quarter of his head blown off; but when I took his photo the remaining eye seemed focussed on me, an unnerving sight. He somehow looked so alive, despite the grey mass of his brains spilled across the grass. We found a book of poems in his knapsack, beautifully hand-written in flowing characters, and illustrated with graceful pen drawings. In front of the book was a family portrait, obviously his wife and children, smiling, healthy, happy.

I looked at the book and the photograph then at the limp bloody body I had taken it from and at that moment I realised in a way I never had before just how disgusting and cruel man really is.

'How can you think of a person who takes a book of poetry to war as your enemy?' I asked a young soldier bending over the body.

'Yeah. It's kinda sad to see his kids' photo,' he replied. 'But I don't forget that could be me lying there now.'

Retreating to the bushes we set out watch posts at each corner and made radio contact with HQ. The rest of the company would come down the valley in a wide sweep to ensure our escape, we were told, but it would be some time before they could reach us.

About an hour later refugees began streaming through the clearing, led by a little boy waving a ragged white flag on a stick. Following him were women and children of all ages, carrying their belongings in rice baskets suspended on sticks over their shoulders — a pitiful parade. When they saw us the women put their baskets down, prepared to rest in the clearing. The soldiers waved them on.

I tried approaching them to get pictures but the 'radio' held me back with a warning: 'Stay here. You never know what they might be carrying in those baskets. They could have grenades. In this valley you trust no one.'

We relaxed our vigilance only when they were well past us.

I couldn't help wondering if it weren't just as dangerous to let them continue their journey, since they could easily report our limited number to nearby VC units.

It was slowly growing darker, and about half a mile away, showing up against the dusky background of the mountains we could see tiny black dots moving from one bush to another. We were only eighteen in number and the Viet Cong could be coming back with reinforcements, to wipe us out. The radio operator tried to contact HQ to check on our rescue party's movements, but could not get through. As night was creeping over the horizon I was getting more and more scared. I felt trapped in those bushes, waiting for something to happen.

The PIO had sent one of his assistants in with me, Rodriguez, an American of Mexican descent, and he didn't make me any happier with his comments about how we might be stuck there for the night. He'd say something cheerful, 'Let's hope they don't find us in these bushes before rescue get here.'

'I'm more frightened of facing the VC at night than in daylight, where I can see what's coming,' I answered. 'As a child my mother sometimes locked me in the huge attic of our house and I've been afraid of the dark ever since.'

The radio made contact. 'They're on their way . . .' and he passed on to HQ the truest message he'd ever relayed: 'There's a pretty frightened little lady here. I think she'd like to get back to headquarters.'

The reply was that General Pearson was trying to send in a chopper to pick me up but the area was too insecure to land in. The platoon leader, a friendly chap who seemed very worried about getting me out of there safely, tried to cheer me up. 'In the dark, it's also harder for the VC to see us,' he pointed out, and passed orders around: 'Keep low and hope they by-pass us.'

A coloured GI to our right commented dryly: 'This is one good time to be black, boy — I jus' close my eyes and they can't see me.' This released the tension as we hid our fears behind laughter, even if my giggling was near hysteria.

Suddenly a soldier waved energetically from the other side of the bushes. The platoon leader and I crawled across and saw the silhouettes of about sixty figures coming across the valley at roughly a ninety-degree angle from where we had observed the other movements. Radio contact was lost again so we couldn't establish if they were our party or not. In the quietness, as we watched, one soldier said soberly: 'If those guys aren't ours, all we have left is a three-word prayer . . .'

That was when panic set in for me. I squirmed out of the bushes, making for the weapons that had been taken from the dead Viet Cong. I took several grenades, a Chinese rifle, and a Russian bayonet, then wriggled back into the bushes and built my small arsenal up around me. I was shaking with fear and my hand trembled as I cupped a cigarette but I was determined they wouldn't get me easily. I was ready to fight them to the bitter end. I kept thinking how stupid I had been to come out, when I could have been comfortably relaxing elsewhere. There was no law that said I *had* to be out in the field so what the hell was I doing here?

'Please, please . . . I want to see Robert again — just one more time . . .' I whispered.

I made up my mind that if I got out of this spot I was going to be nothing but a plain, ordinary housewife for the rest of my life. Scared stiff, I was still muttering curses to myself about my stupidity when I heard someone shout, 'I see smoke. They must be ours: they're burning the hamlets on the way.'

At the same time two FACs appeared, cruising above us.

'They look like angels in the sky,' said one fervent GI as he blissfully looked up at them.

Everyone started to relax then.

When the rescue party came close enough I ran out of my sheltering bushes, shouting, 'You look so darn good I could kiss you all' which met with an enthusiastic 'Start right here' from one of the newcomers.

Tension eased at once and the platoon leader confessed: "My greatest worry was about her and her arsenal — that scared me more than the VC!'

We teamed up with the main rescue patrol and went in a sweep down the valley, burning huts and shelters on the way. On top of the hill, where the men were to camp for the night, an H-13 was waiting to ferry me out of the valley. The men were disappointed I was leaving — but I was too shaky to face another day in that area. Before I left, though, I took a photo of a sight I will never forget. Against the night sky danced bright-flickering fires: Tuy Hoa Valley was burning.

# 14

## *THE PHOENIX*

ᚹᚺᚹᚺᚹᚺᚹᚺᚹᚺᚹᚺᚹᚺᚹᚺᚹᚺᚹᚺᚹᚺᚹᚺᚹᚺᚹᚺᚹᚺᚹᚺᚹᚺᚹᚺᚹᚺᚹ

Back at Brigade Headquarters I ran into General Pearson and apologised for having been such a coward out there in the valley.

'There's nothing wrong with being scared under the circumstances,' he assured me. 'And as long as you make my men feel good by running around the camp with your smile for everybody, you're still doing a great job for morale.'

How nice of him to make me feel so much better about it!

At the office, Lieutenant Appel handed me a letter from Robert. I had radioed a message from Phan Rang that I'd be heading for Tuy Hoa as I expected to stay for more than a week.

My sorely missed woman,

I have just completed re-reading all your letters. Such pain they bring, unendurable. I can see you clearly, I reach out for you, but you are not there. Such sadness. Darling, those letters of ours, each one I write and each one I receive, bring us so near to each other. I know the effect of mine on you — how you'll react, sadness, laughter, desire, love — so much love for us. I am looking at the photos I have of you, all taken since that first meeting when you were borne to me. This is the you which is mine. I love and trust you and know that my future life is tied directly to you and you alone physically and mentally. Sex is very important to me. By sex I mean you and me; without you it's not sex it's just nature's way. Nature I can do without, you I can't.

Rena, from the time I first saw you I wanted you, I loved you. Now after I have possessed you it is much worse.

My love, I lie here reading of your body aching for me, how I would like to press away that pain with my body until our love has run together and we are spent, me to rest, look and love you so dearly.

I'd watch you relax, spent, serene peace on your face — my face. My woman, you can't comprehend my love for you, its magnitude, its intensity, I always tell you in words that are inadequate.

Had a letter from a friend in Aussie who seemed to read between the lines and asks if he can smell romance in the air. Have assured him

119

that there is and that I have asked you to marry me. You did say yes, didn't you, cherie?

Take care of yourself, darling, and return to me safely, my woman.

Your man,

Robert xxxxxx

I took the next Saigon-bound plane, rushed my films of the ambush scene to AP, where I waited till they were developed, I took several prints with me and headed for Vung Tau, though it was only Friday afternoon.

When Robert looked at my pictures from Tuy Hoa and I told him about the events there he didn't look very happy. Again he urged me to leave Vietnam and wait elsewhere for him. I suddenly realised there was another reason for his feelings, a type of jealousy because I had been seeing more action in Vietnam than he had. Men just don't like a woman outdoing them at anything and while I had thought he would be proud of me, he actually disliked my having such experiences.

I was convinced Robert would have faced the same situations much more bravely than I had. It was only a matter of chance that I had been out there, and that nothing had ever happened when Robert was flying a mission, missions for which he volunteered, I now realised, solely to prove he could face the same dangers I did.

I decided it would be better if I underplayed my activities a little instead of boasting about them.

Sunday afternoon on the beach, he said: 'Darling, sometimes I worry about us. I mean, there's so little I have to offer you, and you seem so perfect.'

'For Heaven's sake, Robert,' I said, 'don't get such foolish ideas. I'm full of faults. I try to hide them from you so I won't lose you, because I need you so much. If it makes you feel any better, I'll confess some of my misdeeds. At nineteen I spent a night in jail for hitting a cop over the head with my shoe in an argument about a traffic offence.'

Robert laughed: 'That's not considered a fault in Aussie. Hitting the fuzz is an honourable gesture . . . if you get away with it. Our ancestry you know!'

'I got fined fifty dollars for the assault. But the entire courtroom laughed at the 200-pound copper testifying how I had attacked him "like a wildcat".'

Robert chuckled at the thought.

'That the worst thing you've got to confess?'

'No. I was a prostitute once.'

He looked incredulous and said flatly: 'Come on, now, I don't believe that!'

'It's true,' I said, and watched for his reaction.

'Poor darling, you must have been destitute after Jean left!'

'Yes, but I can't use starvation as an excuse. You know that solid gold pendant I sometimes wear, with the phoenix on it, the one I told you hurts my neck because it's so heavy?'

Robert nodded.

'Well, I earned the money for that in the good old way!'

He thought I was having him on, so I told him the whole story.

'Shortly after my break-up with Jean, in the Cafe Brodard, Jacqueline pointed out Jean's latest conquest. The bargirl's face was coarse and she had horribly protruding teeth. I wondered how on earth Jean could have kissed her. "See the pendant she is wearing?" Jacqueline asked, "that small disc with the dragon on it? She shows it off all over town as a present from Jean." It was a traditional Vietnamese pendant, sold in all sizes, depicting either a dragon or a phoenix. You know the sort?'

Robert nodded.

'Well, to me that medallion suddenly seemed a symbol of my defeat. I raced over to a jewellers at the Eden gallery and picked out the largest medal available, one with a phoenix — the bird that rises from its own ashes. It was huge and vulgar. I paid down the last of my money on it and I needed the equivalent of US $200 for the balance. I was terribly hurt that Jean, after four years together, and after I had helped him out of trouble so often, would prefer this girl's company to mine. It was irrational, but I decided to get even by earning my medal in the same fashion as his latest girl friend had. At the next camp I met a good-looking B52 pilot and asked if he was game to go for a midnight swim at the off-limits beach. We arrived with champagne and cognac in our jeep and I told him I needed $200 and would spend the night with him for that amount. He was certainly surprised and said, 'Didn't think you were the type!'

Robert interrupted: 'And I didn't either. You didn't go through with it, did you?'

'Yes, I did,' I said firmly. 'Like I said, he was surprised but only too willing. We swam, drank champagne — then wandered off into the dunes. I didn't feel bad about it. It was an unreal experience, but nevertheless, a very tender and affectionate one. Back at the barracks he gave me the $200 and I collected my phoenix medallion. I returned to that camp about three weeks later and he asked me if I'd go with him that evening. He had been kind, a good lover, and we had laughed a lot in the dunes that night, running around in the moonlight like children so I said "Why not?" The following morning he came to bring me another $200 and had the surprise of his life when I refused it. I told him that all I had needed was the original $200 and he kept bugging me to know what for, and why I wouldn't take any more money. I just smiled and said: "That's the secret of the dragon and the phoenix" and never told him. By the way, my Vietnamese friends nicknamed me Phuong-Hoang, Phoenix, from then on.'

I didn't know just how Robert was taking it, but I didn't wait to find out as I continued: 'On the other hand, I once turned down an offer of $1000 to spend a weekend with a Special Forces guy.'

He was a huge chap who took a liking to me. He had been in Vietnam for thirty-one months, was highly qualified, spoke several languages, and told me he had a salary of over $2000 a month. He hadn't had a Western woman in all that time, and when I was leaving camp he said: "Please don't be offended but I want you so much I'll give a thousand dollars if you'll spend the weekend with me".

I told him that at that price, I couldn't possibly feel offended — but no thanks, I had my man waiting for me in Vung Tau.

'Just as well. I don't care what happened before I met you but from now on you're mine alone,' Robert said angrily.

# 15

## *TWO SPECIAL FRIENDS*

Six o'clock next morning, and the chopper headed for Saigon.

Below, Saigon River wound like a lazy snake in the valley, sparkling in the sun that penetrated the early morning mist. A cargo ship lay on its side in a bend of the river, disembowelled by a Viet Cong mine. After twenty minutes' flight we arrived at Tan Son Nhut helipad, but it took the cab nearly an hour to get from there to my apartment. These blue and cream Renault taxicabs were remnants of French colonial days, and were repaired by their owners with odds and ends such as Coke bottle tops and bits of wire: there were few spare parts to be had in Vietnam.

Saigon traffic had always been hectic but now, after the big troop build-up it was sheer chaos. The worst part was trying to cross the congested bridges over Rach Cau Bong, nicknamed 'Cholera Creek', when coming from Tan Son Nhut airport towards Cong Ly or Hai Ba Trung Streets. Military vehicles, taxis, new and old limousines, motorcycles and Lambrettas galore, cyclos and uncounted numbers of bicycles all cluttered the streets to form one big immobile mess.

'The field seems like a rest camp compared to Saigon traffic' was one GI's comment.

Traffic signals were completely ignored, with right of way belonging to the biggest bluffer and the loudest horn. A car was never really broken down until its horn stopped working. It wasn't unusual to see two White Mice chatting calmly at a street corner while the traffic jammed itself into immobility and the hornblowing became deafening.

The congestion had one advantage — it did save lives because there was no room for anything but minor accidents. Late at night when streets were clearer, a ride in a cyclo or taxi became a frightening experience. Cyclo-pedallers seldom turned in the direction they indicated; they cut right across the front of cars, to the accompaniment of squealing, protesting brakes. Taxi-drivers simply pushed their horns down and raced, looking in every direction except front. A callous American remarked: 'Build them two hundred miles of freeway: it's the best way of controlling the population explosion, far more effective than the war.'

The traffic wasn't the only thing affected by the US build-up. Nguyen Hue, the Street of Flowers, gradually shed its blooms, which were replaced by shoddy souvenir stalls and black market goods. Asked the reason, a vendor shrugged: 'Flowers are expensive now. They come down from the cool Dalat mountains and the Viet Cong demand road taxes. Flowers, fresh fruit, vegetables, nothing escapes the tax.'

The price of bare necessities, such as rice, soared and each day there were more and more refugees coming into the city, starving and without the means to pay for survival. They shuffled their feet in a monotonous rhythm of misery, their faces void of anything but despair, their shoulders hunched with weariness from carrying their meagre belongings.

A woman once stumbled in front of me and fell, spilling the contents of her rice-baskets on the ground. I helped gather her belongings together, things she had treasured enough to risk slowing down her escape from the war zone: three pots blackened and battered from use, a tin cup, several shabby black pyjamas (the only clothes she had for herself and the child with her), a rusty oil tin with a wick serving as a lamp, a small sack of rice and a chain-store type picture of Buddha in a faded gilt frame.

This woman and child would join other refugees in an alley, staring at dirty gutters, their faces masks of blankness. Somehow they'd manage to scrounge a handful of rice now and then, just enough to keep them from starving to death. The Vietnamese have a reputation for indifference, heartlessness, even cruelty, but there still existed among the poorer classes, the peasants and the workers, some compassion for those considered worse off than oneself.

Relief goods sent in by the ton from outside nations seldom reached the destitute. Supposedly distributed under orders from the Vietnamese Government, the bulk of these goods ended up on the black market, where items plainly marked as gifts from other countries were sold openly. Wealthy racketeers profited while thousands of refugees were starving except for handouts from those not much better off than themselves.

With my journalist's curfew pass, I once wandered the streets after midnight. I passed hundreds of people sleeping everywhere, heedless of enormous rats jumping over their bodies, or cockroaches crawling up their legs into their clothing. Saigon cockroaches are not easily ignored, being 'big enough to throw a saddle on'.

A few, a fortunate few, of these refugees managed to land a job somewhere. That wasn't easy. They had to pay a kick-back to the person providing the job. For instance, a man wishing to work as a cyclo-pedaller had to rent his vehicle from a wealthy proprietor, and if he didn't earn enough to pay the rent demanded, there were plenty of others willing to take his place.

Some owned or rented a toolbox and set themselves up as repair merchants. Their 'shops' were street corners, their clients the city's bicycle riders. Every rusty nail, every tiny sliver of wire was pounced on and hoarded for use.

Out of the ten dollars monthly I paid Chi Hai she gave a kick-back to the maid who had recommended her, and a kick-back to the janitor for allowing her to walk through the door. I wasn't her only employer: she looked after two other apartments in the building, and from her total salaries she herself employed another woman to do the heavy laundry on the roof of the building. The washer-woman gave her services to three other maids in the building — the 'maid's maid', a common institution in Vietnam, where there is always one still poorer than the poor. She also paid her dues to the janitor.

Our janitor spent his day on a couch in the downstairs hallway and his sole work was locking the door at curfew and unlocking it at stipulated times, and switching the electricity on and off according to police orders. He was the husband of the 'original maid' in the kick-back system of this building, and their combined efforts enabled them to live in comparative comfort. The janitor also discovered another profitable angle — switching on a tenant's electricity in forbidden hours in exchange for a few piastres from the tenant.

Such an extensive kick-back system in my building alone: what must it be like at government level?

Despite the people's misery, I was always astounded at the fun and laughter still existing in the streets. Jokes they played on each other were well received, and there were sheepish grins when someone lost his last piastres gambling, approving back-slapping and laughter when a companion got the better of a foreigner.

I was the victim of their cunning once. Sidewalk stalls on Le Loi Street had brand-new French books, amazingly cheap and I filled my arms with bargains only to find on closer examination that all copies had pages missing, or were filled with misprints. Nevertheless, my desk Larousse only cost me a fifth of its normal price, and if I managed to decipher the double print in the K and L section, didn't worry about words beginning with V, W and X, I didn't have too bad a bargain!

Coming down to their breadline level had advantages. Knowing

I was poor also, the neighbourhood people from then on charged me Vietnamese prices only. I once gave a local cab-driver ten piastres for a seven-piastre fare and told him to keep the change. With a grin he handed it back and said: 'Next American I charge 30. You pay no extra.'

The friendliness of the people lasted, even after I got a job and was able to have Chi Hai back. I continued to eat at street stalls where meals were ridiculously cheap compared with the same meals at European-style restaurants — and they often tasted better.

When one of our street's cyclo-pedallers married, his friends spread a blanket on the sidewalk and put huge bowls of food on it. I emerged from the building and they waved me over and handed me a bowl and chopsticks, laughing as I helped myself generously. The groom used to sleep in his cyclo at nights at our street corner, but he proudly showed everyone the canvas cot he had bought for his bride. Few of the refugees had such luxury. Most slept on the ground and considered themselves fortunate if they owned a blanket. The bride was visibly expecting, so there was another resident of Nguyen Van Sam Street on the way. The baby would be lucky: his father would earn enough with his cyclo to feed the family.

The orphans of Vietnam, who were alone in this mass of humanity, learned young to live by their wits and to put up with their lot stoically. One evening I saw one of the neighbourhood's shoeshine boys huddled up against a door next to our building, soaking wet with the spray from gushing monsoon rains flooding the street. I'd seen him about, a bright-faced, open lad who seemed less aggressive than some of his companions.

I nudged him awake, made a sign that he was to follow me. Shyly he sidled into the hall. Immediately the janitor was on his feet, shouting and waving him out.

'No, he goes upstairs with me,' I said sternly, grabbed the boy by the hand and marched him past the startled janitor.

While cooking rice and sliced steak with onions, I discovered his name was Phuong. He smiled timidly and ate his meal. I wondered if he'd protest about taking a hot shower, but the difficulty was getting him out from under it. He shrieked with pleasure and finally I had to turn the tap off decisively. I threw a sheet and blanket on the couch, on which Phuong slept like a log. The following morning he donned his ragged shirt and torn shorts and wandered back into the street.

I went shopping for Phuong that morning — shorts and shirts, rubber thongs, a blanket which an obliging GI bought at the PX. Hunting about for the boy, I checked his usual spots and finally tracked him down in front of a restaurant on Le Loi Street. I took him back to the apartment; language barriers were no problem as he expressively fingered the clothes in disbelief and joy.

I had Chi Hai explain to him that whenever I was in Saigon and the weather was bad he could come and sleep at my place. There was no point in giving him a key as the janitor would never let him into the building during my absence. Besides, I didn't want to encourage him to look on my apartment as his permanent home. My stay in Saigon would not last forever and it was wiser not to estrange him from his buddies in the street. However, we became mates, and the neighbourhood knew it and smiled.

Chi Hai told me Phuong rented his shoeshine kit by the day from a Chinese down by the river. This was one practical way I could help him: I had a carpenter make up a box and a friend fitted it with polish and brushes. Now Phuong could keep all the money he earned.

I almost lost his friendship once. He had been troubled with a toothache and his jaw became hot and swollen. We went to my dentist but as the waiting room was crowded and I was pressed for time I paid in advance, adding enough money for Phuong's ride back, and left him there. Next morning Phuong was waiting in front of my building; he shook his little fist at me and tearfully shouted the only taunt he knew I would understand: 'You number ten! You number ten!' as he pointed to the gap where the tooth had been.

The crowded street roared with laughter.

Apparently the dentist had not explained that this was one of his 'first' teeth, and that another one would grow. All Phuong knew was that one of 'my friends' had stolen his tooth. Also, he hadn't expected it to hurt. I had paid enough for local anaesthetic but it sounded from the report as though it hadn't been given. An explanation and a large ice-cream from the 'North Pole' shop re-cemented our cracked friendship.

Phuong was always around when I returned from a field trip until, a few months later, I suddenly missed him.

Chi Hai was vague about an 'aunt' taking him away. I had my Vietnamese schoolteacher friend Lam ask her about it. Lam explained that Phuong had found a home, with a relative according to the story, but possibly, Lam thought, with strangers who took a liking to him and perhaps saw the chance of making a bit of profit from a boy with his own shoeshine kit and new-found self-confidence.

'Don't worry,' Lam explained. 'If Phuong didn't like being with them he would come back. He is not kept in chains here in the city.

For a Vietnamese orphan, to be adopted by a friendly family is the greatest thing that could happen. To belong to someone, to have "brothers and sisters", that means more than wealth to my people.'

Much later I saw Phuong again. His new hangout was 100P Alley* near Tan Son Nhut. He looked happy and healthy and insisted on giving a free shine to my American companion.

I fed many children after that I but I never 'adopted' one in the way I had Phuong.

There was something special about him.

Lam, who found out where Phuong had gone, was another 'special' friend. There was nothing outstanding about his appearance. He was of average Vietnamese height, about 5′ 2″, slim and always wore a white shirt and dark trousers. When we first met our relationship was stiff and awkward — typical of Asian and Westerner trying to impress and outdo each other in politeness. The ice was broken one evening over a few drinks when we both started clowning and imitating each other's peculiarities in grotesque exaggerations. After we became friends he frequently dropped in for a chat whenever I was in Saigon.

Lam spoke fluent French and English and was interesting to talk to. A philosopher, and apolitical, he had a deep concern for his people's suffering.

One afternoon he came to the apartment and I mixed him a whisky and soda (weak, since, like many Vietnamese, Lam couldn't drink much alcohol).

'What's new around Saigon?' I asked.

'Nothing much. They're still clearing away rubble from the Metropole on Tran Hung Dao. You must have felt the blast if you were in town.'

'I was here and I certainly did feel it! It threw me right out of bed.' I pointed at the corner of my bed, supported by four bricks. 'Look. The post collapsed. The whole building was shaking. I was sure they'd hit No. 2 Police Station next door. I crawled under the mattress with my pillow over my head and waited for the next blast.' (There were usually at least two explosive charges set off each time. In this case, the second one failed to go off.)

'I looked outside and saw No. 2 station still standing. One of my cyclo friends shouted that it was the Metropole. I should have known something was due to happen along Tran Hung Dao — for the last few days the "neighbourhood fleet" detoured via Pham Ngu Lao. They always know when something is planned somewhere.'

*Where the bargirls charged 100 piastres.

'They do — not exactly where or when, just a tip to stay away from a certain area,' Lam remarked.

'It's amazing the Americans haven't got a better information service.'

Lam looked reflective.

'My people are not on their side,' he said slowly. 'They don't want them here. It is only the racketeers and corrupt officials who benefit from their presence. But, oddly enough, *they* are the first to be delighted when Americans get hit. It's a question of our yellow brother scoring one against the foreigner. A white skin, for us, is the colour of oppression.'

'Whose side are you on, Lam?' I asked jokingly.

'My own,' he said drily. 'I know many Americans mean well. There's the medic who saves someone's life, the GI who gives his rations to a hungry kid. People often say, "I don't like Americans but Tom or Joe or Harry is an exception. He's nice." The trouble is, twenty friendly Joes fade into the background when one arrogant imbecile treats my people with contempt. The way they show off with their money in the face of all the poverty! They overtip and overpay with that superior attitude and the recipient accepts, but at the price of his dignity.'

There was a knock at the door.

'Aha, the counsel for the defence — just in time,' I joked, when I saw my friend Russ, an American engineer.

Lam laughed, and Russ looked perplexed.

'We're on our pet subject,' I explained, 'criticising the mighty USA.'

'Oh well, we're used to that by now.'

'We were talking about Americans throwing their money around,' Lam said.

'We might feel guilty about having too much of it and want to help,' said Russ.

'Oh, but you go about it the wrong way.' I interrupted. 'For example, giving a cabdriver 100 piastres for a 10 piastre fare causes inflation. He expects it from every Westerner from then on. Also, unlike us, most Orientals aren't ambitious so, if he has extra money, the cabbie will just work fewer hours. And you guys wonder why taxis are suddenly a scarce commodity.'

'If you're helping by being free with money, how do you explain the present misery?' Lam asked. 'Even during French times my people never ate out of garbage cans. Now many are reduced to just that.'

I recalled when Special Forces friends brought an entire case of T-bone steaks we barbecued and ate on our roof garden. I put the bones next to a tree downstairs for the skinny neighbourhood dogs. A peasant clad in rags, leading a small boy by the hand, beat the dogs to the bones. He bent down, sniffed at them, quickly scooped them up and headed round the corner towards the river.

'What about all the aid from the States?' Russ asked.

'It never reaches the needy,' answered Lam. 'You can buy it all back at the black market.'

'We had to agree to let your government distribute it,' Russ protested.

'True. And now we come to the root of all the trouble: the disastrous American foreign policy in Vietnam,' Lam said sadly. 'You're too shortsighted. To fight Communism you'd have to offer a government that is better for the people. This one is worse.'

Russ admitted, 'They don't even try to hide their corruption. Like the big show they put on for our television when they burned the blackmarket goods on Nguyen Hue under police supervision. Sure a few articles were burnt, but mostly empty cartons. When the journalists left to file their stories the cops put the fire out quickly and rescued what they could. Next day the blackmarket was stacked as usual, with the police collecting their "keep the eyes to the sky" money.'

Lam nodded. 'The peasants and workers are better off under Ho Chi Minh than under a leader like le petit Maquereau.* Here they are exploited by a ruling class. There, as long as they accept the system, they have equal opportunities, a pension if they are disabled, social welfare if destitute.'

'You just said it: as long as they accept the system,' Russ retorted. 'If they don't they are thrown in jail. At least *we* can talk against our system and get away with it.'

'Yes, talk, Russ — but not act. Not even resist passively,' I interjected. 'Just burn your draft card or refuse to train medics for the war and your fate's the same.'

Lam continued, 'I dislike politics, but Vietnam needs communism to get back on its feet. Our mentality is not suited for a Stalinistic extreme, but we could now be the Yugoslavia of Asia, had the Americans refrained from interfering.'

'And China would swallow you up,' Russ stated triumphantly.

'A strong Vietnam under Ho would fight China as fiercely as they're fighting the US and form a human wall against Chinese expansion. History shows that. Our peasants also rose many times when exploited by our leaders and condemned to misery.'

'You couldn't stop 650 million Chinese,' Russ said cynically.

---

*'The little pimp', a popular nickname for Ky who had lived with a bargirl named Phuc before he married Mai. Phuc had a son by Ky.

'China can't afford to be an aggressor — and America should realise she can't either, in the face of all the emerging nations. Once these nations stand on their feet, they'll make sure no country will become powerful enough to swallow them all.'

Lam went on to tell us about a village in Quang Ngai province.

'A patrol of ARVNs came into the village, killed chickens and pigs for food, raped two young girls. They are not wholly to blame for their behaviour. Most of them are reluctant draftees, underpaid, and even that meagre wage is often diverted to the pockets of corrupt officials. So, in a moment of brief power they take vengeance and their victims seldom register a complaint for fear of worse reprisals. A few weeks later a group of PAVNs came to that same village and asked for shelter and food. They ate the rice that was offered, treated the people with respect, and helped them plant their paddies during the day. Where do you think the sympathies of that village lie now?'

Russ stared silently at his cigarette and Lam took a sip from his glass and continued. 'I don't want to whitewash VC actions, but their terrorism is less indiscriminate. They know the propaganda value of refraining from senseless acts of violence. They don't rape, don't loot villages, and if they execute without "cause" they are severely punished by their own cadres. Americans get snipered at, napalm the village, kill 27 women and children — it's an accident. But if civilians get hurt in a VC raid — it's terrorism.'

'What does a simple peasant understand about democracy or communism? Burn his child with napalm, then explain it was for the good of democracy! I talked once to such a man who had lost his wife and two children when Americans bombed his village because some VC had snipered a patrol nearby. The villagers didn't even know VC were in the area. He said, "I don't understand communism but I know Americans hate it. So now I am a Cong!" Americans made more VC sympathisers in this country than communist propaganda could have hoped to accomplish. All the millions the US spends on psychological warfare to win the minds of the people is just so much ridiculous waste! The war costs 30 million US dollars a day — a dollar for each Vietnamese citizen, north and south. Give them the dollar for food and they'll live happily ever after!'

'I agree with some of your points,' Russ said. 'You can't win minds when bellies are empty and bombs destroy villages. I love my country but I don't mind admitting I sometimes wonder on whose side I'd be if I was a Vietnamese peasant.'

'I know if I was starving I'd be slightly to the left of Ho Chi Minh for a bowl of rice.' I said.

They laughed, and seemed to be relieved to get away from a depressing subject.

Lam said, 'You're lucky — you can observe without being compelled to choose sides.' He heaved himself out of his chair. 'Come, Russ, let's take her to the market to eat. We want to preserve her neutrality.'

# 16

## BRASS TALES AND TRUTH

෬෬෬෬෬෬෬෬෬෬෬෬෬෬෬෬෬෬෬෬෬෬෬෬෬෬෬෬෬෬෬෬෬෬෬෬

Robert was always protective when I was around, even about incidents that didn't bother me much. One evening we were having supper at Cyrno's when a drunken GI at a nearby table started cussing in a loud voice. A wrinkled forehead showing his annoyance, Robert glowered at him, muttering, 'If that fellow doesn't shut his big mouth, I'll go over and do it for him!'

'For Heaven's sake, leave him alone. He's probably had enough of Vietnam, and this is his way of getting things off his chest.'

'Just the same, I don't like him talking like that in front of you,' was Robert's stubborn retort.

I tried to jolt him out of that mood. 'You remind me of a colonel who introduced me to his men and added: "While she's here I want no cussing around the camp." I pointed out that this order could make the whole camp mute. After all, I don't faint at the sound of a four-letter word — as I am intruding on a man's world, I'm prepared to accept it on their terms. There are half-a-million English-speaking men in Vietnam, many with only one expressive adjective in their vocabulary. You can't expect them to adapt to the few females running around the country.'

Robert was not appeased. 'In a woman's company, it's simple courtesy for men to watch their language!'

'Most do, but there's always a moment of tension, or sometimes they don't even realise there is a woman within earshot, like the time I was in a camp while Marines were erecting a tent under the supervision of a bald sergeant who was shouting the orders. Somebody goofed and the whole structure collapsed. The sergeant bellowed "You mother-fucking bullshit bastards! I'm gonna send yo'all back to kindergarten".'

'A young private gave a horrified look and pointed, the sergeant jerked his head — and spotted me about six feet away from him. That was one of the funny sights of the war — a tough old Marine blushing. He stamped off in disgust, muttering something about women who should be home washing dishes and diapers instead of making a nuisance of themselves in war zones.'

Robert said quickly, 'I agree with him whole-heartedly. You shouldn't be in a war zone, and you shouldn't be hearing such language!'

'Oh lala, what concern for my tender ears! Don't you worry, darling, those words mean nothing, especially as English is a foreign language to me. To feel that a word is "bad" you have to be brainwashed about it while very young. I'll prove it! Which sounds worse to you — *merde* or *pain?*'

Robert hesitated: 'How would I know? That last one, I guess.'

'See what I mean. In French the first word means "shit" and the second one "bread", but you still wouldn't react to them, even now that you know their meaning.'

'Yeah, I guess you're right.'

'I'll give you an example from this part of the world — one of Thailand's popular vegetable dishes is called gangfuk. In a Bangkok restaurant when I yelled to the waiter, "Got any gangfuk today?" — well, you can imagine how GIs sitting nearby reacted! On the other hand, English-speaking Thais say "Not until now" instead of "not yet" because "yet" is the Thai equivalent of your four-letter word for intercourse. So you see, the whole thing is silly when you look at it properly.'

'I get your argument, still, when we're back in Aussie I hope you'll watch what you're saying. The average person back home is pretty stuffy when it comes to women swearing.'

'I'll try to be ladylike, I promise! But I'll sure miss using good honest language. You know, to me some people never sound coarse even when telling a blue joke. Others can make you feel insulted just the way they say "Good morning".'

Robert said soothingly, 'Well, there's one good thing about you. I've heard you tell some pretty strong jokes but at least I've never heard you swearing badly.'

'That's because you've never seen me really mad or scared. When I've got cause I could make an old Marine blush — with envy!'

I told him what had happened in a chopper bringing supplies and mail to a mortar position in the jungle. The Viet Cong opened fire on us just as we were about to land and they scored several hits — it was a miracle no-one was hurt. I was paralysed with fright and almost cross-eyed from watching holes popping in one side and out the other. The gunners rattled away at the unseen enemy below and I suddenly came to life, reached for an ammo-belt and held it out to the number-one gunner at my right.

'You should have heard me letting off tension then,' I said. 'After landing I was still shaking when the gunner asked, "What were you yelling up there? I couldn't hear a thing . . ." "Just as well," I thought, and said, "Oh, I was only telling you there was plenty more ammo in the box if you needed it".'

After Tuy Hoa it took me three weeks to get enough nerve to go back into the field.

Shortly after eight o'clock on a Monday morning, the heat already oppressive, I left my apartment. At the corner stand I ate Pho, my favourite Vietnamese breakfast (a soup stock with noodles and whatever condiments one chooses to add from chopped goodies displayed in a glass case). I gobbled down the hot broth, grabbed my camera bag and headed for Jim Pickerell's office.

Jim had been a journalist with AP until he opened his own small agency. Flooded with requests from smaller American papers and magazines, he hired me on a retainer of $50 a week and 50 per cent of what he received for photos and stories I produced.

Jim was pretty good to work for, though sometimes he was a little vague. During a Buddhist demonstration he requested good close-ups of peoples' faces when the police threw tear gas, but he didn't provide me with a gas mask, which made lens work rather difficult. The resulting pics showed blurred faces with flooding tears streaming, while their owners were at the same time laughing at my attempts to focus with burning eyes.

This morning Jim had a job for me in An Khe: 'Go to the 1st of the 9th and interview the fellows who were with PFC Strickland on patrol when he was killed. Find out what kind of a guy Strickland was.'

I knew better than to ask, 'Why Strickland?' Jim's answer would have been: 'I'm paying you to get *your* story about him, not handing you one on a platter.'

He gave me a direction sheet and 2000 piastres for expenses and I was off to Tan Son Nhut.

In An Khe the top PIO, Major Smith, looked at me suspiciously. 'Who's the story for?' He thawed a little when I told him. 'Won't be easy, some of the men were wounded and evacuated and others are out on missions.' Smith didn't impress me with his obvious reluctance to co-operate on a fairly routine request.

An hour later I was introduced to Sergeant Donald Williams. We went to a deserted mess tent for the interview. 'You're doing the story because of the letter, I suppose,' was Williams' opening comment. I felt my way; I knew nothing about a letter. The Sergeant's head shook slowly as he said: 'The damnedest thing. Predicting his own death before he went out that day.'

It sounded as though I might get more of a human-interest story than I had expected.

'Tell me about the letter,' I suggested.

'Well, when we gathered his things together we found a letter in his notebook: "Dear Folks, I'm writing this letter as my last one. You've probably already received word that I'm dead and that the Government sends its regrets. . ." I can't remember the exact words but it said something about how he was glad to give his life for the freedom of the United States, and things like that.'

We were joined in the mess tent by Sergeant Nelson Flosi who was also on that fatal patrol, and I heard the rest of the story.

That morning, Lieutenant Teddy Sanford set up a patrol of thirteen men to look for a heavy automatic weapon that had been firing on passing helicopters. When Strickland heard about it he came three times to the Lieutenant, begging to be taken along. He was told the choppers were already fully loaded. Sergeant Flosi was scheduled as radio operator. As his right leg had been bothering him, Strickland saw Major Boyd and persuaded him it would be unwise to let Flosi carry the radio under the circumstances.

'Once before when Strickland was left off patrol he bent the Major's ear for the five days we were gone. From then on the Major let him go whenever possible,' Williams said. 'We walked across rice paddies and fields, and found a couple of deserted bunkers we blew up. Then we saw a Vietnamese running up a hill. We thought he was just a scared villager and didn't shoot. But we were on our guard, especially because everything was so quiet around us.'

Flosi continued: 'We had just covered the hill, with the main body inspecting an empty hut close by, when we stepped into a clearing surrounded by dense bushes. That was when all hell broke loose. Automatic weapons fire came from everywhere. We had no shelter so we hit the ground and fired back with everything we had. John Griffith charged the machine gun with a grenade and killed two of the enemy before he was chopped down. Another machine gun hit David Houston in both shoulders.'

Williams took up the story: 'The right flank charged out of the bushes towards us. That's when we knew they were trained PAVNs from North Vietnam: the VC do their dirty work and leave. They never charge openly.'

'I called for air support,' Flosi said. 'Suddenly Houston got up and started walking across the clearing, streaming blood and staggering like a drunk. He didn't know what he was doing. Strickland saw him, dashed out and grabbed him, and dragged him into the nearest bushes.'

'He never even saw the PAVN a few feet behind him.' As he straightened up, he got a bullet through the back of head and was killed instantly. We got the PAVN.'

When the survivors retreated under fire, Flosi was cut off from the rest. He shot up the radio so the enemy couldn't use it and crawled deeper into the bushes to hide.

'I heard them laughing and shouting while they were stripping the bodies of Griffith and Strickland of anything useful. Then suddenly two gunships rotated above and opened fire. The PAVNs shot back but were forced to retreat. I slowly edged my way to the clearing and saw Houston trying to crawl up the hill. I ran after him and carried him down. Later we picked up the bodies of Griffith and Strickland.'

Williams returned to the letter: 'We felt pretty bad when we found it, especially as he shouldn't have been on patrol in the first place.'

I had my material, but that last phrase, 'He shouldn't have been on patrol in the first place,' kept nagging at me.

After dinner I joined the enlisted men for a few drinks. One of the group had also been on the Strickland patrol and after a few more beers and a formal promise not to use his name he opened up:

'There was nothing supernatural about that letter. Strickland had a death wish, it's as simple as that. Last November he was on patrol at Plei Me and they were almost wiped out. Strickland came out unharmed. He pretended to be dead, and lay there watching while two of his best buddies had their throats slit. Strickland wasn't the same after that. Both men had wives and kids back home, and he kept saying "Why them? Why not me?" He kept begging to go on patrol all the time after that. When we went without him he made such a fuss. It just wasn't normal. We approached the CO, said we thought the Plei Me ambush had been too much and Strickland had cracked up. The CO shrugged it off: "There's nothing wrong with him. He's just got a bit more guts than some of the others around this place".'

I wrote the story from that angle and handed it in. A few weeks later Jim showed me a copy of the *Family Weekly Magazine*. They had changed my title 'Last Patrol' and had called it 'The Story Behind a GI's last Letter to his Mom'. Not a word of the Plei Me ambush and Strickland's death wish. Instead, they'd turned it into a schmaltzy sentimental mish-mash about a young hero who foresaw his death but gave his life willingly for his country.

It sounded like a corny 'Join the Army' pamphlet and made me sick.

The day after my interview with the sergeants I went to the 'golf course'. A young gunner waved cheerfully, his protective vest open and swinging.

137

'Too bad you didn't come out with us. You'd have got some good pictures of the elephants we shot.'

'What elephants?'

'Nine VC elephants transporting mortars and ammunition.'

I'd have no trouble selling pictures of an incident like that to Jim or AP. Suppressing the small pangs of pity for the huge beasts I I had come to like while among the Montagnards (elephants cry tears when they are sad or hurt, a moving sight), I hurried over to the Colonel at headquarters. Perhaps I could arrange transport and get some post-incidental aerial pictures.

'What elephants?' the Colonel barked defensively when I made my request. 'I don't know what you're talking about.'

I was bewildered and suspicious. Pretending to accept his denial I ducked into the briefing tent to look at the situation map. There were three notations in a close area, claiming several elephants. The last recorded were nine in one spot.

The following morning I headed for town to see a French-speaking official who was likely to be 'in' on anything that was going on.

He was not a happy man.

'There were nine elephants killed,' he agreed. 'They belonged to the Montagnards and their sole purpose was the transporting of wood. The Montagnards are very angry. They were all the tribe owned, and much prized. An incident like that can sway any village from one side to the other!'

I spoke to a GI later and he told me they had orders 'from the top' to shoot every elephant on sight. 'Some shoot anything that moves — tigers, buffalo, porpoises at the coast — and call it "cleaning out the machine guns",' he admitted sadly.

With the story verified I headed back to the Colonel. He was furious, partly because he had been caught in a lie. I offered to let the pictures go through with any official caption or version he liked to give, if he would let me go out and take some. But he wouldn't budge and finally I was just as angry as he was and told him that if it hadn't been for his attitude I wouldn't have become suspicious and looked for the real story.

That was the end of the interview with the Colonel.

And the start of trouble in Vietnam for me.

Two days later I joined the officers in their club house. With screened windows and a cement floor it was a pleasant spot in which to spend an evening. In a tent below the club I changed from my dusty fatigues into a silk shift and high-heeled sandals before heading up the hill. I played the slot machine for a while then sat in a circle with several officers.

As usual the talk soon turned to home, their wives and sweethearts.

'You remind me so much of her,' a familiar phrase followed by a photo of anyone from a Valkyrie-type blonde to a skinny redhead. The fact that I had 'round-eyes' and spoke their language was enough to remind them of their womenfolk back home.

'I don't know why the American command doesn't send women here, like the French did,' I commented.

'The French had it made,' one officer stated. 'They had regular, health-controlled brothels with their own women — and the money went back to their own country. Our committees won't face that troops don't live a life of celibacy. So we go to the villages, disease risk and all.'

'The set-up's no secret to the politicians or the Army brass.'

Another commented: 'Oh they know, all right, but they're scared of the fuss some frustrated old bitches back home would make if they did anything about it.'

'Politicians think about votes and the Brass thinks about the next promotion coming up,' said another.

'Yeah, and that's not all. Our Colonel said if he ever caught a married man of his unit going to the bars it would show on his report. So we can't even go where our medics give injections! What's the result? Some sneak out back with women in laundries or tailor-shops downtown and come back with a dose.'

A few more beers and the boys started to sing the An Khe song. Then a young PIO came in and told me he'd been ordered to escort me back to my quarters. Surprised, I checked my watch and said, 'It's only just after nine. Does the club close this early?'

Embarrassed, he said, 'No. But the Colonel wants you to leave.'

'In Heaven's name, what for? He walked through about half an hour ago and said hello but he didn't say anything about leaving. Tell him to come and order me out himself or I'm staying!'

The PIO left but the young officers looked concerned.

'Look, you'd better go, or he'll make us no end of trouble.'

'All right. I'll just finish this beer.'

I didn't get a chance to. Major Smith stormed in and grabbed me by the arm.

'You come with me!'

I shook myself loose, furious.

'Don't touch me!'

Brushing past him I headed for the tent. Smith ran after me and tried to pull me towards the jeep.

'Take your hands off me!' I screamed. 'My fatigues are in that tent, and I'm not going in your dirty jeep in my silk dress!'

I stormed into the tent and he followed.

'I'm staying here,' he announced.

He turned his back on me but I wasn't too angry to fail to notice that he kept his head at an angle.

'Out! Out!'

Several men assembled outside, their boots showing below the tent flap. Smith saw them too and left the tent.

My fatigues on, I grabbed my camera bag and went outside: 'Would one of you men please accompany me through the ravine to my quarters?' Smith promptly yelled that he was taking me there. Captain Roberts grabbed my camera bag.

'Let's go!'

He wore only his fatigue slacks and, barefoot, he and a lieutenant guided me through the ravine.

At the nurses' quarters Smith gave me a dirty look and said: 'That will cost you your MACV card!'

My temper hadn't cooled so I snapped back, 'If keeping my MACV card means having to take crap from a bastard like you, you can shove it!'

The next morning two MPs came to escort me to a plane for Saigon, but not before many of the young officers came to let me know they backed my stand. Smith was very much disliked in An Khe.

The MPs weren't too happy about their job and murmured something about 'orders'. 'Never mind, boys, c'est la guerre.'

In Saigon I contacted Commander Maddison at MACV. He'd always had a soft spot for me and promised to do his best to straighten the matter out.

A few days later he faced me with a doleful shake of his head.

'I'm sorry, I can't help you, Rena. Smith's story was that you were drunk and egging the men on to fight over you. Unfortunately he's got the ear of the command here — your accreditation is cancelled.'

Smith couldn't have chosen a more preposterous story if he'd thought for a month. I was always proud to be equally friendly to all the troops, just to take their mind off the war for a while, and I'd never caused any problem.

No doubt the fuss I'd raised over the elephants was the real reason behind it all.

I went to the Caravelle and cried on the shoulder of my old friend John Harris. He was full of practical advice.

'Look, Rena, there's one thing you've got to learn to live with. You are the type of woman who will have problems. You don't give a damn about being diplomatic. You live by your own code, by what *you* think is right, and you tread on too many toes, like you did over this elephant incident. You should have filed the story away in your mind but not made such a fuss about it in An Khe.' He shook his head at me. 'A few of us will always be your friends. But from others you can expect lots of heartbreak and trouble, unless that man of yours is strong enough to defend and protect you. And I hope for your sake he is!'

John was a straightforward, outspoken chap.

I sighed and kicked off my shoes and he glanced down and grinned.

'He should take you out of here and keep you permanently pregnant — and barefoot, since you appear to prefer that. Meanwhile, how about moving yourself over to PA&E. I heard they want to bring out a fortnightly paper like RMK do, and you might get a job there.'

I dried my tears, put my shoes back on and took a cab out to the Tan Son Nhut office, where I was hired on the spot. Salary was US $750 per month, plus $275 living allowance for Vietnam. I couldn't believe my luck.

I rushed back to John Harris and told him the good news.

'Fine. Make the most of it while it lasts!' was his slightly dampening reaction.

'You old Cassandra!' I teased.

A few days later I was approached by a *Time-Life* reporter, ordinarily based in Hong Kong. He had just returned from an assignment to cover an operation with the 1st Cavalry and when he greeted me by name I groped in my memory to recall him.

'The morning before your trouble I was with Smith when you walked by. I asked who you were and he said, "A freelancer, and a real bitch. But I'm going to cook her goose!" He sounded so malicious I knew something was up and later I went to see if I could find you to warn you but you weren't around and I had to leave on an operation.'

He'd heard what had happened since, and offered to make Smith's remark known in the right quarters. But by then I had my job with PA&E so I let the matter drop.

# 17

## THE VOICE OF THE PENTAGON

'That Smith sounds like a first-class bastard to me,' was Robert's comment when I complained about losing my accreditation. 'But I'd still shake his hand if ever I met him — just for keeping you from committing suicide out in the field.'

I should have known better than to expect sympathy from Robert. He was thrilled that I was forcibly kept off patrols and missions. In truth I wasn't too unhappy about it myself. With my improved salary I was able to save money and our weekends in Vung Tau made up for the lack of excitement in my work.

It was Sunday morning and we were breakfasting at the Grand, as usual. This time the manager, Mr Nguyen Phoc Dang, joined us, to let off steam about the previous week's election. He spoke French, and I translated for Robert.

'Under Diem, at least we had only one family to pay off. Now everyone wants kick-backs,' the manager sighed. 'The police chief's wife complains about the heat in her bedroom without an air-conditioner, the mayor's wife about her son's need for a bicycle . . . and I know better than not to supply them if I want to keep my hotel permit. And those elections, what a farce!'

'Yeah,' I agreed, 'my friend Lam said, "Now we have a choice between two idiots — just like in the US." '

Robert commented about the White Mice going from house to house and literally driving people in herds to the voting booths.

'I saw a cyclist turned around at gunpoint at the edge of Vung Tau,' I said. The manager explained: 'He probably didn't have his identity card stamped at the polls and without this stamp he'd get nowhere.'

'We heard Johnson's speech over AFRS,' Robert said. 'He made a big issue about how many people went to the polls "voluntarily".'

'Sure, just as he claimed 80 per cent of the South Vietnamese are on the side of the government but didn't explain why they have to destroy so many of these to get at the other 20 per cent.'

142

I was glad when Robert suggested going to the beach. Discussions about politics always depressed me and made me doubt if the average IQ in the US could be more than 70 if they swallowed all the crap that was dished out about conditions in Vietnam. We spent the afternoon at the beach and while I was lying on my stomach dozing in the sun I could feel Robert tickling my back. 'We'll join the picnic in a little while,' he said. 'Plenty of beer and steaks. I'm glad you're here. I always get a bit sentimental and loving after a drink or two and I like to have you within easy reach then.'

'Does that mean a walk towards the burnt-out tank a little later?'

'Hmmmmmm . . .'

When we joined the picnic I noticed some fellows walking around me and laughing and I asked Christa to look at my back. Robert had written, with his ballpoint pen: 'If lost, return to R.T.G.' Christa tried to erase the lettering with sand and practically took my skin off. I grumbled about childishness but was actually quite proud to be marked as his 'property'.

Ron and Christa invited us for supper at the Pacific, but Robert insisted on taking them to a French restaurant instead.

'The Pacific is an officers' club, and I don't really like going there,' he said later. As rank meant nothing to me, I had never thought about that aspect.

'But, chou, isn't it expensive to eat in town every weekend?' I asked.

'Never mind. I can always sell my hat to a Yank.' Americans apparently paid up to $30 for Aussie slouch hats, and the Australians had also discovered another profitable sideline: they had village women sew 'VC flags' which they kicked through the dirt, and took to the camp cook to get a bit of blood splattered on; sometimes they fired a shot through the cloth for good measure. Americans paid quite a price for these 'terrific war souvenirs'. It would seem that this generation of Diggers had inherited the well-known 'con tricks' of the fathers and grandfathers who had donned khaki in the two previous wars.

With Christa's help I had an ideal set-up for getting messages to and from Vung Tau via the PA&E communication system, and this helped offset any disadvantages the new job held for me. Compared with my former activities, the work at PA&E was dull, but on the whole not too bad. The staff consisted of a rather ineffectual editor (PA&E's former personnel manager who had married a daughter of the management), Kim, a Korean photographer, two secretaries, and me. My job was to interview company personnel, write up their background, and report on the progress of jobs throughout Vietnam. We had to fill four pages every two weeks.

I could visit camp sites on company travel orders and often managed to get stories for news on the side.

At Qui Nhon, after finishing my routine job, I met a pilot walking towards the airfield. His name was Captain Earl Apperson and he handed me his calling card:

HAVE U-10, WILL TRAVEL
PSY-WAR OUR SPECIALTY
Be a litterbug on a national scale.

He explained: 'I'm assigned to psychological warfare. The U-10 is equipped with a battery of twenty-four loudspeakers which produce an absolutely ear-shattering total of a thousand watts. We send messages from Uncle Sam to Charlie Cong. We also drop leaflets. If you're willing to heave them out for me you can come along for the ride.'

'I'd love to!'

The plane was daubed camouflage-style and he explained, 'The VC hate us and do their damndest to shoot us down. We paint these planes camouflage hoping that if we are downed they'll have a tougher time finding us.'

The tiny, slow-flying craft turned towards a valley known to be a Viet Cong hideout. Farmers working below looked like clusters of mushrooms in their conical straw hats. Accustomed to aircraft they did not look up, until the pilot switched on the loudspeakers, then it was as though a wind had swept through the valley and tilted the mushrooms upside down. Every face looked at our plane, now soaring directly above their heads.

'Your wife and children are now sitting down to eat at your home,' the great voice roared its effective, taped message. 'They are looking with sad eyes at the empty chair at the head of the table. Why don't you go back to them while you still can?' (Uncle Sam forgot that most Vietnamese squat down to eat.)

The leaflets' message was roughly the same, and the sheets were illustrated for the benefit of peasants unable to read.

'Here goes,' said the captain as we lost altitude. 'We're not supposed to fly lower than 1500 feet, but it's impossible to drop the leaflets anywhere near our target if we fly too high, especially on a windy day like this.'

Most of the peasants ignored the leaflets but children were running about, trying to catch the fluttering pieces of paper in mid-air. To them it was a new game — catching pictures falling from the sky.

Another story I picked up on the side was about the spoiled little dog at the camp near Lai Khe. He had joined a patrol, happily yapping and wagging his tail. The men rebuffed him, afraid he'd betray them to the VC, and he rushed into the bushes. Suddenly there was a tremendous thundering boom and the pup ran out, tail between his legs, and headed straight for the camp. He had tripped a claymore mine meant for the patrol which could have wiped them out. After that, the pup was fed on steak, had his own special doghouse and was undoubtedly the most pampered pet in Vietnam.

As my new job took me out into the field camps, there were still some risks. Lai Khe was mortared one night — but at the time a group of us had gone swimming in the pool of a former French plantation further down the valley. The pool was outside the perimeter: we were lucky not to be caught, either by VC or our own MPs.

After the mortar attack all vehicles were ordered to drive without lights — a rather absurd order since headquarters were lit up like a three-ring circus, and the Vietnamese occupying the former plantation hands' quarters could easily report locations of vital targets. The 'no lights' order resulted in the death of a young American, run over by a darkened truck. My reporting of this mishap didn't endear me further to the top brass.

VC mortars weren't the only danger at Lai Khe.

Mr Williams, PA&E's electrical engineer, and I stepped outside the office tent, when suddenly a Vietnamese youth who'd been digging drainage trenches ran towards us, swinging his shovel. For a second I thought he'd run amok, and ducked as the shovel came down a few feet from me . . . crushing the head of a small snake. I shuddered — it was a type the troops called Two-step Charlie . . . 'that's how far you get after one bites you.' (Several Vietnamese told me that lepers are immune to this snake's bite.)

A Vietnamese office employee emerged from the tent, saw the snake suspended from the shovel, looked at my sandelled feet and said drily, 'Do you know what to do if one of those bites you?' Expecting to hear some secret Oriental remedy, I shook my head and he said: 'Sit down calmly, take out a cigarette and flick your lighter. If the lighter doesn't work the first time, forget it.'

I headed back for Saigon the next morning.

The Central office carried quite a few hard-drinking freeloaders, mainly pre-occupied with building flats for their mistresses, and a sprinkling of genuine adventurers. Most women employees were what the troops classified as 'Stateside rejects' and were (to put it politely), a pain in the neck. The four who were swell had been driven there by fate. I took an immediate liking to a skinny, lively, intelligent girl of Australian origin, who had a bottomless reservoir of 'esprit'. Elaine was orphaned at the age of seven (her father died at the horror camp on the River Kwai, her mother several months later). She grew up in a strict, loveless convent. In her teens, she met and married a Thai who had come to Australia to study.

'I was very happy with him while we were still in Australia,' she told me. 'Back in Thailand his family treated me as an outsider.'

She left and came to Saigon to earn enough money to take her two lovely children back to Australia. (The family tried to keep the children but Elaine eventually succeeded in gaining custody, and returned with them to her home country.) Although top secretary at PA&E, she received only about half the salary a mediocre US typist earned. Australians and Canadians were labelled '3rd Nationals' by US firms in Saigon, and thus received less pay than Americans. My own classification would have entitled me to $1,300 a month had I been a US citizen.

I dragged Elaine to Vung Tau with me the first weekend and introduced her to Robert's friends. We had a great time, with Ron and Christa joining the group.

We danced at local joints, ate out together, and at night we would all pile in a jeep and drive to Back Beach where we'd hide the vehicle in the dunes and swim in the nude, each couple the centre of a little private world . . . like South Sea Islanders — happy, laughing and uninhibited.

In Saigon, Elaine and I saw each other often outside the office. One afternoon we were having a drink at the Caravelle when a friend from the US Embassy introduced us to Ralph.

Ralph, dark-haired, tall and with a jolly, friendly face was with the State Department. His surname was incredibly long — 'the longest name starting with Mac in the Washington telephone directory' he boasted — so we simply called him 'Mac'.

He took me to dinner that night. We talked, danced and drank champagne. The next morning — red roses and another invitation to dinner. It became a routine: roses every day, sometimes twice a day, and bottles of champagne.

He was infatuated, and even telling him about Robert didn't seem to make much difference. He didn't want to understand that Robert meant everything, and that he was only a convenient dinner escort.

I guess it was in an effort to impress me that Mac opened up about his work. Every night, shortly after dinner, he had to dash to Tan Son Nhut. I wondered about the odd job that started at eleven every night.

But I wasn't probing when I made an idle comment about it, though I was a little surprised when Ralph said casually: 'It's 11

146

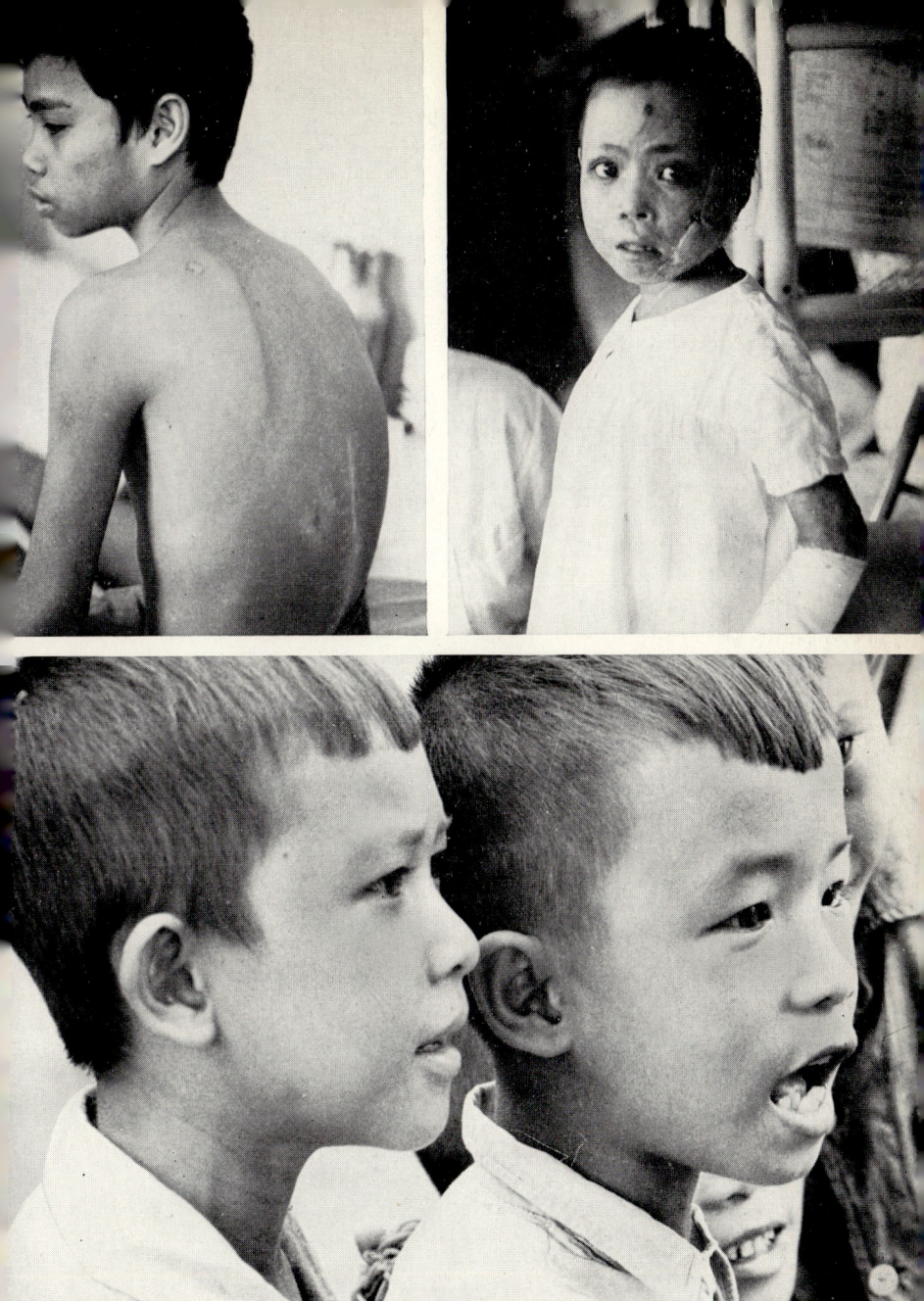

Luong: paralysed for life. Sau: mosquito net or napalm?
Phuong (left) with friends. There was something special about him.

RAAF chopper crashed into an ammunition dump.
'Crop my knees off, mate . . .'

After tramping through dense growth, an Australian patrol rests in
a clearing.
Sunday picnic in Vung Tau dunes for 9 Squadron, RAAF.
(*Photo: Sgt. Bob Curnow*)

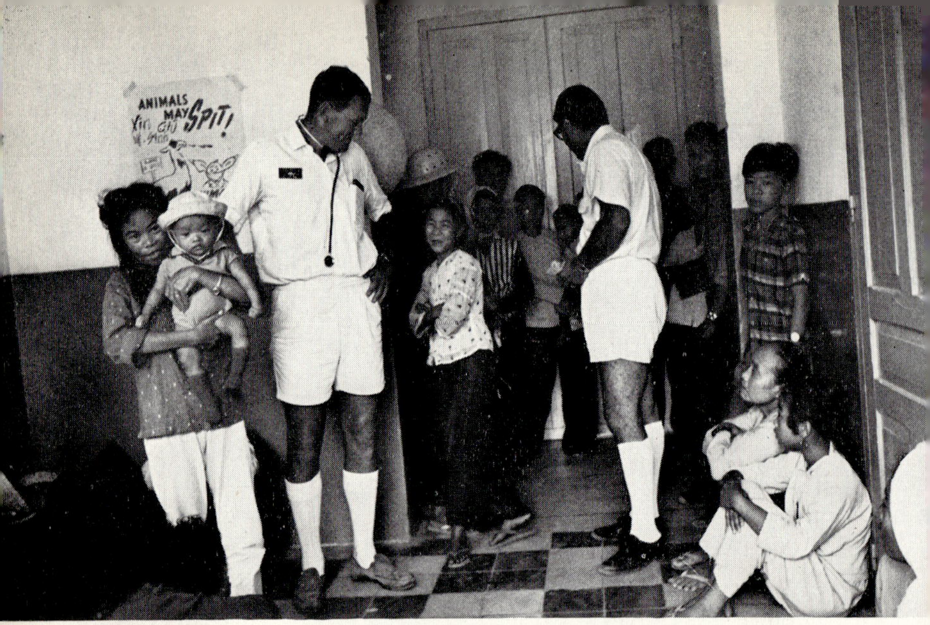

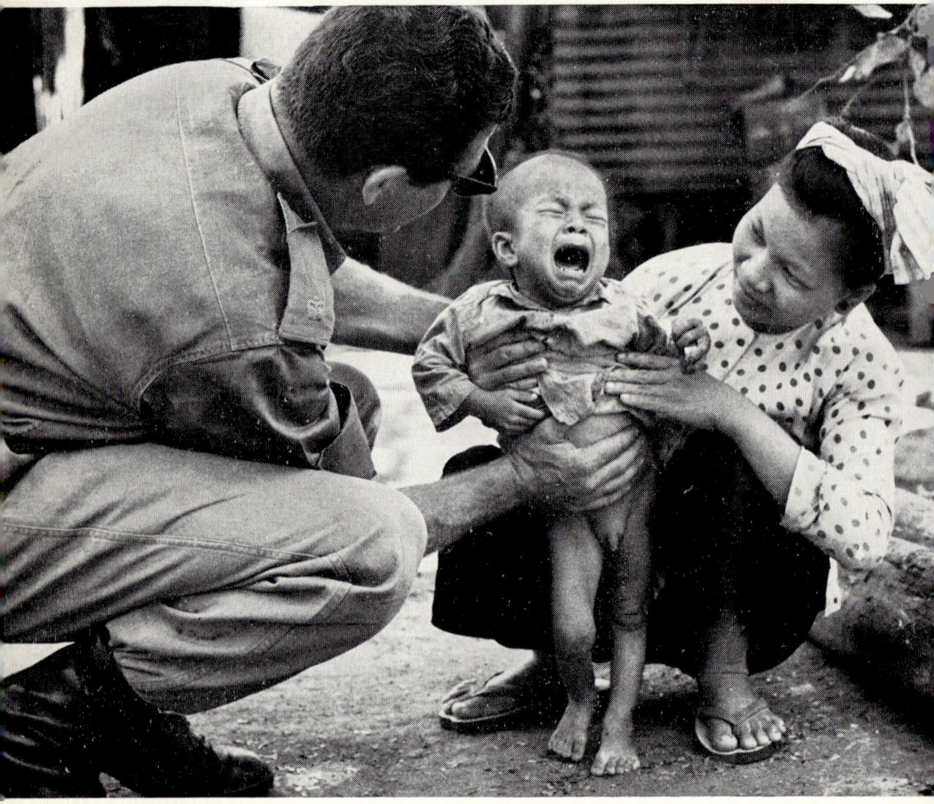

Dr Perrett (left) and Dr Aroney among patients awaiting treatment at
Le Loi hospital.
Major Donohoe advises mother to bring her sick child to the Australian
dispensary at Hoa Long.

a.m. in Washington: the hour they start to wake up at the Pentagon. I operate the coding machine connecting us with Washington.'

He told me about the complex machine on which he sent coded messages from Saigon command to the Pentagon, and received orders in return.

'So you're the voice of Westmoreland and McNamara — all rolled into one!'

'Yes — and you want to know something? I shouldn't even be seen with someone like you — I could get into trouble!'

I didn't take him seriously — but about a fortnight later I received a note by messenger boy.

Mac asked me to come to his place immediately.

He lived on Tu Do Street, just one block from the Continental and I hurried over, racing up the two flights of stairs, the lift being out of order as usual. I didn't know what to expect when I arrived.

A stranger opened the door.

'What's wrong with Mac?' I asked. The man shrugged and said, 'Nothing — he's here.'

He stepped aside and I could see Mac packing his suitcase. Watching him were four men, all strangers to me.

I can smell Secret Service ten miles against the wind.

Mac looked rather white and shaken and I blurted out, 'What's going on?'

His voice was unnaturally stiff as he replied, 'I'm leaving for Washington in a few minutes. I just wanted to say good-bye and thank you for being such good company and showing me Saigon.'

I was aware that this was no normal departure.

'I'll be damned. This is certainly sudden.' Then I caught hold of myself and said quietly: 'I'm sure you'll have time for a cup of coffee before you leave, so we can say good-bye without the audience.'

He clicked his suitcase shut as I spoke and glanced questioningly at one of the men. The man ignored his look and I decided to challenge him. 'Nice of your friends to give you a lift, Mac. Won't you introduce me?'

One of the men spoke:

'You can have ten minutes at the Pagode across the street. But no more or you'll miss the plane. We'll take your bags.'

We hurried across to the Café Pagode and ordered two citron presses.

One of the men followed us and took up what he thought was a discreet stance on the opposite sidewalk.

'What the heck's the matter?' I asked anxiously.

'They're shipping me back because I've been seeing you,' Mac admitted. 'They're CID men. They arrested me yesterday and questioned me all night about what I'd told you and what you've been asking me.'

'Hell, I've never asked anything about your work, and you know it! I loved the roses and champagne treatment — that was all.'

'That's not the way their minds work. Anyway I only hope I can straighten things out back in Washington. I'll give you one bit of advice, Rena — they'll be after *you* from now on. Watch yourself. If I were you, I'd leave here pretty quick. If you make it to Washington, don't forget I'm the longest Mac in the telephone directory!'

I found it hard to believe, but Mac was adamant about the accuracy of his comments.

'You don't know how ruthless they are, nor how they operate. First of all, you talked too much about your husband. Now you're on their blacklist, whether you deserve it or not. Be reasonable and leave before something happens.' He was pleading with me now.

A signal from across the street. I walked back with him to the black limousine, squeezing his hand before they drove off.

'Don't worry, I'll be all right.'

And for three days, I was.

Then came a summons from Tran Hiep Thoi, chief of immigration. I wasn't at all concerned about it. I had applied for renewal of my residence permit some ten weeks earlier. Formalities like that always take an endless time in Saigon. They'd send a stamped receipt saying that the application had been registered, and this was regarded as enough to go on. Often the actual permit arrived just in time to apply for yet another renewal. So I took it for granted that I was to pick up my permit when I entered Thoi's office.

Thoi was a young man to hold such a high position, thirty-five at the most, I judged. He was slim, wiry and not bad-looking but he had a rather conceited manner, and his eyes were insolent. He sat enthroned behind a huge desk squat in the middle of his office.

'Madame Jacobs-Briand?'

He motioned towards the chair opposite his desk.

'Asseyez-vous.'

'Merci.'

He looked at me then busied himself with papers on his desk for several minutes before he started talking, and then it was to rattle off a number of questions.

Where was my husband? What were his activities while he was here? He had a false passport — what about yours? Why are you still using the name Briand? There were other questions, all in the same vein and all equally unexpected.

I answered them as well as I could — told him I had no idea

where Jean was, nor the extent of his involvement with the CIA; that I had never procured false identification myself, that I still used the name Briand for writing purposes and had legally registered it in Vietnam because it was vital to adhere to one by-line for material published.

Finally he said slowly: 'I don't think I can grant you an extension. The American authorities have indicated that it would be better if you left the country.'

At one time that would have stunned me but by that stage I knew how to touch the Vietnamese on a sore spot.

'Oh, that's too bad. I thought you had the authority to renew or refuse my visa. I didn't realise how much Americans were running things these days. When will I pick up my exit visa?'

The ruse worked. Thoi was definitely taken aback. He hurried to recover ground.

'Naturellement, the Americans can only *suggest* that I make you leave,' he said angrily. 'We command in our own country. I will investigate your case further and notify you of my decision.'

The next day I sent my Vietnamese friend, Bai, with $100 for Thoi, the usual 'price' if one struck difficulties about the renewal of the annual residence permit. Bai brought the money back: 'Thoi laughed in my face. He sent a message to you. He said "Tell her I can get money from others".'

Bai was disturbed.

'Why don't you leave Vietnam for a while?' he suggested. 'Go to Hong Kong or Bangkok.'

Robert took the same line when I told him what had happened. He begged me to leave and wait for him somewhere else.

But I was afraid there might not be a somewhere else.

This was war and I wanted to be with Robert as much as possible. We never knew in those days whether there would be a tomorrow.

# 18

## *TROUBLE*

On the Monday following my session with Thoi a friend working at the personnel office asked me to meet her for a drink. While we sat in the Caravelle, she said, 'Two men came to the office today flashing CID identification. The boss told me to leave the room but shortly afterwards he stuck his head out and asked for *your* personnel file. The men stayed with him for about half an hour. I thought I'd better warn you — something seems to be up.' Half-jokingly she added, 'Have you done anything wrong? Are you a French spy or something?'

From that day on I couldn't do a thing right at PA&E and eventually I was transferred to a different department — as a typist. Some typist! It took me about two dozen attempts to produce my first semi-neat letter!

But I wanted to stay near Robert and was prepared to enlist the aid of anyone I could think of. I asked a friend at the US Embassy to intervene on my behalf, promising not to say anything against the US presence in Vietnam again.

Another summons from Thoi arrived, but this time there was a form of face-saving compromise. He wanted me to sign a statement agreeing to notify him if Jean ever came back. I obliged without hesitation. I was quite sure Jean would never return to Vietnam. After I'd signed, he gave me a permit — for one month.

'You can have it only on a monthly basis from now on,' was his comment.

Then he asked me to have supper with him that night.

'I'm sorry. I can't accept. I am engaged to an Australian in Vung Tau.'

'But you dine out with other men. You are constantly seen about town!' he protested.

'Only for work. They're colleagues who help me with my articles or people I have to interview for the PA&E news.'

'You mean that they are Westerners and you don't wish to go out with a Vietnamese.'

'Don't be absurd. You know quite well that I have dined often with Vietnamese friends, even next to cyclo drivers on the streets where the likes of you would never be seen!'

I hesitated, then softened the harshness of my outright refusal. After all, maybe all he wanted was to be seen in my company socially. 'I have already accepted an invitation to dinner tonight . . . maybe some other night.'

Thoi took me up on that three nights later, escorting me to a very plush restaurant in Cholon. He ordered perfectly: exquisite dishes like sharkfin soup with asparagus, pigeon in a mild, clear broth, steamed fish with ginger and greens, chicken in oyster sauce. Before, during, and after the meal he drank cognac from a waterglass so he was quite drunk when he suggested going for a digestif to a quiet little place nearby. I thought he meant a small bar or one of the concealed opium places which abounded in that neighbourhood. I wanted to return home but he was insistent that the evening be 'rounded off'.

We arrived at a huge, austere house in a side street and he rang the bell. Shuffling feet approached, a square slid back and two narrow slants squinted at us. The owner recognised Thoi and opened the door.

I thought it must be an opium den. I'd visited one before and had memories of the sickly odour. I'd even taken a few puffs and been violently ill afterwards, cured of any desire to repeat the experiment.

We followed the bent back and shuffling slippered feet towards the rear of the house. A door was pushed open and there, brightly neon-lit, was a room with apple-green walls — and a double bed, table and chair of chrome and plastic, a sink which held two glasses, a comb, soap and towels.

'Oh, non!' I exclaimed and gave a shudder.

The old man looked proudly in my direction. By Vietnamese standards, the room was ultramodern and clean, probably the best in the establishment. Frantically I wondered how I could get out of this situation without making Thoi lose face. My thoughts raced — and I pointed at the neon light.

'I cannot stand neon lights!' I said firmly (and this was true enough). 'We'll have our drink somewhere else!'

I turned and headed for the exit.

I heard Thoi jabber in Vietnamese — at least I had given him an excuse to proffer to the old man. Then he quickly followed me out into the street.

In the car I said decidedly, 'I want to go home.'

'But you promised . . .'

'I promised to go to dinner and to a bar for a drink!' by then I was screaming at him. 'What do you think I am — a piece of meat? To take me to such a ghastly place, thinking I'd lie down out of gratitude for my visa! And don't give me that line 'because you're a Vietnamese', either. It has nothing to do with anyone being black, white, red or yellow. I've had lovers of other races before — but without sneaking down alleyways for secret meetings!'

Thoi didn't say a word in response to my outburst, and drove me home.

The next morning I contacted the British Embassy and told them what was brewing — they thought I'd be wise to leave the country.

All Saigon whispered.

People seemed to be sure I was an agent for *somebody*. Nobody knew who that somebody was, nobody cared, but they all whispered about it. The French simply nicknamed me: 'la James Bond'. It was recalled that eighteen months previously I had passed on a warning that the My Canh (Floating Restaurant) was going to blow up. One of my street friends had told me, knowing it was a favourite eating spot of mine. Nobody believed me at the time — but a few days later it happened. Then people were suspicious of my 'connections'. (Forty-two people were killed in the explosion, and a fortnight later the My Canh re-opened, ironically heralded by a large placard which announced 'Service as good as before'.)

In the middle of this Jean returned from Paris, quite suddenly, with a new and legal passport under his name, Bernard Jacobs. He had been granted amnesty and had no difficulty in obtaining his papers. He bore me no grudge. In fact, I had done the right thing in forcing him to re-assume his own identity. He said he had missed me and wanted me to go to South America with him.

Completely detached when talking to him, I had no feelings left, not even of hatred. I told him quite candidly about Robert, and made it clear that it was too late to make amends. I also told him about the paper I'd signed for Thoi, and that I'd have to report him to protect my own skin.

Jean asked for two days in Saigon to attend to some 'unfinished business'. He claimed I owed him that much, since at the time I destroyed his passport an American crony had hinted that the best solution would be to have me killed by someone. But Jean had protested at going that far!

I was on pins and needles, and sent a message to Robert via Christa. Within hours I had my reply — Robert had written a letter at the hangar and handed it to a Saigon-bound pilot who dashed into the PA&E office with it while his plane was being loaded.

My love,

So Jean is back — true to his form. Rena, what does he have to do to you before you wake up? When he's through with you, your life won't be worth five cents. Don't succumb to his influence. If I was at your side I'd soon straighten out that Jeanboy one way or the other. When we are together he will not harm you ever again. Don't help him in any form — he doesn't deserve help after the rotten deal he gave you.

I'm glad to hear you very sensibly contacted the British Embassy when you received Thoi's summons. I am sure that Thoi acts on behalf of the CIA, and hope they are not making things more difficult for you. If so, let me know immediately. Should anything happen to you I would never forgive myself if I could have been of help. Promise! Such elements are very callous, and powerful at getting their way. I don't want you exposed to this. If need be, go straight to Australia to friends of mine. I'm sure their influence would be much less there. The ideal situation is for me to marry you, then they can all go to hell. Rena, I worry about you, away from where I can protect you.

Cherie, in a way I can understand the trouble you are having. Americans want you out of VN for political reasons. You were very pro-French, naturally, and their policies are of assimilation and co-existence with the Viet Cong. You let your feelings on the subject be known to me and possibly many others. You must know that the way you spoke up made you actively against the US enforcement of their Vietnamese policy and under those circumstances they will not let you remain here. There may be truth in what Jean said about being approached on the subject of your permanent removal. Rena, these people aren't fools. Your criticism will have brought you many enemies and your remaining safely in this country seems out of the question now.

Rena, I have never been interested in politics. Has it been an active part in your life as well as Jean's? You say that I should care about the path nations take. Up till now it has not been necessary for me to ask myself questions on the rights and wrongs of different types of government movements. I hope it stays that way.

When we return to Australia I shall make you forget everything else except us. You and me and our lives shall be all, and your only worry in life will be to keep me happy and contented and fed, and that will be easy, cherie, by returning my love with your need for me. I shall make a wish: 'Please let Rena be pregnant.'

We have so much to give each other, darling, some good, some bad. But I want to give it all and accept it all. That is to be my life. Darling Rena, there is a void gaping in me today, dark, deep and empty, and only you can fill that space. Please make me complete again, my woman. Beloved, I only hope that you are well and no harm has befallen you over Jean's visit. I am awaiting my next news of you, Rena, so very anxiously. My love and my life to you forever. Please be well for me and if there is a God let him protect you to deliver unto me.

My woman,
Your man,
Robert.

153

Robert's letter reassured me; but I still couldn't bring myself to pick up the phone and betray Jean's presence to Thoi. As promised, Jean was ready to leave Saigon two days later and he phoned, suggesting I come to the airport to make sure he was really gone. I went — but Jean didn't leave that day. Instead he was arrested . . . and Thoi yelled at me for not having notified him.

'He's still my husband. I didn't have to denounce him,' I said.

'You denounced him before! And you destroyed his false passport!' Thoi was bewildered.

'That was different. He was trying to force me to leave the country and I was fighting back. This time he didn't come with intent to do me harm, and I'm not vicious without cause.'

Thoi told me my husband was in jail but that he would be free if I was co-operative. I wasn't prepared to go that far for Jean and said so, notified the French consul and left it to them to sort Jean's affairs out. Jean was escorted to a plane a few days later but his departure was kept secret and Thoi continued to tell me how I could obtain his freedom. Though he could have had his pick of Saigon's most beautiful young girls, the man had become obsessed with getting me into the hay! I told him quite bluntly that for all I cared Jean could rot in jail.

I was alone in the apartment a few evenings later when a knock came on the door. Unsuspecting, I opened it, knowing the janitor would not let strangers in. It was Thoi, dead-drunk, staring at me with bloodshot eyes. As soon as I opened the door he walked right in and dropped into my armchair.

'I want to talk to you. Bring me a cognac, please.'

'I am going to bed.'

'But I must talk to you.'

I went into the kitchen and poured a cognac then sat down on the couch across from him. He came over to sit next to me and I immediately switched to the armchair.

He stared at his drink for a while then told me he had received a letter from the CID (Criminal Investigation Department) requesting that I be told to leave and that he would be in trouble if he helped me any further.

'All right. Give me my exit visa and I'll leave. I'm tired of all this. If it hadn't been for Robert I'd have gone long ago.'

Thoi rambled on about how he'd like to help me but, unmoved, I told him to forget about it — it was obviously causing him trouble. Suddenly, and without any warning, he was kneeling in front of me, embracing my legs.

Looking up, he said: 'Madame, vous etes si belle. I have to make you my mistress. Or — how does Mme Thoi sound to you?'

Controlling a sudden urge to giggle, I pushed him away: 'Madame Thoi is at home with all the children and that is where you are going now!' (I knew all about his family — his son was in a class a teacher friend of mine conducted.)

I freed myself from his clutching hands, went to the door and held it open. To my horror, Thoi, still kneeling, committed a most obscene act. Sickened, I ran towards the bathroom, yelling at him in disgust: 'Salaud! Cochon!' When I ventured out again he was gone and the door of my apartment was ajar.

I knew that was the end of my stay in Saigon. Sober the next day, Thoi would never forgive me for being a witness to his making such a spectacle of himself.

Shaking with nerves, I packed a bag and took a taxi to TSN. Too late for regular transport, I found a pilot willing to chopper me to Vung Tau in an H13. I went to tent row where Robert lived and found him playing darts at the Ettamogah Hotel, the unit's clubhouse.

He came outside immediately, worried at the sight of me trembling and crying, and we sat in a ditch, where he held me tightly as I blurted out, between sobs, what had happened.

Robert was very still when I finished. Then he spat out: 'If that guy ever touches a hair of your head, the Viet Cong will have themselves another man!' His words shocked me so much I stopped crying. Robert, a dedicated Australian, making such a statement! That proved how deeply he cared. And suddenly the troubles meant nothing as I was flooded with the warmth and security he brought me.

We drove to town in a weapons carrier and that night he held me tenderly, just stroking me, without making love, because he knew that it would have been beyond me just then.

The next day he asked me not to return to Saigon again, and said he'd look after my needs until I left for Australia.

A few days later I was feeling desperately ill with an attack of malaria. (I had had my first attack only weeks after my arrival in Vietnam.) Robert and Christa took excellent care of me. Robert bought me a beautiful white ski jumper at the PX at Vung Tau, one of the things imported from Hong Kong for soldiers to send home as presents. Even in the heat of Vung Tau I was glad to wear it when I had my 'cold spells'.

By then Elaine had arrived with news of a summons from Thoi descending on PA&E, claiming I was illegally in the country and demanding my whereabouts be reported immediately.

It was time to leave Vietnam.

Robert decided that I should go first to Las Vegas for my divorce, then to Australia to wait for him. With a heavy heart I took leave of him and my friends and returned to Saigon, where I was warned that Thoi was planning to throw me in jail. I had to go to his office for my exit visa, but had two Special Forces friends accompany me. A wise precaution, for while they waited outside for me, Thoi locked the door and chased me around his desk.

I raced to the door and hammered against it and my friends hammered back from the outside. Thoi could do nothing but unlock the door and I darted out still minus my exit visa.

I packed a few clothes, giving the bulk of them to Chi Hai, together with a $10 bonus, grabbed my camera equipment and negatives and jammed them into a small suitcase, hurriedly packed books, souvenirs and paintings and left them with Jacqueline for safekeeping. With the help of my two Special Forces friends I was ready to leave within an hour.

We loaded my things onto a jeep while the neighbourhood, who knew Madame was in trouble with 'the authorities', stood watching silently. A few of them approached and wished me 'bonne chance' among them my favourite cyclo pedaller, a little fellow with a crippled leg who had a special pedal built on one side of his cyclo. His wife was a huge Khmer woman from the Delta, and they lived with their small son at our street corner, sleeping on a canvas bed.

It wasn't until I was ready to go, with Chi Hai crying on the sidewalk, that I realised what I was leaving behind. Locals like the cyclo driver had become friends, while Chi Hai the little woman who hushed like a shadow through my place, had taken care of me like a mother.

We drove to Jacqueline's college and I stayed at her flat inside the compound. My Special Forces friends radioed Vung Tau and Robert obtained leave and came to Saigon. Jointly we went to the British Embassy but they said there wasn't much they could do in the face of Thoi's determination. They agreed that I must leave the country somehow and suggested a military flight. A friend wrote out travel orders on PA&E forms for a MAC flight to Alaska and Travis. The flight wasn't leaving for two days, but Robert couldn't stay away from Vung Tau that long — the last night we were together at the college we didn't sleep.

We held each other silently, because there wasn't much we could say. And even when we made love it was a continuation, an extension of our despair and I clung to him feeling that the future held nothing but doom. The feeling still lingered next morning. When he left at 6 a.m. for duty at Vung Tau I cried bitterly and told him I felt this was the end for us.

He tried to snap me out of it.

'Nonsense, my darling. You'll make it safely to Aussie, because I need you so much. You have to be strong, for me and our babies. And I hope you have one of them in your little belly right now.'

But he also had tears in his eyes as he spoke.

The next morning I boarded the jet, with Elaine and Russ standing by to notify the British Embassy if anyone interfered with my departure.

I didn't breathe freely until the brilliant coastline of Vietnam disappeared below the silver wings of the plane. I looked back at the two hills of Vung Tau and prayed: 'Please, let Robert leave safely too, even if he is not coming back to me.'

Because right till that last look at Vietnam I had a premonition that I was losing my man, leaving him behind forever as the plane travelled into the empty sky ahead.

# 19

## WAKE TO NIGHTMARE

xxxxxxxxxxxxxxxxxxxxxxxxxxxxxxxxxxxxxxxxxxxxxxxxxxxxxxx

Jacqueline had sent a cable to friends in San Francisco and they whisked me away from Travis Airport to a plush restaurant at Fisherman's Wharf where I promptly repaid their kindness by falling asleep from exhaustion. When the waiter came to take our order they nudged me. Disapproving glances told me that onlookers thought I was drunk but I could hardly walk around and tell everyone that public cat-napping becomes a habit in a war zone.

The following day I continued my journey to Las Vegas and filed for my divorce. The six weeks' waiting period I spent in a trance-like state. After two years in Vietnam Las Vegas seemed so unreal. But it wasn't like waking from a nightmare to find yourself in fairy-land; quite the opposite.

I had previously been enchanted by Las Vegas' glitter but now it struck me as a nightmare, as something evil. Certainly I enjoyed the odd show and good dinners but often I would be watching people gambling in the casinos, laughing and shouting — over-dressed, over-jewelled, over-fed women — and suddenly a bitter surge of rage would creep up inside me until I felt like hammering away at those smug faces and shouting, 'Don't you know what's going on out there in the *real* world? Don't you know that right at this moment your countrymen are pouring napalm over innocent children? And that right at this moment one of your own boys is getting his throat slit . . . all so that you can go on over-dressing and over-stuffing yourselves and feeding coins into your silly slot machines?'

People who learned I had been in Vietnam asked me what it was really like there but when I told them the truth they didn't understand — or didn't want to understand — and looked at me as though I was crazy, or called me a Commie.

In the end I stopped going out and stayed at my small studio apartment at the Golf Manor. Even there I wasn't free of trivia. Other women awaiting their divorces came with what were to them world-shattering problems: who gets the villa with the pool and who the country house, whether they should return a brooch which belonged to *his* mother, or how the lawyer compromised on the number of times *he* could visit the youngsters, until, fed-up, I finally told them how foolish these things really were.

Unexpectedly, Jean appeared on the scene, descending from Mexico City and trying to stop the divorce, first by blustering, then by turning on the old familiar charm. When neither worked, he capitulated — graciously enough.

I was happy to find I was pregnant, though the doctor warned me that I had better relax and get my nerves calmed down. I was keyed to breaking pitch in those weeks the only thing that kept me from going insane was the arrival of Robert's letters. He sent me one every day.

I also wrote to Robert daily, but I didn't mention that there was, indeed, a Ulysses on the way. I didn't want to build up his hopes about the baby until I had stopped having troubles with it. But I did write of the agonies I was going through thinking about the war, and how something must be done to stop all that massacre; how resentful I felt about the indifference of the average American, and that I hoped I wouldn't feel the same in Australia. One day I was so far down in the dumps I even wrote saying I'd leave for an island where I could be completely alone!

After my divorce was finalised I returned to San Francisco to stay with Linda, a Canadian friend, until I was ready to leave for Australia. I was kept busy shopping for maternity dresses and baby things, and splurging madly on items like lovely flowered sheets to take to Australia with me. It was one of the happiest times I had spent for a long, long time. The one small cloud was that I had been without a letter from Robert for nearly a week . . . however, since mail did bank up at times, I didn't let it worry me unduly, though I watched for mail deliveries eagerly.

Finally, five letters came at once, all in the familiar beloved handwriting. I opened one at random. I started to read it, and at the first few lines I am sure my heart stopped beating for a time:

Dear Rena,

I am sorry I didn't arrive at this decision before.

Goodbye, Rena, our life together has finished. There is too much between us, too much in the lives gone past.

Rena, I had never met a woman like you in my life. You knew all the answers, had been through so much more of life than I ever will. You could say I am just a small country-town hick. I am not reaching for the stars — a quiet life in Australia would never last for us. You wish to shape the world. Go ahead — I wish to remain one of those countless millions you scorn . . . the ones with their heads in the sand. My ambitions would be too small for you, my conquests too insignificant. I came to you at a time of need for both of us. But, without sex, our lives are miles apart, on different planes.

Rena, I still think deeply of you, and always shall. But love and marriage do not automatically go hand in hand. I have arrived at the conclusion that our differences are too great and would in the end lead to our parting.

Here's hoping you once again land on your feet.

> Good-bye, good luck,
>
> Robert.

Shattered, I refused to believe what I read, and with a trembling hand I opened the other letters. They had been mailed earlier — the last one four days previously to that fatal one — and they were as loving and tender as all his earlier letters had been:

Rena, let me tell you one thing. I love you, my woman, and nothing will change me. If you don't receive any mail, it's delay of kinds, nothing else. You are the one and only woman I have asked to marry in my life, you are the one I want for my wife and the mother of my children. . . .

. . . Each letter from you makes this parting just a little easier to bear whilst I read your words to me. Then the terrible loneliness follows, the dull realisation that you are thousands of miles and months away from me. Please let them both pass swiftly. . . .

I used to lie awake looking at you, at every little part of you, desiring you so strongly, feeling would flow from me, a beautiful, bitter-sweet feeling and I wanted to drown you with my love, lock you away in my body for me alone. Now, the feeling is just as strong, my love, the memories sharper. I love you, Rena, my mistress, my wife, my body, my soul, I love you. . . .

It hurt so much, reading of his love and longing and promises, knowing by then that they were history, something that had died within hours. I couldn't even find tears. I walked quietly out of the place and through the drizzling rain, automatically putting one foot down, then the other, like a robot. I stood at the ocean front staring into the waves for an answer and somehow later that night found my way back to Linda's place. And I still couldn't cry when I told her.

'Why don't you write and ask why?' was her practical suggestion. 'That letter doesn't seem to give a real reason.'

But I couldn't think of anything to say. Finally I wrote the only thing I was capable of writing then, the one and only poem I ever wrote in my life:

WITHOUT YOU

Walking drab streets
Leading to nowhere
The grey sky encircles
A world of emptiness and loneliness.

I search passing paces
They have nothing to tell me.

Through fog the Golden Gate
Unreal
Like the dream I reached for.

Wind sweeping the Bay,
Mournfully calling
Why, oh why?

Waves chasing waves

Lucky waves
Travel to that faraway shore
And gently touch my beloved
Lucky waves
Not expected to land on your feet
When thrown from your Alcheringa.

Two weeks passed and I tortured myself looking for an answer. I sought a reason — maybe I shouldn't have written so strongly about my feelings against the war. But then, he had always shared them with me in Vietnam. He had spoken out strongly against Australian involvement there. That couldn't be the reason. Another woman? I had written to both Elaine and Christa, asking not to be spared. Their replies came, and they were as puzzled as I was. There was no other woman and I knew it couldn't have been kept a secret in Vung Tau if there was. But Robert had refused to discuss the matter with anyone, they told me.

Once again the familiar envelope — but all it held was a single sheet, with a short poem replying to the one I had sent:

Neaptide memories
Borne on the waves of time
Cast onto the depths
So beautiful
So bitter
Shall fade into the past.
Have faith in the coming of the ebbtides.
They bring new and exciting worlds for you to conquer.

That was all.

I decided to stick to my plan of going to Australia — I wanted my baby to be born there. I would see Robert on his return. I wouldn't get married for the baby's sake, but I hoped he might live with me.

I had sold a long article about Vietnam to *Maclean's* magazine in Canada and they had asked if I'd go back to get material on an article about the children of Vietnam. I would have rushed right back but the one thing that stopped me was the baby, that miniature Robert I was so looking forward to.

Then another blow struck. My malaria returned and I miscarried.

A few days later with a one month visa I received on the strength of a written assignment from *Maclean's,* I was on a plane bound for Saigon. With huge sunglasses and a kerchief as a flimsy disguise I made it through immigration without being challenged. My passport was in my maiden name so there was nothing to connect me with the notorious Rena Briand whose name was undoubtedly well known to every immigration official.

I headed for the Vung Tau-bound Caribous at 3rd Corps ATCO. But things had changed in the short time I had been away. War had become a red-tape affair.

'Travel orders?'

I had none and I had no intention of going into Saigon or to MACV for an accreditation.

A pilot would have taken me, but a colonel ordered me off.

'I've come nine thousand miles to see my fiancé, and you ask for travel orders! All right. I'll take a bus to Vung Tau and if I get captured by the Viet Cong you can send patrols out looking for me and get ambushed if you prefer it that way!'

I was luckier at the helipad. One of the sergeants there was an old-timer I had known and he looked the other way over non-existent travel orders.

As we approached Vung Tau it seemed as though my heart was beating louder than the clattering rotor blades above us, and by the time we made our landing I was trembling with nervousness. I stood inside the court of the villa and waited for Robert to arrive, wanting to confront him in privacy.

I will never forget how he looked while he was walking towards me. There was such hurt in his eyes, such incredible hurt.

I was the first to speak. 'Hello, my love.'

'Hello. Why did you come back here? Thoi is still in power. You are so foolish. Oh, darling, why did you come back?'

'I had to, Robert. I had to find out why. I'll wait for you upstairs.'

When he came back from supper we walked towards the villa,

Children at Quy Hanh orphanage on seesaws built by Diggers.
Near Baria, a boy signals Lindie and me to turn back; the mountain area
was occupied by VC.

Prince Sihanouk's guard is wary about camera lens.
My unwanted travelling companion.
Polish delegation at Angkor. 'Among the demons, please!'

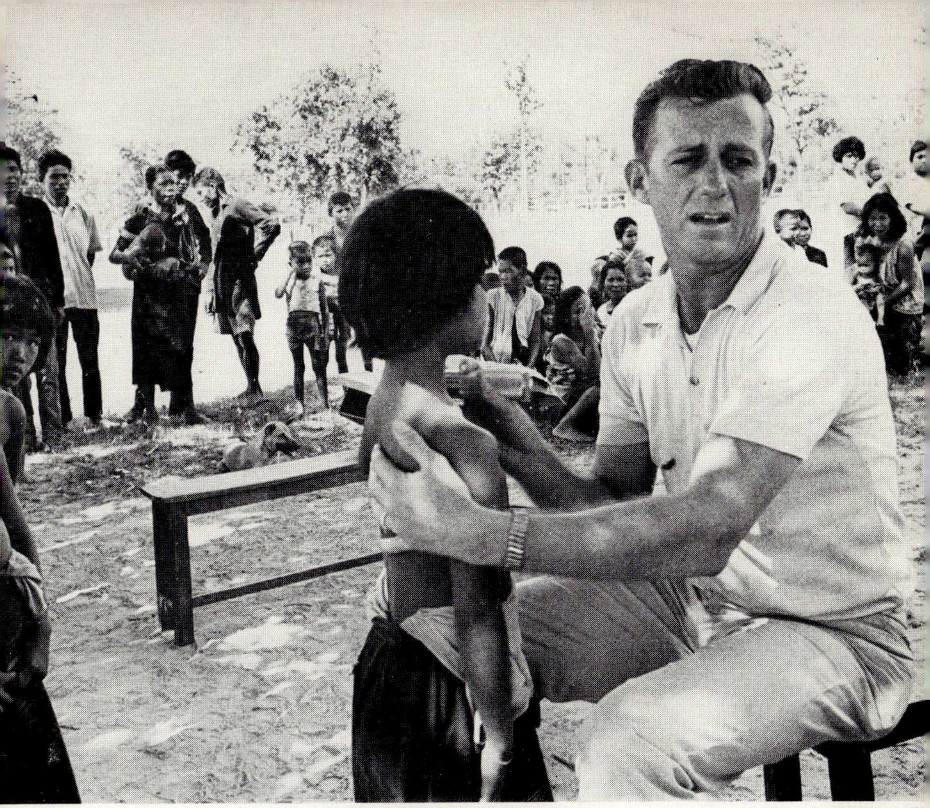

Buddy Kirtley shows strain while treating patients in the heat of N.E.
Thailand.
Honorary Buffalo Manure Washer-offer at work.

Transvestites of Bugis Street. 'She' could fool anyone.
Stripping seems a favourite pastime of Aussies on R & R.

where Ron and Christa had restored the bed in the storage room, and we sat down to talk.

We talked for hours.

To me, his excuses seemed feeble.

'. . . when I heard Jean had joined you in Las Vegas, I worried in case he'd talk you into going back to him . . . Your getting so upset about American politics — I don't want to be mixed up in politics back in Australia . . . and when you sent that letter about moving to a lonely island — I was sure you'd leave me sometime, so I decided if I must lose you, I'd sooner lose you now than later.' (Who hasn't at least once in his lifetime expressed the desire to get away from it all — but how many of us actually go to live on the deserted island of our dreams?)

We talked and talked until I realised the real reason for Robert's change of heart — his emotions for me had become so strong he couldn't cope with them any more and they terrified him. He was frightened and that was why he broke off our engagement. He was a typical bachelor at heart and now that show-down time had come he was too scared to face up to the responsibility.

He was genuinely sorry when I told him about the miscarriage, and there were tears in his eyes. He said he had wanted a baby very much — he would have taken care of both of us. And he said he still loved me very much.

We made love that night and many other nights during my one month stay in Vung Tau. We had as much need for each other as ever and he often murmured over and over again that he loved me. Sometimes he tried to stay away, telling me it was no good and that we shouldn't see each other again. And sometimes he was spiteful and said things to hurt me, and I knew this was because he couldn't forgive me for nearly having 'trapped' him. Other times he seemed to hate me for the hurt he had caused . . . and that he couldn't undo without losing his precious freedom, but this mood never lasted more than a day or two.

And I was happy when he wandered back again. I loved him so much I was quite willing to have him on any terms, and I still wanted another baby. I didn't care much about tomorrow . . .

# 20

## SCARS OF THE FUTURE

Robert and our problem was in one compartment of my life in those days. In another was the work I had come to do — the story of the Children of Vietnam.

Investigating the fate of many youngsters in the war was heartbreaking and difficult work.

'War victims? We don't have any,' a German doctor told me. 'There are only "victims of accidents".'

He showed me a pathetic girl covered in burns.

'Sau was hurt when her mosquito net caught fire,' he said straightfaced. Then he confided: 'Her entire village probably doesn't own a single mosquito net but the people have to say it was an accident or wounds caused by the Viet Cong or some such story, otherwise they won't get treatment, and officials and interpreters threaten them. So — they tell lies to get help. We *know* Sau's burns are caused by napalm but, *um Himmel's Willen,* don't write that, or we'll never get a chance to treat such children again. Besides wanting to help them, we also do research on the best methods of treating such cases. Sau will be as good as new when she leaves here, physically, that is.'

The ship *Helgoland* was the only hospital I visited that had spotlessly clean sheets and only one patient to each bed. And I knew there were thousands of sick and wounded who would gladly have lain on the ship's deck if only they could get help.

Peter Arnett at AP's Saigon office was good about supplying me with background information. He told me of a child hurt in an action near Can Guic, an area the GIs called a 'Free Fire Zone'.

An American squadron blasted its way through the trees, exchanging shots with guerillas in foxholes and bunkers; the forest of banana trees gave way to a paddy, and there came a sudden yell: 'Get the medic! Get the medic for the kid!'

A small boy looked blankly at a blood-streaked patch where a chunk of flesh and bone had been torn away from between his wrist and fingers. Beside him stood his mother, a young brother, and a sister.

The medic wrapped the wound, carried the boy a quarter of a mile to a dry dyke and sent an urgent radio message to evacuate the child before it was too late to save his hand. There was only an occasional whimper from the boy, and an excited chatter in Vietnamese from the mother and sister, the intervals filled with the steady drumming of rifle fire and automatic weapon sounds from a little further on. The fierce firing prevented the Medevac from landing and while the group waited the blood soaked through the bandages. Still the little boy didn't cry. 'He's a brave little kid. It must be hurting him something awful,' said the medic.

When the shooting subsided, Medevac took the family on board. Another small victim for the hospital was on his way.

At an orphanage the sister in charge showed me a scarred little girl. Pham lived with her mother in a small hamlet in the midst of rice paddies. One day a whisper went through the village, telling of men clad in black pyjamas and carrying weapons who had moved into a hut outside the hamlet. Worried, Pham's mother spent a sleepless night then decided to seek the comparative safety of the city. She loaded two rice baskets with the few treasured possessions they owned and took Pham by the hand to set out for Saigon on foot. They were among the unlucky ones — fate led them along the path just as firing broke out between Viet Cong and ARVN troops and they were caught in the crossfire. The mother threw herself over her little girl and worked her way through the mud, seeking the safety of a nearby dyke. There was an explosion, and a scream: a grenade had landed beside them, driving several pieces of shrapnel into the mother and blasting Pham into unconsciousness, with her right leg torn, and shrapnel fragments biting deep into her soft flesh. The firing ceased abruptly and the mother carried Pham painfully back to the village. Pham survived — but she is scarred for life. They didn't even know which side threw that grenade, but to Pham it doesn't matter.

At the Le Loi Hospital in Vung Tau the surgical team from Prince Henry's Hospital in Sydney was at work, treating children with a variety of ailments. Their skills were on call for many reasons: to operate on a harelip, to save the life of a boy so badly burned it was a miracle he survived, to check a suspected plague victim. Dr Perrett pointed out an eleven-year-old boy, paralysed for life, victim of a bullet that had lodged near his spine.

'VC? Americans, I believe,' Dr Perrett said in response to my question. I asked a French-speaking Vietnamese friend to get the story from the boy himself. Luong was skinny, as his meals consisted of rice supplemented by vegetables. However, he was tall by Vietnamese standards. One day he wandered into some nearby woods to look for edible roots and wild fruit. He was wearing the traditional black pyjamas and straw hat. He didn't know that an American patrol, searching for Viet Cong hideouts, was also in the woods. A soldier spotted the black-clad figure and shouted a warning. Unable to understand, Luong panicked and ran through the bushes towards his home. The bullet hit him in the middle of the back. Once more a helicopter took a child to hospital . . .

Pham, Luong and the little boy from the Can Giuc area have been 'compensated'. (Luong, who will never walk again, received $US75.)

The amount of compensation is determined by a committee consisting of a province official, a Vietnamese military officer and an AID man or US adviser.

Payment is in a single lump sum. There is no 'follow-up' assistance. The degree of injury has little bearing on the amount of compensation paid which is judged solely by the social standing of the victim. The child of a peasant woman who lost a limb received less than $US100 . . . the son of a village chief who lost three fingers was paid $US1700.

I tried to discuss the obvious anomalies of the compensation system with an American officer, quoting Luong as an example. If he had not been injured, he almost certainly would have improved his family's standard as he grew up to earn a man's wage. I was brushed off with — '. . . name another war where a country made any effort to help innocent victims.' I also talked about Luong with an official of OCO* the new collective control (CIA control) over AID organisations. When, after half an hour of subtle brainwashing I still didn't see the 'good' in it all, he stood up and said, 'It is very difficult to agree (sic!) with somebody who doesn't agree with the American policy!' and walked away stiffly. His phrase was such a classic I roared with laughter, despite the tragic subject of our discussion.

It is true that some organisations try to improve things, and I saw many soldiers share their rations, touched by the skinny little limbs and hungry, begging eyes. But this is no more than the proverbial drop in the ocean. And official help, such as giving a child an artificial limb, doesn't excuse having bombed him 'accidentally' in the first place.

No statistics are released about child casualties of the war. Life expectancy for many Vietnamese children is very short, whether through illness or injury. In fact, it is estimated that four out of

*Office of Civilian Operations.

every six Vietnamese children do not reach the age of five. Hospitals are overcrowded, as many as six children to a bed. And mute proof of child mortality lies in the countless small graves dotting the country.

UNICEF's Mr Klausener, a Swiss, told me that about one million children had been killed or wounded in the period from January 1961 to December 1966. One million children!

'I talked to someone at OCO,' Mr Klausener said, 'and told him to leave Vietnam and find another banana republic. Vietnam is too muddy for the US — they'll sink. He answered "We're up to our necks in it and we'll stay. We'll beat the VC at their own game. We're going to cut off their pricks and we're going to cut up their women and children. We can stand it!" ' Klausener added: 'They are brutal. Some US soldiers are brutal, too, even to children. Most children who are hurt die before they reach a hospital, because the Vietnamese evacuation system is so poor. And in many cases soldiers kill badly wounded children. They call it mercy killing, but I say it's to hide how many innocent victims there really are!'

There are war casualties other than those killed or injured. In 1966 there were more than two million refugees in South Vietnam and it was estimated that approximately half of these were children.

Some eighty orphanages had registered orphans totalling eleven thousand. Most of the children had been placed there by relatives contributing to their support. The majority of bona-fide orphans do not have the luxury of life in an orphanage and survive as best they can. A few are 'adopted' by a family, others beg, or steal . . . or commit suicide.

In Vietnam it is still a shameful thing to be a child fathered by a foreigner. Products of hasty or ill-considered affairs are often abandoned near military installations, at churches, or simply by the roadside. When the French were in power they fed and clothed the ones fathered by their troops and took them to France for their education. Under French law any man who acknowledges paternity automatically confers the right of French citizenship on the child without being obliged to marry the mother. There is no such provision for children fathered by the troops currently stationed in Vietnam.

Some prostitutes, however, seem pleased at having a métis baby girl. A bargirl proudly showed me her little curly-headed daughter. 'Thanh very pretty. Will sell GI beaucoup Saigon Tea. I take care Thanh now. Thanh take care me later.' To her, the pretty daughter is an old-age insurance.

Elaine discovered Anh while she was collecting material for an article. Fathered by an American Negro and deserted by her prostitute mother, the child is spending an unhappy childhood void of affection at a Catholic orphanage in Saigon. Elaine told me about her. 'She seemed acutely aware of the fact that she was different. She stood apart, looking very old and wise, while the others were playing. She has all the dignity of a blue-blooded Bostonian lady, the pride of a Viking — and her face is arrestingly beautiful.' Possibly Anh's maturity came from an instinctive knowledge that life had put all its hurdles in front of her: she was half-black, half-yellow, illegitimate, abandoned. 'If she was less intelligent or proud, she'd be able to accept the situation,' Elaine said, 'but she already realises that being half-Negro she will never be welcomed by a Vietnamese family as a daughter-in-law; therefore she will spend her life as a servant or drift into prostitution.'

My friend made a move to forestall this dismal future facing Anh. She wrote to *Ebony* magazine, offering Anh's story and picture free of charge, including a health and school report to support her claims about the little girl. Her hope was that a US Negro family might adopt Anh, but she never received a reply from the magazine.

'Do you want to see Anh?' Elaine asked. 'I'm taking some presents to the orphanage for her this afternoon.'

I went and was just as impressed by the beautiful solemn child, whose eyes shone a little brighter when Elaine handed over her gifts. But later, while other children laughed and shouted, little Anh's face still remained serious.

'She has never smiled . . . nor cried,' a Sister remarked. 'She doesn't know how.'

I never ceased to be amazed by the children's will and ability to survive, their unquenchable spirit of fun, despite poverty and hardships. Usually the youngsters ganged up in groups of about six to eight members. I got to know one such group in Vung Tau. They spent most of their time on the beach — two of them sold hats, one peddled sunglasses and cheap trinkets, two girls sold pineapples. Once I saw them fill a discarded purse with sand, put it on the road and hide behind some bushes. An American soldier picked up the purse, opened it and threw it away in disgust. The children jumped out, gleefully laughing and teasing him.

The dream of every lonely boy roaming the streets of Saigon is to belong to 'Gia Dinh Don Bosco' (The Family of Don Bosco), an orphanage run by a Brazilian priest, Father Generoso Bogo. The plump, friendly man in the black cassock once led a straggling band of 400 children through the savage jungles in an exodus similar to that of the *Inn of the Sixth Happiness*.

Until the Communists took over the North, Father Bogo had an orphanage in Hanoi. His charges were swept up from prisons and police stations, where their solitary struggles for survival had landed them. Many sneaked out at night to serve as messengers for the Viet Minh. Father Bogo couldn't stop them without getting into trouble with the Viets, but he finally kept them so busy during the day they were too tired at night for anything but sleep. After the Geneva Conference, Father Bogo headed south. The children had to decide for themselves, and all but fifty went with him.

Emperor Bao Dai, in the southern part of the newly-divided country, offered them refuge in empty rubber storage barracks near the Cambodian border. The French Government made Dakotas available to air-lift them to Ban Me Thuot, but from there on the Father and his four hundred youngsters were on their own. On foot they walked miles through close-grown jungle.

'It was a terrible ordeal,' Father Bogo said. 'We found the barracks in a ramshackle condition, and so small the children were crammed like sardines. Even worse, the area was infested with mosquitoes, snakes, rats and other plagues, and we had to walk three miles through thick jungle to get water. There was no fresh fruit or vegetables and it wasn't long before many children developed beri-beri. Before us lay six months of misery. Thank God, a warm-hearted French settler brought our weekly rice rations from Ban Me Thuot. The older boys cut trees and built classrooms and terraces around the warehouses. They also discovered a wild edible vegetable which they called Brand Air Plane . . . their plane ride had made quite an impression on them. Somehow we survived.'

The jungle offered new interests for the street urchins of Hanoi. Every morning when a boy sounded the bugle, thousands of monkeys came out of the jungle, curious about the noisy invaders of their domain.

'It was really very funny,' Father Bogo recalled. 'The boys and the monkeys would imitate each other. In the evenings, we built campfires and friendly Montagnards joined us. I gave them half a dozen rifles I had "lifted" from the army, and in exchange they brought us half of each animal they shot. They let the boys take rides on the village elephants — quite a welcome break. Truly wonderful people, the Montagnards.'

Lack of vitamins and disease told on the children. Father Bogo kept pleading for healthier surroundings and eventually was allowed to establish himself in the old abandoned tram terminal at Go Vap. The older orphans again helped construct what is now a first-class orphanage. When villagers stole some of their materials, the Viet Minh training came in quite handy. The older boys organised guards and equipped the children with sticks and bricks. The intruders received a thorough beating and didn't bother the orphanage again.

'By the way,' Father Bogo said, a twinkle in his eye, 'I didn't hear a thing that night!'

Father Bogo now has some 550 children in his charge. He keeps his best pupils on as teachers, and the others leave when they have been trained in a craft and have a place of employment. He said: 'There would be no point in raising them and turning them loose to steal for survival. Some of my boys are trained metal workers, some carpenters, interpreters, musicians . . . a few play in bands of local night clubs. It's an honest living!'

Father Bogo takes orphans of any origin or religion and his work has earned him the respect of even the Viet Cong, who are often in the Go Vap area. In 1965 two Italian journalists were stopped by the Viet Cong, but allowed to proceed immediately when they said they were heading for the Family of Don Bosco. 'My dead comrade's son is at the home,' one Viet Cong said in French.

The Father, understanding the Vietnamese mentality, knew the children suffered mostly from not belonging to anyone, so he formed little groups into 'families', with a reliable older student appointed as 'father'.

'Thus the staff is relieved of having to deal with every minor problem, he said. 'We had one funny incident — as usual, we gave the "fathers" the Care parcels to distribute. They came to us complaining about bad American soap that wouldn't lather. The "soap" was small round cheeses . . . a delicacy reserved for the rich in Vietnam. I only wish they would send us more of that "bad soap" and fewer bullets and bombs!'

# 21

## THE AUSSIES

~~~~~~~~~~~~~~~~~~~~~~~~~~~~~~~~~~~~~~~~~~~~~~~~~~~~~~~~~~~~~~~~~~~~

I sent off my story to *Maclean's,* unaware that another Canadian magazine had beaten them to the market with an article on Vietnam's children. I had two weeks left before my visa expired, and certainly was not prepared to see Thoi about a renewal.

Wanting to remain close to Robert till deadline I obtained permission from Colonel Logan to visit various Australian units: 'Only for the day, mind you. Sorry — no women reporters allowed overnight at field camps or on long-range patrols.' Regulations had taken over the war at last and these restrictions killed my chances for good action shots. But I considered myself lucky to be allowed to work at all, for Colonel Logan must surely have been aware that MACV wasn't looking kindly on me. I spent most of my days leaving early for Nui Dat, Xuyen Moc or Horseshoe Hill, chatting with the boys and taking photos, going on short patrols or APC missions.

I always felt safer with Australian troops than with Americans. Contrary to popular rumours, the American units were not lacking in bravery by comparison but the Australians seemed to have had a more thorough training in jungle warfare. This I first noticed when an Australian private pointed to my rings and bracelets in my early days and said firmly: 'Sorry — but that glittering stuff stays behind!' He explained that the reflection of the sun on them could betray our location through jungle leaves. It made sense; shortly afterwards I changed my US aluminium dogtags for Australian ones covered with green masking tape.

Possibly because they are fewer in number there is a closer relationship between Australian combat troops and their command, an essential factor for morale. The tremendous gap that can exist between the US fighting man and his superiors often makes the former feel betrayed. Australians also fight the Viet Cong at their own level, realising that ambushes set in dense jungles accomplish more than wholesale airstrikes, which often find only civilian targets left in the area.

I once asked an Australian why they seldom called for air support.

He gave me a wry grin and said: 'Hell, who wants to get hit by the Yanks? I'd sooner do me own fightin'.'

At the hangar one morning I was having a cup of coffee, hoping to see Robert, when Lieutenant Ted Munday, on whose chopper I was scheduled to leave, called: 'Hurry up, Rena — you can get more coffee in Nui Dat!' Ted was carrying his gear across the air-strip and I yelled back: 'Warm the bird up — I'll be right out.' I dashed to the waiting line of helicopters, jumped into one with rotating blades, and was fastening my seat-belt when the pilot turned his head: 'And where is the young lady going?' I realised I was aboard the wrong chopper. 'My mistake! I'm going to Nui Dat. Where's my chopper?' The pilot just grinned: 'No sweat . . . this one is heading there too. Save you changing over.'

Both choppers lifted into the air together and clattered along in unison. Suddenly the gunner on my right gesticulated wildly and yelled into his headset. Black smoke billowed and eddied into our open door.

My stomach fell. 'We've been hit . . . Oh, God, we've been hit . . .'

Time seemed endless until I realised that the smoke was coming from the other chopper, flowing from flames licking at its tail. Horrified, we watched it crash from 1200 feet right into the middle of an ammunition dump. Our pilot pushed his steering lever straight forward and we followed the stricken chopper down, landing beside it. Vaguely I sensed men running through smoke and dust as I instinctively pulled the lens cap from my camera. Munday's co-pilot, Lieutenant Phil Cooke, tried to push me away, worried the wreck would explode, but dust and sand had extinguished the flames. A crew member stumbled by me, shaking and trembling. Another explained: 'Poor bastard. It's his third crash in ten days.' I felt shaky, too, and when someone took my photo, I warned: 'Crop my knees off, mate, or you'll blur the picture.'

We loaded our chopper with the additional crew and weapons and headed back for the hangar. An anxious crowd was waiting, relieved and amazed to find us all unhurt.

After a few minutes' rest, another cup of coffee and a cigarette the crew prepared to take off again.

'Still coming with us, Rena?' asked one of them.

I didn't really want to but I knew they'd feel worse if I chickened out so I stubbed my cigarette and said: 'Sure, I'm coming' and hoped my voice sounded as casual as I intended.

As I walked out, Robert came over and took me by the shoulders. 'Haven't you had enough yet? For Heaven's sake go to Aussie and wash dishes and nappies instead of playing the little heroine around here.' He was the old Robert again: loving, worried about my safety.

From Nui Dat, I left for Hoa Long in a jeep with Major John Donohoe, who was in charge of the Australian Civil Action programme. 'The area was liberated only six months ago, after years of Viet Cong domination,' the Major explained. I wondered what sort of reception we would get. To my surprise, at the village centre we were surrounded by children jumping and smiling, shouting greetings to the Major. I soon discovered the reason for their excitement.

Australian soldiers were building a playground, with gaily coloured swings and seesaws made from scrap metal. 'This'll keep them busy and off the streets,' Major Donohoe remarked with a smile 'You know, if I get those kids on my side, I may convince the parents that we are not all bastards.'

This wouldn't be an easy task in Hoa Long. The lack of able-bodied men in the village proved significantly that these were still fighting with the guerilla forces in the nearby hills. And when the Australians had dumped a few dead Viet Cong on the square as a warning, it didn't endear them to the widows and relatives who had to look upon the torn bodies of their deceased.

Major Donohoe had a few rules for his men which directly concerned the children: 'I never allow sweets to be thrown to them from our vehicles when they pass,' he commented. 'Apart from the safety angle, the children lose self-respect by picking up food from the dirt.' He had other methods of winning the friendship of the children: he arranged for helicopter trips to Saigon zoo or Vung Tau beach, where they were treated to meals and sweets. He picked up a little deaf and dumb girl, the daughter of a Viet Cong prisoner in a South Vietnamese camp. The child smiled and stroked his cheek with loving confidence.

A loud-speaker boomed from a vehicle stationed at the roadside: 'Slow down, Yank, this is a 15 mile speed zone.' The Major had instigated speed limits for the protection of civilians, and planned to build by-passes for military vehicles.

We walked to the gloomy mud house of a village elder so that the Major could consult him about erecting a bamboo fence around the village. Major Donohoe took no such actions without first consulting the villagers. 'The old man says he does not really understand the purpose of such a fence,' the interpreter translated, 'but he says if you say it is good for the village then it must be so.'

While we drank fragrant tea offered in grimy-looking cups, the Major arranged a monthly payment of $20 for a sick widow. The money was to provide for her children while she underwent a long-overdue operation. The Australian civil action programme is the only organisation providing relief payments of this nature: 'Others would wait until the mother died and then maybe take care of the kids,' the interpreter said with sarcasm.

When we had finished our tea the old man bowed, and we continued our way through clusters of banana trees towards a miserable looking hut standing withdrawn from the main village. There we delivered a wheel chair for a crippled boy. His father thanked us emotionally in broken French.

I glimpsed one face that was not welcoming — on the way back, the hostile look of one woman reminded me of the danger lurking on this seemingly peaceful mission. The Viet Cong had put a price on Major Donohoe's head, proof of how effective his work was.

That evening a Land Rover drove me back from Nui Dat, with two guys riding shotgun. The command had grounded all RAAF choppers until they could be thoroughly checked. There had been too many crashes recently, most likely from metal fatigue.

That night Robert was very loving and we talked about my impending departure. 'Do you want me to stay in touch with you?' I asked anxiously. He was due to return to Australia a month later.

'I'll give you the address of my sister in Fremantle,' he answered. 'You can write to me there. I'll go directly to her place when I get back and I'll be spending my two months' leave with her. If you need anything, let me know.'

He asked where I intended to go, and suggested my getting a job in one of Australia's larger cities.

'Give up this crazy life. Get a normal job — in sales, or something like that.'

I told him I'd consider it but said that first I wanted to go to Cambodia to try to get a visa for North Vietnam.

'I want to get out of this racket but I'd like to leave as a success, not a failure. I want to get one really good, top-flight story, then I'll quit.'

The mention of Hanoi brought strong protests from him and he talked hard trying to persuade me to forget about it. But I knew that if I went directly to Australia, I'd chase him — and that wouldn't be good policy.

I wanted him to have time to think about us in his normal surroundings. Then when he'd had a few weeks to himself I'd see him again.

His concern about my proposed trip to Hanoi was balm to my wounds. I reasoned that if he still worried that much about me then he must still love me, and my hope was that eventually he would find the courage to face family responsibilities. I fell asleep peacefully in his arms with that thought in my mind.

As choppers were grounded I spent the next day on Back Beach.

There I met an attractive Australian girl, Lindie McGregor, who had recently come to Vietnam the hard way, by hitch-hiking from London with forty-six pounds of rucksack on her back. When Lindie found out that I accompanied Aussie troops on short patrols she begged me to take her along. Colonel Logan gave permission.

Lindie had infinite trust in the good of mankind. A trust bordering on naïveté perhaps — but it was a kind of 'guardian angel' that protected her through sticky situations. She seemed completely unaware of the dangers surrounding us. To her, patrols were a great walk through the countryside. I pleaded with her to walk *exactly* where the man in front had stepped. Her eyes showed astonished disbelief when I said: 'I'd hate you to trigger off a booby trap and blow us both to pieces.' It was as though I should know such things just didn't happen.

The troops were astounded whenever she turned up — a genuine real-live, dinki-di Aussie girl — not up on a stage, but right out there sharing their rations in a foxhole.

'Things can't be too bad if you still come here to visit us,' was the comment of Bill Wilson at Xuyen Moc. He was resting on his 'bed' — a plywood sheet under an outslung poncho, with a 'Home Sweet Home' sign pinned to a nearby tree trunk. 'Please — can I take your photo? Mum will think I'm going troppo if I write home about you without proof to back me up.'

Lindie was going to hitch-hike home via Bangkok and Singapore and as my visa was about to expire I decided to go with her as far as Phnom Penh and do an article on her on the way. I had no idea I was going to get more of a story than I hoped for.

After a long last night with Robert, Lindie and I headed for Saigon. We spent a night at Elaine's place, a small bungalow near Ton Son Nhut, down a tiny alley leading off a small alley leading off the main alley leading off a street leading off Cach Mang, the main drag — and on top of all that, hidden by a huge bamboo fence! Thoi, I thought, couldn't find that godforsaken place even if he tried . . . it was hard enough for those who knew its location!

The next morning the two of us hitched a chopper to Cu Chi, an American base camp halfway between Saigon and the Cambodian border. We invented a rendezvous with our Australian boy friends in a nearby village to get past camp gate-control. Cu Chi's main road was ankle-deep in mud. Passing natives looked curiously at us and at the police station where we checked the road map the officer said drily: 'Bonne chance!'

We hitched a lift on an American convoy going to Tay Ninh, balancing on a truck with a load of lumber. GIs passing in a jeep gave us disbelieving stares, then recovered in time to toss up some cold beer — very welcome. A few miles further on MPs stopped our truck. Again we received startled looks when we said we were hitch-hiking to Phnom Penh and Bangkok. They contacted headquarters by radio and asked for the Colonel: 'Sir, we just picked up two girls, one Canadian and one Australian, outside Cu Chi. They're hitch-hiking to Bangkok. What will we do? Over.'

There was an immediate response: 'I don't believe. Repeat, don't believe. Over.'

'It's true, sir. We wouldn't kid you.' the MPs voice was almost a whine. I grabbed the microphone: 'It is true, mon colonel. And if we're not allowed to go on the convoy, please say so and we'll go by local transportation.'

A moment's silence, then the Colonel ordered, 'Continue convoy. I'll come to check this out for myself. Stop the convoy when you see me land. Over and out.'

Some ten minutes later the chopper clattered overhead and landed on a grass patch. The Colonel, surprisingly young for his rank, checked our papers, listened to our story, then passed the buck to his Brigadier.

The Brigadier's response was crisp and short: 'We have no regulations for preventing females of foreign nationalities from hitch-hiking through insecure territory,' and he went off the air after an abrupt, 'Good luck to them!'

We continued with the convoy until Go Dau Ha, where the road to Tay Ninh branches off. We jumped off the truck and walked into the village. We noticed the atmosphere immediately. There were no soldiers about and the looks and comments we got from the villagers were far from friendly.

This was 'Charlie Country'.

We were only a few klicks from the border, so clambered into a three-wheeled taxi, paying 50 piastres (about 40 cents) for the journey.

Unfortunately Lindie's visa had expired and the Vietnamese customs officials would not let her cross. She tried to talk her way through, then to bluff her way through by walking across to the barrier to the Cambodian border post. The Vietnamese official shouted and waved his gun. Worried he might shoot her, I stood in front of him, saying I'd try to get her back. She returned of her own accord — the Cambodians had refused her entry. I begged her not to be stubborn, afraid the official might contact Saigon and that Thoi might find out I was there.

Finally I persuaded her to return to Saigon and we boarded a Lambretta going back to Go Dau Ha. An old man joined us and sat next to the driver. A mile further on the Lambretta suddenly pulled off the road and stopped by a large hut. About twenty men came out and surrounded us. They were unarmed, but I was sure they were Viet Cong. Most of them were very young, but a mean-looking middle-aged man stepped forward, stuck his hand right under my nose and said aggressively, 'Bonjour, madame!'

'Bonjour,' I replied, my throat suddenly very dry. 'Lindie is Australian!' I thought in horror.

I knew that showing fear would be the worst thing, and was relieved to see Lindie utterly calm, smiling shyly at the surrounding men. The older man questioned me in pidgin French and I answered in the same way, a mistake, as he accused me of speaking French with an American accent. My mad outburst at this seemed to pacify him a little, and afford the others considerable amusement.

I claimed we were Canadian schoolteachers at the Marie Curie College in Saigon. He immediately asked me where it was located, and seemed satisfied when I promptly said: 'On Cong Ly'. Then he asked to see our papers and I nearly panicked. If they saw Lindie's Australian passport, their obvious move would be to take her captive and march her as 'bait' through Phuoc Tuy province, ambushing any Australian search parties who came looking for her.

I told him coldly that we had no passports and asked, 'Now, can we continue to Saigon or not?'

The old man in the front seat said something in Vietnamese, and I was able to understand a few words: khong My (Not American), Phap (French), Gia-na-dai (Canadian).

Reluctantly the man stepped back, gestured to his companions to do likewise and we started off. For the rest of the trip to Go Dau Ha, the old man talked to me. He was surprisingly fluent in French and no doubt our freedom was largely due to his intervention.

Lindie's usual attitude prevailed throughout this rather sticky situation as though detached from her current surroundings. Rather naively she said: 'I don't think they could have been Viet Cong. They didn't have any weapons.'

'Twenty men don't need guns against two unarmed girls. And during daylight the Viet Cong usually hide their weapons so that they won't be spotted from the air.'

She still wasn't convinced.

'They wouldn't have done anything to us. There were too many peasants travelling along the road.'

'In Cong territory peasants have their own health rules . . . they never notice *anything*.'

From Go Dau Ha we took a local bus. Squeezed between peasants, chickens, and baskets we reached Saigon after several hours of travelling over rough roads.

The next morning I left on a plane for Phnom Penh — the day my visa was due to expire. Lindie left a few days afterwards by plane for Singapore. By the time my article about Lindie appeared in an Australian magazine, Go Dau Ha and the border post had been over-run and were 'officially' in the hands of the Viet Cong.

# 22

## A PATCH OF PEACE

The smiles at Phnom Penh airport made me forget Saigon with its suspicious and special madness. It was good to be again in a land of peace where people's main interest was having a pleasant day, instead of being pre-occupied with saving someone for democracy or for communism. Streets were clean and lined with bright houses in well-kept gardens; there were no roped-off sidewalks, no refugees living in gutters.

Le Royal, the main hotel, had a fair-sized pool, an excellent pavilion restaurant and the surrounding park contained small bungalows hidden behind trees with flower-laden branches. The desk clerk asked how long I intended to stay. As a room cost seven dollars (US) a day I told him I would have to look for a less expensive hotel. He smiled and said: 'We have rooms for three dollars — they are not renovated, have cold water only, and a ceiling fan instead of air-conditioning.'

'That'll do!'

The large tiled room with bath would have cost me at least ten times as much in Saigon.

At the poolside, shaded by parasols marked 'Air France' or 'Fly Czechoslovak Airlines', sat Cambodians, French, Americans, Russians, Germans (from East and West), Swiss, Red Chinese, Poles — relaxed, contented faces. There was also the inevitable 'spook' who eyed everyone with suspicion over his latest edition of *Time* magazine. I wondered if the CIA got a reduction for keeping permanent bookings at Le Royal, like Air France for their crew.

In the pool I saw a girl who looked vaguely familiar. She was Irena Zur, the interpreter for the Polish delegation of the ICC* in Saigon. Irena was on vacation and we decided to explore Phnom Penh together when the heat subsided. She wore a tiny bikini and

*International Control Commission, which was set up at the Geneva Conference in 1954, comprises Poles, Canadians and Indians. Based in Saigon, Phnom Penh, Vientiane and Hanoi, the Commission investigates and records incidents which violate the Geneva Agreements.

later changed into a dress which would have been chic in Paris, London or New York.

Strolling through the city we passed groups of tourists from East and West, a surprising number from European countries behind the Iron Curtain. Most visitors from Slavik countries were younger than their American counterparts, their women wearing less make-up and costume jewellery, but the men's trousers were the same baggy cut as the Americans', and they also carried cameras (East German or Russian makes, instead of West German or Japanese). We agreed that Phnom Penh was easy-going and wonderfully relaxing after Saigon's maelstrom. In the shops there was courteous service instead of pushy 'hard-sell'.

Even the samlo* pedallers tipped their hats with a friendly 'merci, madame' for a fraction of what we had paid in Vietnam and there were no shouted insults.

We stopped at the North Vietnamese Consulate where I applied for a visa. We sat in the main hall on green plastic armchairs, a ceiling fan turning above. A man served tea. On the table was a ceramic bowl with two open packs of cigarettes. One brand was 'Dien Bien' (Phu) the other 'Tu Do' (Freedom), both from Hanoi, and both tasting the same as the cheap Cambodian ones I had bought at a stand.

After a few minutes' wait a middle-aged wiry man entered. I expected to be handed endless forms to fill out but all he did was write my name on a pad.

'Our chief of the Delegation of Journalists from Hanoi, Mr Bao Dinh Giang, will be here in a few days and will see you then,' he told me, and he let me swap my cigarette pack for one of the Hanoi ones.

Back on the street, a young boy approached us with books and magazines under his arm: *Mao's Thoughts*; pamphlets showing the result of the bombing in North Vietnam, *Assassins of Children*; the Russian publication called *The Struggle in Vietnam*; and outdated editions of *Time, Life,* and so on. He was one of many refugees who found a home in Phnom Penh, preferring to earn a meagre living there to returning to their war-torn home country. Mr Pham Van Quang, the representative of the NLF, lived on Samdech Iem, near Boulevard Norodom, and his entire area was practically a colony of Vietnamese refugees.

Despite signs of communist influence, there were also balancing ones from America — neon signs saying 'Howdy — the friendly drink', Coca-Cola was as popular here as in most other parts of the world, and the wrapper on rolls of locally-produced toilet paper

*Cambodian for cyclo.

showed a Western stage-coach scene and was named 'Good View Brand'.

Back at Le Royal I went to the bungalow where the Canadian Commission resided, introduced myself and asked if they could possibly wangle an invitation for me to attend Prince Sihanouk's Festival of the Sacred Ploughing in Angkor. To get good photographs I would have to follow the immediate entourage but I couldn't present myself as a journalist — foreign correspondents are strictly forbidden to enter Cambodia without a special permit, and I had arrived as a 'tourist'.

The Canadians were cautious and vague about being able to help but Irena got me an invitation from the Polish delegation. The Poles were so contrary to our Western conception of them. They lived in the best hotels and ate only in air-conditioned restaurants, refusing to join me for local food. They drank Coca-Cola without ice ('it might not be purified') and smoked American cigarettes while I puffed local brands. They opened the cigarette packets at the wrong end, to avoid touching the filter, 'because of germs'.

At the poolside Irena and I were joined by two Yugoslav engineers, part of a team constructing a dam in Cambodia. They invited us to dinner at their air-conditioned villa, and had such comforts as their favourite cheese flown from Yugoslavia in a Thermos container. They discussed cars endlessly.

'I think I'll buy a Citroen when I get back home,' one said.

'Listen to my Comrade Capitalists,' I couldn't resist jibing. 'Talking about a Citroen while I struggle along with native food and bargain rooms!'

They grinned. And the name Comrade Capitalists stuck.

The next day a Cambodian acquaintance took me in his car to visit a refugee camp situated close to the Vietnamese border. We drove first to the village where Lindie and I had tried vainly to cross. There my friend bought whisky smuggled in from Vietnam. The village was a veritable bazaar for Phnom Penh residents, offering liquor, weapons, GI uniforms, rations, ilghters, radios, watches, even a US jeep hidden under branches in a backyard. Anything the PX and black market in Saigon lacked could easily be purchased this side of the Cambodian border.

To reach the refugee camp we left our car and walked. At the the camp, herded in primitive shelters hammered together from any available material, were hundreds of refugees: mainly old people, women and children, quite a few of them wounded and scarred from the war. American sources claimed these camps were hide-outs for guerillas but in these pathetic groups I didn't see a single able-bodied man who would have met any kind of recruiting requirement.

The following morning Irena and I were picked up by three members of the Polish delegation at 6 a.m. and we left for Angkor in a chauffeur-driven, air-conditioned Pontiac. The road led through villages built on stilts in the lush green Mekong Valley. People were chatting on their porches. A woman was washing her baby in the same pond another cleaned her dishes in. Both baby and dishes were rinsed off with rainwater from a terracotta container. Cattle grazed lazily under trees and water buffaloes waded in the Mekong.

'They are definitely backward by our standards,' Irena commented, 'but they are so friendly and helpful. They are warm — like the glow of oil lamps in their villages.'

Angkor was of breathtaking beauty.

I had been disappointed visiting the Pyramids in Egypt, so impressive on Cinerama screens but in reality just commercialised heaps of stone with a drab chamber in the middle smelling of urine.

But Angkor was different.

It is a place of majestic beauty where one can spend hours without passing groups of tourists yelling 'How lovely' in a variety of languages. And there are no guides shrilly repeating what pamphlets describe anyway, then stretching out a greedy, demanding hand at the end of their recital.

Unfortunately the temples are not well guarded and many sculptures have been decapitated for the benefit of wealthy collectors. It's sad that people have such beauty destroyed so they can use a fragment of it to decorate an over-filled house, even though the smiling face of the stone head is so alien in its new surroundings.

In Angkor no two temples are alike in layout or detail, very different from Western cultures which usually fall into definite recognisable periods with the same basic design and structure common to each period.

Unfortunately only stone-built temples survived the fires and termites which destroyed all other buildings.

We first visited Angkor Vat, one of the architectural miracles of the world. We followed a long road of huge stone slabs through the park towards three pineapple shaped towers silhouetted against the soft blue of the sky. (Two additional towers were hidden behind the ones on each side.)

As we ascended the stairs a group of Vietnamese in olive green jungle uniforms devoid of insignia emerged from the temple. North Vietnamese, or members of the NLF on leave — the Poles eyed them with curiosity and they shot hostile glances in our direction. I grinned and said, 'Small wonder — with your cameras dangling over your well-fed bellies you look like American tourists to them.' A typical middle-aged couple from the US took no notice of the

Vietnamese — no doubt to them they were just another lot of Asians . . . who all look alike, of course . . .

Irena lit incense in front of the Buddha.

'Just in case. I made a wish and it might come true.'

The delegates shook their heads in amused tolerance.

After lunch at the Auberge des Temples we drove to the complex of Angkor Thom, with four-faced towers marking the entrance in the outer wall. A bridge led across the moat, lined with a double row of gods and demons, pulling a huge naga snake in a perpetual tug-of-war.

I asked my Polish friends to pose for a photograph: 'Against the demons, please. This picture is for a capitalistic publication!'

The road led through dense jungle which suddenly parted . . . and there in front of us was Bayon. Serene faces stared at us as if demanding an explanation for our intrusion. It was overwhelming. Some fifty-odd towers each crowned by huge grey stone faces looking in the four directions. We were mesmerised by the stony gazes.

We climbed through narrow corridors and wandered over deserted terraces. Even close-up, the faces guarded their secrets.

'Look — they are absolutely identical. And yet — they seem to smile when touched by sunlight, and look melancholy in shadow . . .'

'Yes. I wouldn't want to live here. They would drive me insane,' Irena said.

The lower galleries were lined with reliefs. Many depicted the life still practised in today's Cambodian countryside: the same tools, the same type of habitation, the same hunting and fishing scenes, the same musical instruments. Other panels showed war and its cruelties: elephants trampling bodies, prisoners being eaten by alligators.

'Methods have changed but the misery of war is still the same,' commented Irena.

I was delighted to recognise a panel of which I had found a dusty, but authentic rubbing in a Saigon junk shop. It showed a procession carrying a coffin on a ship, and in the water below, among alligators, turtles and fish, floated a human figure whose lower part had changed into a fish, while out of its hands grew a lotus blossom. It probably symbolised death and re-incarnation. (One of the 'Stateside rejects' at PA&E who saw it told all Saigon that I had a pornographic Oriental scene on my wall; I studied it for hours without being able to see what she evidently saw in it.)

My favourite temple was Ta Prohm, which the French had very wisely refrained from restoring. A bare passage had been cleared and there one could still stray, crawling over piles of stones and roots of giant trees to discover devatas* hidden by jungle growth. We disturbed two cobras in their siesta while we explored.

There we glimpsed an inkling of what the French explorer must have felt when he was hunting for insects and suddenly saw phantom faces staring at him through the jungle. (Nobody believed him at first, thinking it had been a trick of his imagination, the result of a fever.)

A day after our arrival the crowds poured in for the festival. Busloads of peasants camped and cooked under the trees and the grounds of Angkor Thom resembled the scene of a gypsy convention. Limousines bearing flags brought the important guests and the tempo of the festivities heightened. The festival itself was the most colourful event I ever attended. There were about 30,000 spectators lining the cordoned-off area on the terrace of the elephants when Prince Sihanouk arrived, flamboyant in shimmering regalia, carried in a hammock. But though there were no armed guards posted, the crowds cheering him with heartwarming enthusiasm kept respectfully on their side of the crimson cord held by small boys.

Thanks to my Polish friends I was able to get inside the cordon and raced with other photographers after pictures of the procession. At one stage I found myself next to a pleasant-looking Vietnamese quickly shooting off film. He glanced at me during a lull and asked whether I was a journalist.

'No,' I lied, 'just a tourist.'

We chatted briefly then were both kept busy photographing the Prince leading the decorated oxen pulling the holy plough around the terrace; behind followed a dainty princess sowing the symbolic rice. Musicians and dancers performed in multi-coloured costumes, sword-dancers swung their enormous sabres and a parade of decorated tractors passed in the background, American makes slightly outnumbering the less-sturdy Czechoslovakian machines. After the symbolic ploughing the oxen were led to a row of silver bowls filled with the various crops that Cambodia produces.

The crowd fell into an awed silence as the oxen bowed their heads. A murmur rippled through the close-packed rows.

'It's the rice, they say,' a nearby Cambodian translated for us. Then he added, 'and the beans. A good harvest is promised for whichever crop the oxen eat.'

There was jubilation whenever a soft nuzzle touched a bowl and, carried away by the crowd's enthusiasm, I was shouting encouragement to the beasts.

In the heat of the afternoon Irena and I relaxed at the room the Polish delegation had at the Grand Hotel while the delegates at-

*Female deities.

tended a reception Prince Sihanouk was holding for diplomats. Suddenly the door flew open without a knock and a young bearded man stormed in.

'This is one of our rooms,' he shouted. 'You must move out immediately!'

We didn't know who he was but Irena calmly told him there must be a mistake, that the room belonged to the Polish delegation and that we were their guests.

'This will cause an international incident!' was all our self-invited visitor called as he turned and raced off down the hallway. Flabbergasted we went to the desk to ask what was going on.

In the hall the armchairs were taken by a group of elderly tourists, their bags next to them, and the desk informed us that our stormy intruder was a Mr Lass, tour-leader for the American OHI tours. Unfortunately there had been a mistake in his reservations. Apparently he should have had the room at present occupied by the Polish delegation, also those of the Swedish and Spanish Consuls and some other diplomats. When the diplomatic corps returned from their luncheon there was a quick discussion then the members agreed to vacate in favour of the touring group.

As Siemreap was over-run with visitors for the festival Irena and I lodged in the Auberge with the Spanish Consul and two Polish delegates sleeping on mattresses on our floor.

'Lass didn't have to behave like such an ass over the matter,' I said rather heatedly, 'storming into the room and shouting "international incidents"!'

'It's no wonder Americans are welcomed only because of the dollars they bring to countries like this!' the Spanish Consul said drily, and a delegate said, 'Speaking of money, Rena, I wonder if you would buy for me some carvings I saw in a store? You speak French — so you will get them cheaper. If I ask for them in English they will charge American prices!'

It was the old story of the double-price standard I had already encountered in Saigon; similarly, in Phnom Penh, Irena paid 350 riels for the identical silk sampot I bought for 250 riels.

That evening the Royal Ballet performed in front of the lighted ruins of Angkor Vat — a scene of 1001 nights as seen through what resembled snow but was actually millions of insects and moths lured from the jungle by the strong floodlights.

The tourists left after the festival and we enjoyed a couple of days of quiet wandering through the temples before returning to Phnom Penh.

After my return from Angkor I called in at the North Vietnamese consulate and was told that Mr Giang had arrived and would see me in a few minutes. I was sipping tea, but dropped my cup into the saucer when he entered the room. We both laughed . . . Mr Giang was the Vietnamese photographer who had spoken to me in Angkor.

'Alors . . . you sometimes pose as a tourist, sometimes as a school teacher,' he chided. 'But I could tell you were a journalist by the way you changed your lenses while chasing after Prince Sihanouk!'

His reference to my posing as a school teacher was confirmation that the men who had stopped Lindie and me were in fact NLF members. Mr Giang knew plenty about me — that I had lost my MACV accreditation, my ordeals with Thoi. He promised to recommend the issuing of the visa, but warned it might take time and I would have to be patient.

As I was leaving, I said, 'If you know so much about an unimportant person like me, your information service must be excellent. If the American telephone system in Vietnam worked half as well as your jungle drums they might have won this war by now.'

'The Americans will never win,' he said. 'They are supporting a government of mercenaries which exploits its own people.'

I joined Irena at the poolside and told her of my interview with Giang.

'I hope it won't take too long for the visa to come through. I can't wait here forever,' I said.

I noticed the hotel manager was racing around the pool like a hornet and there was a camera set up at one corner. A waiter was busy changing Air France parasols for ones market 'Fly Czechoslovak Airlines'.

'What's happening? A revolution?'

'They're making a tourist film — for our side of the Iron Curtain,' laughed Irena.

About a week later I decided to try to reach Hanoi on my own via the Ho Chi Minh trail from Na Phao (Laos) across the Mu Gia Pass to Bai Dinh, in North Vietnam. I carried a small rucksack containing a few clothes, my camouflage poncho liner which served as a blanket, my cameras and plenty of film. I knew that infiltrators would stop me on the trail sooner or later so I had several pamphlets from North Vietnam and the addresses of Mr Giang and Mr Quang on me. A Cambodian friend drove me close to Stung Treng and from that point my transport was local buses, sampans on the Mekong, ox-carts and my own two feet. The first night I camped in a pagoda on the outskirts of a small village and was so exhausted I was asleep by dusk.

The second night I spent at the home of a French-speaking Laotian with whom I had struck up a conversation while eating in the market place. He was intrigued by my adventure, and invited me to his house. His wife and seven children just stared at me in silent awe but I won the toddler over by rocking him on my knee, and following his approval I was accepted as part of the family. I slept in the corner of the main room on several blankets which they put down to serve as a mattress. During the night I woke twice to find the boy (aged about ten) looking at me — he had come to peep at this unbelievably strange sight of a foreign woman sleeping on the floor of his house.

About four o'clock the next day I spotted a pagoda quite removed from the nearest hamlet. A river flowed sluggishly at the bottom of the hill. Trees were thick, so that only the ornamental roof peeked out from the growth. I climbed up, with several monkeys following me via the branches, chattering excitedly. In a clearing below the pagoda stood two small stone buildings with narrow doors, the windows bare slits in the walls.

A young bonze in an ochre robe sat on a wooden bench and at my approach he hastily disappeared inside. I continued on to the pagoda, a small rectangular building with three huge wooden arched doors on each side, its crumbling plaster a light yellow. The doors were all securely locked and if it hadn't been for the disappearing monk, and a cat and kittens curled beneath the bench I would have thought the place was deserted. I sat on the earth steps and waited. Presently I heard some movement from inside the cottage and a murmuring, then a short, stocky man of about sixty appeared with a bunch of huge keys in his hand. He pointed to my camera and said: 'Photo pagode' and smiled. Thank goodness he speaks French, I thought, and said: 'Oui, très jolie pagode!'

He went ahead and unlocked the door which screeched on its hinges. A musty smell of stale incense hit me as I walked towards the huge bronze Buddha surrounded by smaller wooden Buddhas. Dead flowers hung their dehydrated petals in various containers, burnt-out incense sticks stuck like porcupine bristles in bowls filled with sand.

The caretaker opened all six portals, sweating with his efforts. Proudly he pointed to the walls and the ceiling. The entire pagoda was covered with painted scenes from the life of the Enlightened, in brilliant colours. Orange predominated with royal blue as the main background. They were elaborate and ornamental, with placid pink faces, gowns of flowing softness, flowers like licking flames, pink plump hands with long nails, stiffly holding various vessels. Had I seen the pagoda when I first arrived in Asia I would have thought it ugly but I had been in the East long enough by then to find it fascinating. I gave the old man some coins for lighting incense in front of the Buddha, which pleased him enormously. The sickly-sweet smell of freshly-burning incense was preferable to the stale one.

I pointed to the mat in front of the Buddha, the only covering on the bare stone floor, and said with a querying note, 'Moi dormir ici . . .?'

'Demander, madame, demander.' He trotted off to seek permission. When he returned he was accompanied by three monks who surveyed me silently, keeping their distance.

'Correct, madame, dormer ici!' said the caretaker and I unpacked my rucksack, draped my poncho liner on the floor and ate a banana from the bunch I had bought earlier at the market.

Later that evening it became very gloomy inside, the only two windows being in the wall opposite the Buddha.

It was quiet, the sort of quiet which amplifies the slightest noise. There were eerie, faint movements in the pagoda. I was half asleep when suddenly something brushed my leg. I jumped up . . . and heard a tiny 'maouw . . .' I laughed but couldn't go back to sleep. The smell in the pagoda was sickening and I could still hear noises that could not have come from the cat.

'If only I wasn't so alone . . . if there was someone to laugh the noises off with . . .' I groped in my rucksack for my automatic, slightly reassured by the feel of its cold steel in my hand.

But the loneliness continued, and I cried. I thought about Robert and hated him intensely because I blamed him for my being in this situation. What right did he have to build up my hopes for a quiet home, for children, for all the things I wanted and then, for no valid reason, change his mind and leave me more confused and insecure than before? I hungered for companionship, and cursed my boasting about making it on my own to Hanoi. If I hadn't opened my big mouth, I could go back. I didn't want to spend more frightening lonely nights.

I fell asleep eventually and woke at daylight, still feeling exhausted. I decided to freshen up at the river and reached into my rucksack to take out the Aussie sweat cloth I used as a towel. I touched something strange and for a few seconds my fingers explored its hose-like surface. Then it moved under my hand and I screamed — a blood-curdling yell which brought a bonze running into the pagoda. I ran towards him and he froze and stared in horror. (A woman is not supposed to come within touching distance of a bonze.) I remembered just as I was on the point of flinging my arms around his neck for succour! I pointed to my rucksack and he carried it outside, reached in and brought out a rock-python about eight feet long. He gently deposited it on a bush.

Over a jug of very sweet rich coffee and a cigarette my nerves calmed a little. But that was the end. No matter how much teasing

I took about turning back, I was going to the nearest village to catch any transport headed in the direction of Phnom Penh. I had calculated what to do if I met infiltrators, or any 'normal' situation like that. But sharing my rucksack with an eight foot python, that was too much!

# 23

## SECRETS IN THAILAND

Back in Phnom Penh a friend introduced me to Charles Meyer, a French journalist who handled press matters for Prince Sihanouk. He was born in Wissembourg, 6 km from my hometown and we became friendly reminiscing about the beautiful Vosges mountains, our favourite wines, the old castle ruins we had played in as children.

Charles Meyer checked with the North Vietnamese about my visa after my return from Laos. He told me they wouldn't let me in while the bombing was so intense. My finances wouldn't permit me to wait, and after Charles promised to keep in touch and notify me when the visa came through I left for Bangkok. I had given my press credentials to Elaine, who had promised to bring them to Bangkok on her next visit to her children.

I arrived at Don Muang airport with my crossbow strung over my shoulder. A friend spotted me there, gave me a lift into town and introduced me to Mr Rockefeller, owner of the Plaza Hotel and the Plaza Court. Mr Rockefeller suggested I stay at the flat of an American who was absent for several weeks on TDY (temporary duty). The Plaza Court was a huge, luxurious compound for US officers and dependants, equipped with air-conditioning, hot water, swimming pool, restaurant and bar and a playground for children. I accepted the offer gratefully, a rent-free place in which I could await Elaine's arrival suited me fine.

Bangkok, camera-wise, was a veritable feast. The temples, the floating markets, the palaces, the canals with their boats: an overwhelming choice of subjects. I often ran into Americans I had known in Vietnam so I was never lacking escorts to restaurants and nightclubs. Elaine arrived three weeks later with my papers and I prepared to leave Thailand. It was time to make tracks to join Robert and find out what he had decided about our future.

Before leaving I planned to spend a weekend at Pattaya, a beach resort on the southern coast of Thailand. The invitation had come from the purchasing agents for the US Air Force in Korat. In exchange for large orders given to the B&C Co. on Petchbury Road, they were the frequent guests at the weekend villa of the company's owner, Mr Boonchana Kitpanich, a wealthy Bangkok businessman, called 'Mr B.' for short.

Boonchana represented everything that was distasteful to me. He picked us up in his air-conditioned Mercedes. On the way to the villa we discussed the problem of the CT* in the Kalasin Mountains. 'I am not surprised they have a field day in that area,' I remarked. 'The people there are so poor anything they offer must be an improvement. Bangkok is as expensive as New York to live in — and the average yearly income in the Kalasin Province is thirty-five US dollars. Taking into account the better-than-average salaries of the Government officials many people don't see five dollars a year. If communism is to be blocked in that area something should be done to improve their lot.'

Mr B. had a very simple solution: 'We should wipe out the people of North-East Thailand. They're not Thai, they're animals. They paid tribute to us for centuries.'

I could find no answer to such a statement. It is easy to cope with someone expounding on the 'superiority' of a white skin but a statement like Boonchana's can come only from someone completely devoid of all human compassion and neither sarcasm nor logic ever reaches such people.

Typical of Mr B.'s treatment of his employees was his abrupt 'Sing something!' snapped at the embarrassed little Thai girl he had brought along to keep one of the Americans company. And his gardener has to approach Mr B. on his knees if he wishes to address him!

There are many Boonchanas, if you scratch the veneer of Bangkok's pseudo-sophistication. Statistically the prostitution and VD rates surpass even those of Saigon. It is fortunate from their point of view that there are enough GIs to be blamed, conveniently overlooking the fact that local co-operation is necessary for its spread.

The locale of the villa did much to restore my good humour and as I swam in the fantastically clear waters around the islands off the Pattaya coast, surveying the wonders of the Gulf of Siam through my diving-goggles, I shed some of the miasma that had surrounded me.

On our way back to Bangkok, after a delicious meal of Thai seafood, Boonchana asked me how long I intended to remain in Thailand.

'I'm leaving in three days. My visa is about to expire and I understand it is nearly impossible to renew it here.'

*Communist Terrorists, the Thai equivalent of VC.

'Give me your passport. I'll have it fixed for you with no problem,' was his immediate reaction, but I told him I was leaving anyway.

The next morning when I started packing I found that the red leather bag which contained all my money, my jewellery and some negatives was missing. The flat had not been burgled: my radio was still beside the bed, my Hermes Baby Typewriter on the corner table in full view. I notified the manager but he strongly advised against calling the police: 'They'll swarm all over the place, take what's left, and expect money for responding to your call. Have no illusions about recovering your property here. The culprit was probably one of the waiters who brought food to your flat.'

I immediately sent an SOS to my bank in Europe then headed for the Immigration Department to arrange an extension of my stay. They wanted a $1000 bond — in cash. Patiently I explained all over again that my money had been stolen and that I couldn't leave until my funds arrived. They shrugged their shoulders and went on with their work, ignoring me. I had no money for bribes; therefore I was of no interest.

As a last resort I thought of Boonchana. I should have known better: Mr B. was a businessman and expected favour for favour.

I decided to sit it out till my money arrived then bribe the border guard to overlook my expired visa.

Meanwhile I met Peter Arnett from AP's Saigon office who suggested I take up a bit of work. 'Come to Sakon Nakhon with me. I have to interview the Governor there. We'll have to be careful though because the Thai officials are rather hush-hush about what is really going on in their north-east.'

Verification that 'something' was going on came before we left. We tried various car rental firms but when told of our destination, suddenly they were not sure whether a car was available or not. One promised, but didn't show up. After trying in vain for a full day to make a booking, the desk clerk at Peter's hotel finally found a private driver who was willing to take us — for a price. He was probably in bad enough financial trouble to take the risk. He was so nervous we had a most hair-raising ride.

Up to Khon Kaen the road was fairly well used even at night. There were several roadblocks with check-points where cars were searched for weapons intended for the CT. We arrived in Khon Kaen, spent the night at a hotel and continued our journey next morning. The road became rougher, with odd stretches under construction but there was still a fair amount of traffic up till Kalasin. After that, through the mountains, it was completely deserted. We drove, winding through dense forest, without meeting another vehicle except two trucks carrying Thai soldiers armed to the teeth,

and cut you up just for the hell of it?' I asked.

'Sure, sometimes we don't feel too good about being used as sitting ducks out here,' he agreed. 'At one tambol the medic left by the rear door when the CT were shooting a village official in front. He got chewed out! We're not supposed to leave our posts. If the medic had been killed out in the woods it could be blamed on bandits. There are plenty of them in this area.'

The medic stationed in Ban Duasikhanchai spoke fluent Thai. One day a team of ten terrorists moved in front of the dispensary with the leader calling out: 'Come out, American. We know you are there. We won't hurt you because you help our people but we want to talk to you.' The medic came out and had to listen to half an hour of propaganda and criticism directed against the US Government before the party moved on.

Usually the villagers warn the medics if the CT teams are in the area. Ray Glodek of Hoyt's team was alone in the medical centre at Kham Takhra when some villagers hurried up to warn him of an approaching CT team, 'Turn your lights off and keep very still,' they instructed him. Three days earlier the policeman stationed there had been killed just outside the village so Glodek spent a sleepless night waiting and watching. The next morning the villagers told him that a team of eleven CT had come to execute the same policeman and that they had spent hours convincing them the man was already dead.

A French missionary who brought a very sick woman to the Annamine was outspoken. 'The CT teams have only limited supplies but succeed in using these as effective propaganda aids. If only the Thai Government would realise that they'd save themselves a lot of trouble in future if they'd go all out to help the people now but they're concerned with only one thing — filling their own pockets. I'm afraid they'll pay a high price for their negligence soon.'

Amongst the Thai people themselves idealism can be found on a small scale. Some of the interpreters helping the medics are volunteers . . . like Tawatchai Tinmatistan (called Tommy for short) the Wanon Niwat interpreter, who volunteers to scrub children with medicated soap to combat skin diseases . . . a task far below his standing by Thai reckoning. The medics worked hard, from dawn to nightfall, holding sick-calls at schools and hamlets in the area, checking the entire population for possible diseases. They hand out vitamins, treat minor ills, and in an emergency amputate limbs. They teach hygiene and show the villagers how to dig wells to obtain purer water.

In one hamlet of some 1200 people they found the entire population suffering from dysentery, with a death toll of eight in three days. They checked the water supply and found the drinking water came from a river where water buffaloes wallowed. The medics blasted two wells, chlorinated the water supply, and within four days the dysentery epidemic was over.

'Skin diseases are a problem here,' Buddy told me. 'We could clear some of them up if we had adequate supplies of soap, but the Air Force doesn't fly soap in, and the villagers can't even afford proper food, let alone luxuries like soap.'

Robert Peltier, the team's dentist, said, 'Teeth are fairly good here, due to lack of sweets, but many suffer from gum diseases such as periodentitis, and women who chew betel want me to pull out perfectly good teeth just because they are indelibly stained black.'

'We have to fight ignorance and superstition at every turn,' Myron explained. 'Some mountain tribes never wash — they believe in bad spirits below water and are not willing to disturb them. Others put stuff like buffalo manure on sores and end up with a major inflammation.' (This resulted in a job for me — I was elected 'Honorary Buffalo Manure Washer-offer' and scrubbed the kids with medicated soap and water.) Ignorance produces many odd situations — such as villagers exchanging a red pill for a yellow one that a neighbour has because they like the colour better.

The peasants, though poor, bring fruit and corn and whatever they can afford, to show their gratitude. 'We must take their gifts,' the team explained, 'even when we know they represent quite a sacrifice on their part. If we refused we could offend them. Some of the presents liven up the Annamine: the centre has parrots, minah birds and a monkey who tries to bite the maids at every opportunity. The team treated the sick wife of a carpenter, and he made them a beautiful sun-chair. The throat of one old woman was so swollen she had difficulty in breathing. When they cured her she said simply, 'Let me kiss your footprints in the sand,' the highest compliment in the Thai idiom.

In one tambol we discovered a baby close to death. The mother had been paralysed since the birth and the grandmother had tried to suckle the infant from her own withered breasts. The entire family was moved to the health centre: I showed the grandmother how to prepare a bottle with powdered milk and vitamins. At first nearly too weak to suck, the baby was soon able to clutch the bottle firmly with his skinny fingers. After two weeks of treatment the mother was able to move her right arm a little, and her visiting husband had tears in his eyes when she showed him what she could do. He bowed to us, his hands clasped over the back of his head, a greeting normally reserved for the King of Thailand.

I was becoming accustomed to the routine of the team's work, and reluctant to face the fact that I would have to leave. For once I felt

I was really doing something worthwhile. I thought about Robert, and decided to write to him at his sister's address, telling him what I was doing in Thailand. If he cared enough about me, if he had overcome his scruples and fears about getting 'hooked', he'd write back asking me to join him. And if he had decided against a reunion it was better for me to work among the medics where I'd have no time for loneliness and self-pity.

The medics offered to drive me to Nong Khai from where I could cross the Mekong to Vientiane, renew my visa for Thailand, and return to the centre. But the Laotian immigration authorities refused my entry without a visa.

'Ridiculous,' I said to Myron. 'I've been to Laos from Cambodia minus visa. I've been several times to visit Bangkok from Saigon in the cockpit of R&R planes without passing controls. Now I come the official way, and have only problems!'

The one thing left for me to do was to return to Bangkok, hoping my money had arrived. On our way back from Nong Khai to Udon Thani we gave a lift to an Air America pilot with his wife and two children. They invited the medic and me to lunch at the Air America club on the Udon air base. The couple was stationed in Vientiane and had come to spend the weekend with friends whom they met after the luncheon. Myron had some business at the base and left me at the Air America 'Rendez-Vous Bar'.

'You wait here — I'll be back in about an hour to pick you up,' he said.

In the bar was the huge man I had seen earlier at the Green Beret Club in Sakon Nakhon. I walked up to him and said: 'Hey — are you following me or am I following you?'

He gave me a dirty look.

About twenty minutes later while I was playing darts with AA pilot Walt Darran, I felt a hand on my shoulder and heard someone say: 'Follow me. I want to speak to you.'

A tall, pale, arrogant man in his mid-thirties stood behind me. Surprised, I asked Walt: 'Who's this?'

'Chief of Security.'

From the moment I entered Air America Security office I became suspect No. 485 and felt I had ceased to belong to the human race. Though I protested vehemently that I came as a guest of one of their own pilots, that I had no idea the base was off-limits for the Press, and that I had taken no photos while I was there I got nowhere at all. I opened my camera, removed the film and handed it across, asking him to have it developed. But I might as well have saved my breath as he didn't intend to believe anything I said.

After a time I lost my temper, especially when he insisted that the camera, and I, would have to be handed over to Thai intelligence.

'If your base is so damn secret, how come I was allowed through your front gate?' I challenged him. 'I didn't crawl in under the back fence! I had my camera in full view and your guard didn't say a word.'

I was battering my head against a granite block.

'As far as I'm concerned you're a suspect and an unauthorised person on the base,' the Security Chief said coldly. 'And all I want is to get you out of my hair.'

With that he called the Thai intelligence.

I had been in South-East Asia long enough to know what to expect: hours of questioning with the same things being asked over and over again — and that was what followed when the Thai intelligence officer, a Mr Wichar, arrived with an assistant and two armed policemen of the tough, border control types who have a reputation for corruption and brutality. They discovered my visa had expired, which didn't help the situation.

I suddenly thought of the bag I had left in Myron's jeep. It contained my Browning, for which I had no registration for Thailand, *Mao's Thoughts* with the inscription from my North Vietnamese friend, and six morphine injections I always carried in Vietnam in case anyone was badly wounded and which I had brought along thinking of the possible bombings during my proposed trip up the Ho Chi Minh trail. The contents of that bag were enough to send me to a Thai jail for years. They could hang three charges on me — carrying a firearm without a permit, carrying Communist propaganda and carrying narcotics.

I was almost sweating blood thinking that Myron, unable to find me, might easily hand the bag over. I kept begging frantically for him to be notified of my whereabouts. I knew he wouldn't give me away to Air America, knowing they were the private Air Line of the CIA. USAID people in North-East Thailand who were attached to the CIA were always raising a stink about the 606 ACS teams not being fully qualified for their jobs despite, or perhaps because of the fact that they were much more popular than most stuffy USAID personnel. But my begging to see him was in vain. (Fortunately Myron heard what happened, knew the contents of my bag, so quietly took it back to Wanon Niwat and forwarded it later via an Air Force chap to Bangkok.)

The Thai decided to take me downtown — and I was informed that they would set me free and return my camera once we were off the base. I knew better. The car drove straight to the Udon police station and swung into the courtyard. The endless questioning began again while they examined every article I had on me. I didn't need to understand Thai to guess what they said about some photos taken at Vung Tau beach with Robert.

I winced when the fat policeman grabbed my Nikon F and tried to jerk the lever . . . that camera had been my income and my survival kit for the past two years. It was like seeing a friend mal-treated.

I kept asking for permission to contact my Embassy but Wichar said they wouldn't let me go until I was 'cleared'. I was horrified at the thought of staying at the jail or detention room, whatever it was, attached to the police station. Everyone was crowded into the barren room which held no furniture of any kind. People squatted on the floor to attend to their natural functions, or to eat the food brought in by a relative, or bought from a vendor. No meals were supplied to anyone confined there and I wondered what happened to those who had neither relatives nor money.

I protested that I was used to European food and purified water and that if I didn't get these I would be terribly ill (I could lie like a trooper if it meant saving my skin!). The prospect of having me ill on their hands might have been more than they were prepared to face — they finally decided to let me stay at the Udon, where Thai officers and American advisers had their quarters — providing I gave a formal promise that I wouldn't attempt to escape. Keeping my fingers metaphorically crossed, I treated the promise in the same way as the promise that I would be free as soon as I left the base.

They handed over my purse, which contained about eight dollars, but refused to give back my camera or papers. They also refused to give me a receipt for them: 'You don't need a receipt . . . you'll be back tomorrow.'

The British Embassy handles Canadian affairs in Thailand but, either by accident or design, I couldn't reach them by phone from the Udon. I went to the hotel bar to see if I could enlist the aid of anyone there, but they were all strangers to me, and reluctant to become involved. Again I felt so deserted, so lonely, desperate to be near Robert, the one person I knew who would stick to me through all this, and help me.

I swore that I would stay close to him for the rest of my life if I got out of this jam, even if he wouldn't marry me. Who gave two hoots for a certificate, anyway?

I wrote two letters to Robert, one to his sister's home, and one to the address of a friend of his in Richmond, New South Wales. An American civilian promised to airmail them for me, but he must have been a 'plant' as I learned later that neither letter reached its destination. Finally a Puerto Rican sergeant managed to contact the Embassy on my behalf and came back with the guarded message,

'It would be better if she were in Bangkok'.

No one came to escort me back to the police station next day but I noticed the policeman, complete with his pistol, at the corner and the two civilian Thais I'd seen the previous day followed me to the dingy nearby restaurant.

Three days after my arrest I finally found a GI willing to take the risk of getting me to Bangkok: a coloured sergeant from Chicago. He listened to my story, then arranged for a taxi to back into the courtyard behind the restaurant. The outhouse was in the courtyard, and my watchdogs must have thought I was making another trip there when I headed that way. I slipped into the taxi, lying down on the floor. The GI hopped into the seat. With his boots on my bottom, since there was no place else to put them without arousing attention, we made it through the checkpoints around Udon. Spotting a US uniform in the back of the cab, the guard simply waved us through; but at one point halfway between Udon and Bangkok, one guard opened the door and saw me crouching on the floor. I had the presence of mind to pretend to be looking for something I had lost, and grinned up at him, shrugging my shoulders and saying some of the few words of Thai I knew 'Ha Din Sor' (looking for a pencil). He stared at me on the floor, then at the GI; his slanted eyes were almost round with astonishment but he closed the door and waved us on. I breathed a sigh of relief; apparently my escape hadn't been reported as yet.

The GI kept handing me bananas and lit cigarettes for me during our long bumpy ride to Bangkok. I really appreciated his help; he had taken the cab after a full day on duty and would have to return immediately to Udon. I still thank him wherever he may be now.

Ten hours later I stretched my sore limbs in the garden of the British Embassy. Over at last!

But it wasn't quite that simple.

The British Embassy contacted their liaison officer in the Thai government, Colonel Chawalit, and three days later Her Majesty's Consul, Mr Boyes, told me: 'Udon is very upset because you left without permission but they say if you come back you will be fined a small sum, your articles will be returned and you will be free to leave.'

'Go back there? Like hell I will! I'd rather walk barefoot along the Ho Chi Minh trail than return to Udon!'

'Hmmm . . . I wouldn't advise either course of action,' was the Consul's dry comment. 'I suggest you hang on here for a while and we'll see what we can do.'

I hung on for a month.

My passport and papers were transferred to the office of the Thai CID in Bangkok and I went there regularly, always with a friend or the helpful Mr Boyes.

I'd received a telegram from overseas telling me that a money order had been forwarded six weeks earlier but it never reached me. I lived solely on the bounty of generous and sympathetic colleagues who were on a payroll.

The Thai CID were very bland. They kept telling me it wouldn't be long before things were straightened out. In the meantime they were sure I didn't mind being in beautiful Bangkok, free to enjoy its sights. Sure I was free. Free to go to Max's Bar on Patpong and bum drinks off CIA agents there, free to wander about. But without my camera equipment I wasn't free to work. And I was getting very tired of sponging on friends and begging the return of things that were legitimately mine.

The US Embassy in Bangkok agreed that AA had no right to confiscate my camera equipment and hand it over to the Thai police. The Consul said he would see what could be done about it. A month later my passport and papers were finally handed over to me with the suggestion that I leave Thailand immediately. I could stay, of course, *if* I was prepared to face charges of over-staying my visa, which might land me in a local jail. I brought up the question of my camera equipment and Colonel Chawalit promised to hand it over to Mr Boyes as soon as it arrived from Udon.

Two days before my departure I met an Air America pilot I had known in Saigon. We went out for an evening and at the seventh bar and seventeenth martini I asked why there had been such a fuss made about my being on the Udon base.

'Hell! You mean to say you don't *know*?' he asked. 'They are are loading weapons for Laos there — and that could be claimed as a violation of the Geneva Agreements.'

I left Thailand and arrived safely in Singapore two days later. I sought out the second secretary at the US Embassy there, thinking I could enlist his aid in getting my camera equipment returned. In the most unfriendly terms he refused to help, saying: 'We are not responsible for what employees under Government contract might do. You knew we wouldn't help you — why did you bother to come here?' And on that note I was ushered from the Embassy. 'It doesn't need communist propaganda to turn a person anti-American,' I fumed at him. 'You guys do a pretty good job of that yourself!'

Unable to work without my vital camera I lived in a cheap Chinese hotel in a room costing 55 cents a night. I ate from the local street vendors at 10 to 20 cents a time. As in Saigon, the meals from street stands were delicious and varied, as Singapore has so many vendors of different origins, all producing their own specialties.

I enjoyed the colourful city, free of the corruption found else-where in most of Asia. I felt I could again breathe, and didn't worry about persecution from the CIA, who had earlier learned that they could not meddle in that city. During the four weeks I waited for my camera equipment to arrive at the British High Commission, I had a pleasant stay, making many friends of European and Asian residents. Even the crowd of transvestites from Bugis Street extended an afternoon invitation to a villa they occupied, an honour seldom bestowed on a female! By the time my belongings arrived my money had also been forwarded from overseas and I managed to get a booking on the *Centaur,* headed for Australia.

The voyage was relaxing, with a friendly atmosphere on board. Again, I was surrounded by people who seemed so remote, who hadn't the vaguest idea what went on elsewhere. For them, the earth's axis was lubricated with beer and the future of the globe depended on which cricket team won the Ashes. And yet I envied them at times, their minds free of the horrors of Vietnam —horror which I shall never be able to forget.

The ship's first stop was in Broome, and as the red sandy shore rose out of the lapis-lazuli sea before us, my heart beat faster and I looked for the first time on this continent . . . this land my man had told me so much about.

And I wondered what this strange shore would hold for me.